ASHEVILLE
& THE GREAT
SMOKY MOUNTAINS

JASON FRYE

Contents

DISCOVER

Asheville & the
Great Smoky Mountains

There's an energy in the mountain town of Asheville that you don't find in many other places in North Carolina. For more than a century, Asheville has been a hive of progressive thinking and a surprisingly cosmopolitan level of living. With all the writers, artists, musicians, dancers, and other eclectic personalities that have inhabited this town, it's easy to understand how it earned the nickname "Paris of the South."

Surrounding Asheville are The Great Smoky Mountains. Drawing more than 10 million visitors annually, the Smokies are laced with hiking trails, rivers, and waterfalls and populated with diverse wildlife—from rare salamanders to huge elk. The diversity is second only to the sublime mystery of the area. Throughout the 521,085-acre national park, you can find spots so remote they have stood undisturbed for untold lengths of time.

You'll also find people as varied as the landscape they inhabit and histories as wild as the mountains themselves. Come join them.

Clockwise from top left: sidewalk dining in Asheville; the Biltmore Estate in Asheville; horse at the Cades Cove Riding Stable; biking in Cades Cove; tubing at Deep Creek; view of downtown Asheville.

5 TOP EXPERIENCES

1 **Admire Historic Architecture:** Downtown Asheville is full of beautiful art deco and beaux arts masterpieces. Go check them out (page 22)!

2 **Hike in the Smokies:** The best way to explore the woods, peaks, and waterfalls in the Great Smoky Mountains is by foot (page 98).

3 **Taste Craft Brews:** Asheville's brewery scene is at the top of any beer geek's list (page 51).

4 **Seek Outdoor Adventure:** Zip-line, paddleboard, or bellyak—there are tons of options for outdoor fun in Asheville (pages 32 and 33).

5 **Honor Indigenous Culture:** The Cherokee people have lived in the Smoky Mountains for thousands of years. Learn about their history and traditions (pages 110 and 112).

Planning Your Trip

Where to Go

Asheville and the Southern Blue Ridge

Asheville's a town chock-full of creative types: Artists, chefs, brewers, and musicians find inspiration here. A top **beer destination** and one of the South's **premier food cities,** Asheville is filled with **galleries, boutiques,** and the general weirdness you expect from bigger cities. **Art deco architecture**, the famed and lovely **Biltmore Estate,** the wildly creative **River Arts District,** and a renewed embrace of **Black creators** and entrepreneurs are a few of the reasons to visit. Its location between the Blue Ridge and Smokies gives easy access to the mountains, especially the **Great Smoky Mountains National Park**, where recreation opportunities abound.

Great Smoky Mountains

Straddling the border with Tennessee, **Great Smoky Mountains National Park** is a land of ridges, rocky rivers, virgin forests, and tumbling waterfalls. The **most-visited national park** in the United States, it's a hot spot of trails, **waterfalls,** mountain vistas, and 500,000 acres of wilderness to explore. Visit appealing little towns like **Bryson City, Dillsboro and Sylva,** and **Maggie Valley** as well as the tribal seat of the Eastern Band of the **Cherokee,** a **casino,** and the first (and only) **fly-fishing trail** in the United States.

the Smoky Mountains

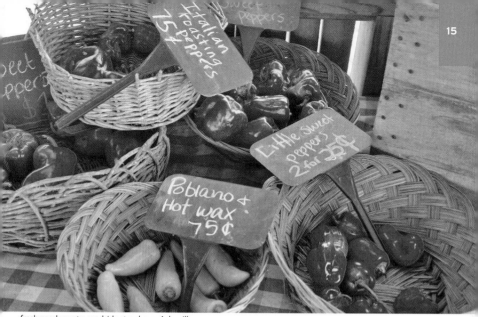

fresh produce at a roadside stand near Asheville

Know Before You Go

Spring debuts in the Southeast as early as late February, then creeps into central North Carolina and up the coast, reaching the mountains a little later. Temperatures are a consistent 60-70°F by mid-April.

Summer is high season: Traffic is slow in the mountains. Heat and humidity can be brutal, so the cooler mountains draw visitors from far and wide. Rent your mountain cabins far in advance for the choicest of stays.

Autumn begins in the mountains. **Fall foliage** accounts for the mountains' second high season, running late September-early November; it's busiest in October, when cooler weather offers relief after sweltering September.

Winter is milder here than in many parts of the country, but many businesses in the mountains reduce their hours or close entirely.

Weather can change on a whim. It pays to layer, as temperatures in the 80s can drop into the 60s at night. **Pack** for chilly weather in the mountains, even in the summer.

Cell phone signals are consistent, but there are rural pockets in the deep mountains where cell service and 4G, 5G, and LTET connectivity is spotty.

Getaway to Asheville and the Great Smoky Mountains

Day 1

ASHEVILLE

Begin your journey in Asheville, where you'll find streets lined with galleries, one of the nation's largest collections of **art deco** architecture, and a growing array of **chefs, brewers, and mixologists.**

Head directly to the **Biltmore Estate.** Tour the **Biltmore Winery,** watch the **blacksmith** at Antler Hill Village make music with the anvil, and find lunch at **Cedric's Tavern.** Head downtown and check into **ASIA Bed & Breakfast Spa,** freshen up, and get ready to roam.

Dine downtown at **Cucina 24** or at **Wicked Weed Brewpub,** then head to nearby **Orange Peel** for live music. Make one last stop at **Sovereign Remedies** for a nightcap.

Day 2

ASHEVILLE CONTINUED

Start your day with breakfast at **Early Girl Eatery.** Window shop at **Malaprop's Bookstore** and **Woolworth Walk** art gallery, and don't sweat lunch: a food tour with **Eating Asheville** will fill you up and point you in a direction for dinner. Walk off your food tour at the **Asheville Art Museum** while you debate whether to dine at **The Admiral, Cúrate,** or **Jettie Rae's.**

Day 3

ASHEVILLE TO CHEROKEE

The winding section of the **Blue Ridge Parkway** between Asheville and the southern terminus in Cherokee is quite beautiful. Before you hit the road, down a giant biscuit at **Biscuit**

Pack Square Park in downtown Asheville at night

a trail bridge in Great Smoky Mountains National Park

Head. Continue down the Parkway and take in the view of **Mount Pisgah.** Hike to **Devil's Courthouse** and stop at **Richland Balsam Overlook,** the highest point on the Blue Ridge Parkway.

Be sure to visit the Waterrock Knob Visitor Center for a four-state view and panorama of the **Great Smoky Mountains.** Head into Cherokee for the night where you can gamble, visit a spa, and grab a bite at **Harrah's Cherokee Casino.**

Day 4
CHEROKEE TO GREAT SMOKY MOUNTAINS NATIONAL PARK

Before you start your short drive to **Great Smoky Mountains National Park,** visit the **Qualla Arts and Crafts Mutual** in Cherokee. Stop at the **Museum of the Cherokee Indian** across the street and the **Oconaluftee Indian Village** just up the hill. During the summer months, catch an evening performance of *Unto These Hills.* Head into the park, **reserve a campsite,** and prepare for exploring and hiking tomorrow.

Day 5
GREAT SMOKY MOUNTAINS NATIONAL PARK

Take the 30-mile Newfound Gap Road through the park into **Gatlinburg,** Tennessee, eat lunch, and head back to North Carolina. You're as likely to see a bear as a deer on this stunning scenic road, and you'll also pass a number of trailheads. Trails range from short jaunts to overnight hikes leading deep into the forest. The trails in **Cades Cove** and around **Clingmans Dome**—the highest point in the Smokies—are popular. The **Appalachian Trail** crosses Clingmans Dome, so take a stroll here if for no other reason than to say you've hiked on the AT. Fervent hikers may want to consider spending a few more days exploring the park.

Asheville and the Southern Blue Ridge

The "Paris of the South" was built on a series of hills around the confluence of the Swannanoa ("swan-uh-NO-uh") and French Broad Rivers, commerce found its way here in the 18th and 19th centuries via water routes and a mountain stagecoach road. In the late 1800s the town experienced a boom as railroad lines began to bring vacationers by the tens of thousands. It was around that time that George Vanderbilt, scion of the massively wealthy Vanderbilt dynasty, began building his mountain home, the Biltmore, just south of downtown. From the 1880s to the 1930s the mountain town underwent a long and rapid expansion, eventually becoming a small city in its own right.

Surrounding Asheville are mountains and hundreds of years of folk traditions, with folk art, music, dancing, and customs that survive

Highlights

Look for ★ to find recommended sights, activities, dining, and lodging.

★ **Downtown Architecture:** In the early 20th century, wealthy visitors left their mark on Asheville's downtown, a district packed with art deco and beaux arts masterpieces (page 22).

★ **North Carolina Arboretum:** One of the most beautiful garden spaces in the country, this enormous collection is worth a visit. Don't miss the special Bonsai Collection (page 23).

★ **Biltmore Estate:** Asheville's most popular attraction is not only an awe-inspiring palace and symbol of the Gilded Age; it's also a collection of great little restaurants, shops, and a popular winery, all in a beautiful riverside setting (page 26).

★ **Folk Art Center:** Learn about the master craftspeople of the southern Appalachians and purchase gorgeous handmade items such as traditional weaving, woodcarving, and fine-art furniture (page 30).

★ **Hiking:** Hit the trail at the North Carolina Arboretum, Biltmore Estate, or Blue Ridge Parkway; there are plenty of trails to choose from (page 31).

★ **Live Music:** You'll hear great music everywhere here, from buskers on street corners to the nation's premier live music hall (page 35).

★ **River Arts District:** Asheville's reposed warehouses have become a lively collection of art galleries and studios, restaurants, and breweries (page 44).

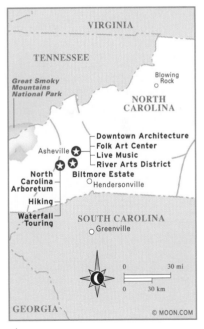

★ **Waterfall Touring:** Head to Brevard and Transylvania County to see how many of the 250 waterfalls here you can visit (page 70).

Asheville

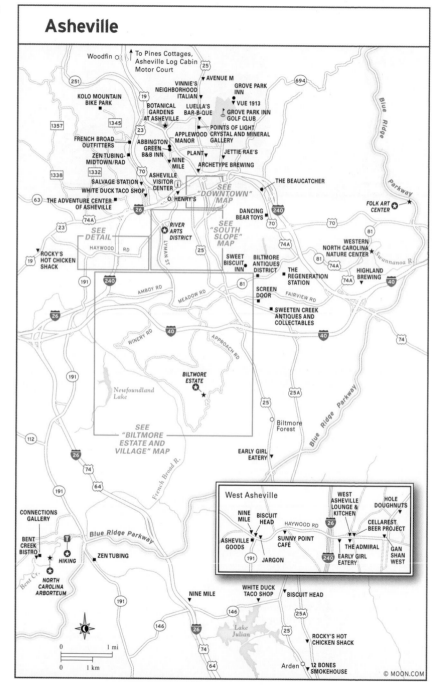

Woodfin ○

To Pines Cottages,
Asheville Log Cabin
Motor Court

251

25

AVENUE M

VINNIE'S
NEIGHBORHOOD
ITALIAN

GROVE PARK
INN

694

KOLO MOUNTAIN
BIKE PARK

19

VUE 1913

BOTANICAL
GARDENS
AT ASHEVILLE

LUELLA'S
BAR-B-QUE

GROVE PARK INN
GOLF CLUB

1345

1357

23

APPLEWOOD
MANOR

POINTS OF LIGHT
CRYSTAL AND MINERAL
GALLERY

FRENCH BROAD
OUTFITTERS

ABBINGTON
GREEN
B&B INN

PLANT

JETTIE RAE'S

ZEN TUBING-
MIDTOWN/RAD

NINE
MILE

ARCHETYPE BREWING

1338

1332

70

SALVAGE STATION

ASHEVILLE
VISITOR
CENTER

THE BEAUCATCHER

WHITE DUCK TACO SHOP

O. HENRY'S

SEE
"DOWNTOWN"
MAP

240

63

THE ADVENTURE CENTER
OF ASHEVILLE

26

DANCING
BEAR TOYS

70

70

FOLK ART
CENTER

74A

23

SEE
DETAIL

RIVER
ARTS
DISTRICT

SEE
"SOUTH
SLOPE"
MAP

74A

81

WESTERN
NORTH CAROLINA
NATURE CENTER

HAYWOOD RD

25

Swannanoa R.

19

ROCKY'S
HOT CHICKEN
SHACK

SWEET
BISCUIT
INN

BILTMORE
ANTIQUES
DISTRICT

81

74A

HIGHLAND
BREWING

191

240

81

THE
REGENERATION
STATION

74A

40

AMBOY RD

MEADOW RD

FAIRVIEW RD

SCREEN
DOOR

26

WINERY RD

40

APPROACH RD

SWEETEN CREEK
ANTIQUES AND
COLLECTABLES

40

74

191

BILTMORE
ESTATE

Newfoundland
Lake

Blue Ridge Parkway

112

SEE
"BILTMORE
ESTATE AND
VILLAGE" MAP

25

25A

Biltmore
Forest

26

74

EARLY GIRL
EATERY

64

191

West Asheville

WEST
ASHEVILLE
LOUNGE &
KITCHEN

HOLE
DOUGHNUTS

CONNECTIONS
GALLERY

NINE
MILE

BISCUIT
HEAD

HAYWOOD RD

26

CELLAREST
BEER PROJECT

BENT
CREEK
BISTRO

T

ASHEVILLE
GOODS

SUNNY POINT
CAFÉ

THE ADMIRAL

ZEN TUBING

HIKING

191

JARGON

240

EARLY GIRL
EATERY

GAN
SHAN
WEST

NORTH
CAROLINA
ARBORETUM

Bent Cr.

NINE MILE

WHITE DUCK
TACO SHOP

BISCUIT HEAD

191

146

25A

26

Lake
Julian

25

ROCKY'S HOT
CHICKEN SHACK

146

74

64

Arden ○

12 BONES
SMOKEHOUSE

French Broad R.

Lyman St.

0   1 mi

0   1 km

© MOON.COM

today. Old-time Appalachian string-band music (not to be confused with bluegrass, although bluegrass is alive and well here too) thrives in the hills and hollows among the descendants of the region's early settlers, whose songs, instruments, and techniques have been passed down over many generations. Four- and five-string banjo pickers, guitarists, fiddlers, and other musicians have migrated here from all across the globe to be part of the music traditions and the thriving music scene. Asheville is one of the best places in the world to hear old-time and bluegrass music as well as a sidetrack genre known as mountain swing.

One of the epicenters for visual arts in the Southeast, Asheville draws from centuries-old Appalachian folkways and traditions like woodcarving, weaving, and other arts and merges them with elements of the modern craft and fine arts movement. The results from these seemingly disparate elements being put in Asheville's pressure cooker together is a vibrant set of studios and galleries where art and craft of all sorts have a home. Arts organizations such as the Southern Highland Craft Guild (www.southernhighlandguild.org) help preserve the traditional arts, while places like the River Arts District and a number of small guilds, groups, and galleries support contemporary artists.

All of this makes Asheville feel like a countercultural center. Elements of Haight-Ashbury circa 1968 mix with Woodstock, the Grand Ole Opry, Andy Warhol's Factory, and a beatnik vibe, but with better food, to create an electric atmosphere.

PLANNING YOUR TIME

Once the last leaf drops from autumn trees, many mountain towns close until spring. Asheville is vibrant year-round (although the pace does ease quite a bit when the snow falls). In winter, Asheville is less expensive; rooms at hotels, inns, and B&Bs are plentiful; and reservations at the hot-ticket restaurants are easier to score. Fortunately, the breweries and cocktail lounges don't slow down, and some of the best bands roll through town in winter months. The city will see snow several times throughout the season, but it's not generally a problem, despite the fact that it does occasionally shut down the Blue Ridge Parkway, and some of those higher mountain roads can be impassible.

Once spring breaks and bunches of wild-flowers start to show up in earnest, so do the warmer-weather visitors. This is a prime time for wildflower hikes and visits to waterfalls (which can be quite impressive with snowmelt and spring rains), plus there's an energy to the city as everyone and everything begins to wake up after the dark of winter. Spring at the Biltmore Estate is marvelous thanks to their outstanding gardens that are thick with tulips.

Summer, of course, is a great time to be in Asheville, as the elevation brings cooler air on the same day it will be sweltering across the Piedmont and Sandhills. Summer also brings a number of festivals and special events, and it's the time when the greens and blues of the Blue Ridge are most vivid. Fall colors arrive at slightly different times each year, so you'll want to keep an eye on leaf forecasts for ideal getaway times. Generally speaking, however, you can plan to see leaves start to turn in mid-September, peak in mid-October, and finish by the second week of November. Fall is prime season to visit Asheville, so make lodging reservations early and expect some delays on scenic routes like the Blue Ridge Parkway.

Asheville's proximity to Great Smoky Mountains National Park (GSMNP) makes it a natural launch point for trips into the park. Visiting the Smoky Mountains brings the same seasonal concerns as visiting Asheville. Fall is peak season and crowded with leaf-peeping visitors; things slow down in winter and pick up in spring as the wildflowers

---

Previous: Asheville; a bonsai on display at the North Carolina Arboretum; the River Arts District is a must-see for artists and art lovers.

begin to bloom. Then summer brings the hikers and national park enthusiasts back in full force. The elevation of Newfound Gap Road, the only road across GSMNP, is such that it can have weather-related delays or closures, so keep this in mind when planning a visit. The **Blue Ridge National Heritage Area** (www.blueridgeheritage.com) has a number of valuable trip-planning resources, but a preferred resource is **Explore Asheville** (www.exploreasheville.com), the Asheville Convention and Visitors Bureau's website. The site's creators and the people at the **Asheville Visitors Center** (36 Montford Ave., 828/258-6129, www. exploreasheville.com, 8:30am-5:30pm Mon.-Fri., 9am-5pm Sat.-Sun.) take a lot of pride in their town and can help steer you toward new and old favorites in the area. For planning a trip to the Smoky Mountains, you'll find many resources through **Great Smoky Mountains National Park** (GSMNP, 865/436-1200, www.nps.gov/grsm); of course, you'll also find a number of resources through Asheville's local visitor services.

Asheville

SIGHTS

Getting around Asheville isn't much of a problem once you get oriented, and getting yourself oriented is no problem. Downtown Asheville sits at the center, on the crest of a couple of hills, and it's here we find the largest concentration of hotels, restaurants, and bars. Just south of downtown is the South Slope and an assortment of places to eat and drink. The French Broad River flows to the west of Downtown, and the River Arts District sits here, between downtown and the river. In the warehouses and industrial facilities are hundreds of art galleries. Across the river is West Asheville, a destination with its own vibe and set of restaurants and breweries. The Biltmore Estate, and Biltmore Village (an actual miniature village built to support the workers on the estate, gardens, and house), sit at the foot of South Slope. South of here is I-40 and the rough dividing line between South Asheville and the rest of the area. To the north of downtown you'll find the University of North Carolina Asheville and residential neighborhoods. The Blue Ridge Parkway wraps around the eastern and southern sides of the city.

Downtown

In Downtown Asheville, pick a parking garage, or park at your hotel, and stow the car, then head out by foot. From Pack Square at the heart of Downtown, you're only a few blocks or a few minutes away from galleries, boutiques, breweries, restaurants, and places to stay.

TOP EXPERIENCE

★ DOWNTOWN ARCHITECTURE

As beautiful as Asheville's natural environment may be, the striking architecture is just as attractive. The Montford neighborhood, a contemporary of the Biltmore, is a mixture of ornate Queen Anne houses and craftsman-style bungalows. The Grove Park Inn, a huge luxury hotel, was built in 1913 and is decked out with rustic architectural devices intended to make vacationing New Yorkers and wealthy people feel like they were roughing it. In downtown Asheville is a large concentration of art deco buildings on the scale of Miami Beach. Significant structures dating to the boom before the Great Depression include the **Buncombe County Courthouse** (60 Court Plaza, built 1927-1929), the **First Baptist Church** (Oak St. and Woodfin St., 1925), the **S&W Cafeteria** (56 Patton Ave., 1929), the **Public Service Building** (89-93 Patton Ave., 1929), and the **Grove Arcade** (1 Page Ave., 1926-1929).

The **Jackson Building** (22 S. Pack Square,

built 1923-1924) is a fine example of neo-Gothic architecture with a disturbing backstory. According to legend, on the day of the stock market crash in 1929 that started the Great Depression, one of the wealthiest men in Asheville lost it all and leaped to his death from the building. Three or four (depending on who's telling the story) more of Asheville's wealthiest followed suit. What is known to be true is that there's a bull's-eye built into the sidewalk in front of the building as a morbid monument to the story.

ASHEVILLE ART MUSEUM

The **Asheville Art Museum** (2 S. Pack Square, 828/253-3227, www.ashevilleart.org, 11am-6pm Tues.-Wed. and Fri.-Sun., 11am-9pm Thurs., $15 adults, $13 over age 60, $10 students, free under age 6) recently underwent two years of renovations to add new exhibition space and a fresh approach to their collection. They've been around since 1948, and in the intervening decades have enriched the art community of Asheville by displaying works by some of the most important, influential, and up-and-coming artists of the 20th century. The permanent collection includes a wide array of media and styles, including photo portraits, ceramics, statuary, and beautiful modern pieces. A large collection from the nearby experimental school, Black Mountain College, shows the highlights of works created by faculty and students.

South Slope and River Arts District

Restaurants, breweries, and nightlife make the South Slope a distinct destination. The former warehouses and industrial spaces turned art galleries make the River Arts District a great spot to spend a few hours, but the breweries and restaurants here make it easy to spend the day.

West Asheville

In West Asheville you might have trouble parking as this once entirely residential neighborhood continues to evolve. Popular restaurants and breweries, a number of boutiques and shops, and some vibrant murals make this a great place to grab a bite or spend the bulk of your weekend away.

★ NORTH CAROLINA ARBORETUM

The enormous **North Carolina Arboretum** (100 Frederick Law Olmsted Way, 828/665-2492, www.ncarboretum.org, 8am-9pm daily Apr.-Oct., 8am-7pm daily Nov.-Mar., Bonsai Collection 9am-5pm daily, admission free, parking $16 cars, $50 RVs) is considered by many to be one of the most beautiful in the country. The 434 natural and landscaped acres back into the Pisgah National Forest, just off the Blue Ridge Parkway. Major collections include the National Native Azalea Repository, featuring nearly every species of azalea native to the United States as well as several hybrids, and the special Bonsai Collection, comprising more than 200 bonsai plants, many of the staff horticulturists' own creation.

Bicycles and leashed dogs are permitted on many of the arboretum's trails. Walking areas range from easy to fairly rugged, but with 10 miles of trails, you will find one that suits your skill level. To learn more about the history of the arboretum and its plants, as well as the natural history of the region, join one of the guided tours (1pm Tues. and Sat.). These two-mile walk-and-talk tours happen rain or shine, so dress for the weather. The arboretum also has a nice café, the **Bent Creek Bistro** (828/412-8584, 10am-4pm Tues.-Sun., $4-9), and gift shop, the **Connections Gallery** (10am-4pm daily).

Biltmore Estate and Village

The area around the Biltmore Estate includes the estate itself but also Biltmore Village, where workers on the estate, grounds, and home lived during and after construction. The estate is a kingdom unto itself, with a winery (it's the most-visited wine tasting room in the United States, incidentally) and brewery in

Downtown Asheville

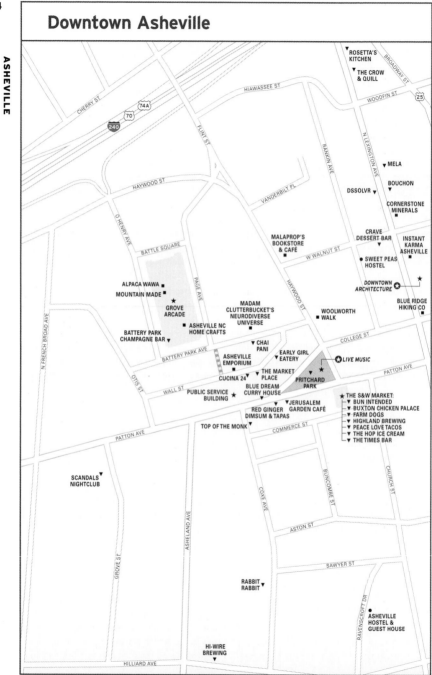

ROSETTA'S KITCHEN

THE CROW & QUILL

HIAWASSEE ST

WOODFIN ST

MELA

BOUCHON

DSSOLVR

CORNERSTONE MINERALS

CRAVE DESSERT BAR

INSTANT KARMA ASHEVILLE

SWEET PEAS HOSTEL

DOWNTOWN ARCHITECTURE

BLUE RIDGE HIKING CO

MALAPROP'S BOOKSTORE & CAFÉ

W WALNUT ST

WOOLWORTH WALK

COLLEGE ST

ALPACA WAWA

MOUNTAIN MADE

GROVE ARCADE

MADAM CLUTTERBUCKET'S NEURODIVERSE UNIVERSE

ASHEVILLE NC HOME CRAFTS

BATTERY PARK CHAMPAGNE BAR

CHAI PANI

BATTERY PARK AVE

ASHEVILLE EMPORIUM

EARLY GIRL EATERY

LIVE MUSIC

CUCINA 24

THE MARKET PLACE

PRITCHARD PARK

PATTON AVE

BLUE DREAM CURRY HOUSE

PUBLIC SERVICE BUILDING

WALL ST

JERUSALEM GARDEN CAFÉ

RED GINGER DIMSUM & TAPAS

THE S&W MARKET:
- BUN INTENDED
- BUXTON CHICKEN PALACE
- FARM DOGS
- HIGHLAND BREWING
- PEACE LOVE TACOS
- THE HOP ICE CREAM
- THE TIMES BAR

TOP OF THE MONK

COMMERCE ST

SCANDALS NIGHTCLUB

PATTON AVE

COXE AVE

BUNCOMBE ST

CHURCH ST

ASTON ST

SAWYER ST

RABBIT RABBIT

ASHEVILLE HOSTEL & GUEST HOUSE

HI-WIRE BREWING

HILLIARD AVE

WOODFIN ST

FIRST BAPTIST
CHURCH

CHARLOTTE ST

OAK ST

N MARKET ST

0   100 yds

0   100 m

THE GOURMET
CHIP COMPANY

E WALNUT ST

N SPRUCE ST

COLLEGE ST

BOTANIST
& BARREL

SOVEREIGN
REMEDIES

LAWYERS ALLEY

BUNCOMBE
COUNTY
COURTHOUSE

LAWYERS WALK

BROADWAY ST

VALLEY ST

DAVIDSON ST

AC HOTEL
BY MARRIOTT
ASHEVILLE
DOWNTOWN

CAPELLA ON 9

Pack
Square
Park

KIMPTON
HOTEL ARRAS

DISTRICT 42

BARGELLO

MARJORIE ST

THE JACKSON
BUILDING

HORSE + HERO

FRENCH BROAD
CHOCOLATES

RHUBARB

S MARKET ST

S SPRUCE ST

ASHEVILLE
ART MUSEUM

25

EAGLE ST

CÚRATE

WHITE DUCK
TACO SHOP

MAST
GENERAL STORE

BENNE
ON EAGLE

S LEXINGTON AVE

NOIR
COLLECTIVE

BILTMORE AVE

WORKSHOP
LOUNGE

THE FOUNDRY
HOTEL

S CHARLOTTE ST

ASTON ST

S SPRUCE ST

Triangle
Park

S BEAUMONT ST

MAX ST

LAZOOM
COMEDY TOUR

S MARKET ST

25

ORANGE PEEL
SOCIAL AID &
PLEASURE CLUB

HILLIARD AVE

© MOON.COM

Biltmore Estate and Village

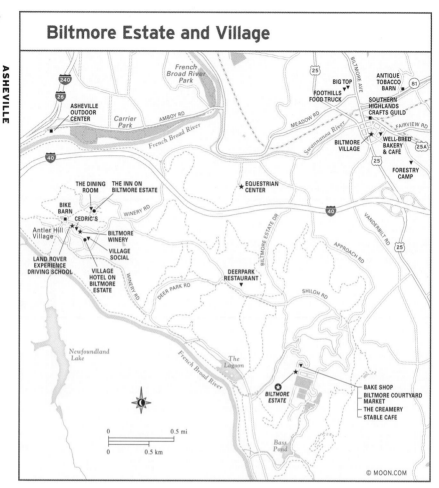

© MOON.COM

Antler Hill, amazing gardens and that stunning house at the center, a vineyard (it's on the other side of the estate, the working side), nearly a dozen places to eat, a pair of inns, a whole slew of outdoor activities to get into, and so much space. It's a beautiful place to explore. And Biltmore Village is no exception. This lovely little grid of brick and stone cottages is charming as can be and full of boutiques, galleries, restaurants, and more.

★ BILTMORE ESTATE

Much of downtown Asheville dates to the 1920s, but the architectural crown jewel, the

Biltmore Estate (1 Lodge St., 800/411-3812, www.biltmore.com, ticket office 8:30am-4pm daily, house 10am-5pm daily, gardens 9am-7:30pm daily, admission $66-86, additional fees for activities), predates that by decades. It was built in the late 1800s for owner George Vanderbilt, grandson of Gilded Age elite Cornelius Vanderbilt. Like many of his wealthy Northern contemporaries, George Vanderbilt was first introduced to North Carolina when he traveled to Asheville for the mountain air and nearby hot springs. He found himself so awestruck by the land that he amassed a 125,000-acre tract south

One Day in Asheville

Only have one day to devote to Asheville? Here are the city's must-see, must-do, and must-eat attractions:

MORNING

Start the day with some great breakfast grub from **Sunny Point** in West Asheville. Spend the morning **exploring boutiques and galleries** like those in the **Grove Arcade** and **Woolworth Walk,** taking time to stroll by examples of Asheville's notable **downtown architecture,** including the First Baptist Church, the Jackson Building, and the **Buncombe County Courthouse** before joining a **Hood Huggers Tour.**

AFTERNOON

At lunchtime, make your way over to **S&W Market** for chicken sandwiches, *bao,* tacos, and a beer from **Highland Brewing. Buxton Hall Barbecue,** a few blocks off downtown on the South Slope, is another good lunch option. After lunch, get a new perspective on the city by boarding the **LaZoom Comedy Tour** bus, floating down the French Broad River with **Zen Tubing,** or by heading out for a hike or woodsy walk at the **North Carolina Arboretum** or at any of a number of trailheads along the **Blue Ridge Parkway.**

You could spend the afternoon at the **Biltmore Estate,** a three-mile drive from downtown. Enjoy the first part of your afternoon at Antler Hill Village for a wine tasting at the **Winery,** and then lunch at the **Bistro,** making sure to leave at least three hours to tour the house and gardens before they close at 4:30pm (3:30pm in winter).

EVENING

Head back downtown for the evening, kicking the night off with a pint at **Hi-Wire** or **DSSOLVR,** or cocktails from **Sovereign Remedies.** When you're ready for dinner, try **Cucina 24** for Italian, **Benne on Eagle** for a splendid meal of African diaspora-inspired cuisine, or Mediterranean at **Jerusalem Café.** Walk dinner off with a stroll—a number of buskers will entertain you. Grab a nightcap at **Crave Dessert Bar** or a chocolate at **French Broad Chocolates.** If you're in town on a Friday, check out the drum circle at **Pritchard Park.**

of Asheville where he would build his "country home" and enjoy the area's restive and healthful benefits. He engaged celebrity architect Richard Morris Hunt to build the home, and because the land and the views reminded them of the Loire Valley, they planned to build the home in the style of a 16th-century French château. The Biltmore Estate was once the largest privately owned home in the country. Vanderbilt also hired the esteemed Frederick Law Olmsted, creator of New York City's Central Park, to design the landscape for the grounds, gardens, and surrounding forest, a project nine times the size of the New York park for which he is famous.

A three-mile-long approach road leads through manicured forests, revealing bits of the landscape and hiding the house until you are upon it, creating a sense of drama and wonder for arriving visitors. While the Biltmore Estate's original 125,000 acres are now greatly diminished—the estate comprises a little more than 8,000 acres today—it's easy to see just how big it was; standing on the South Terrace and looking south and west, everything in view was once part of the estate. A large tract of the land was sold to the federal government and has become part of the Pisgah National Forest; what remains is immaculately manicured.

Construction of the home was done primarily between 1888 and 1895, although there were a number of projects that continued up through World War II (when part of the home was turned into a bunker to store part of the National Gallery of Art's collection). Many are astounded at how long it took to complete the home, but think of the house this way: Approximately 5,000 tons of stone were used to build it, there are 65 fireplaces and more than 250 rooms, the square footage is nearly four acres, and they put up a 35-foot Christmas tree in the banquet hall. The numbers don't lie; this is a house unlike any you've been in. Most of the house is open to visitors on self-guided tours, and other parts—like the roof and some servants' areas—are accessible on behind-the-scenes tours. As astounding as this may be, it's nothing compared to the art collected here. There are paintings by Renoir, James Abbott Whistler, and John Singer Sargent; a collection of European antiques including Napoleon's chess set; and room upon room of masterwork in tiling, woodworking and carving, masonry, and stone carving. For its time, the Biltmore was a technological marvel, with electricity, elevators, central heat, and hot water. And we haven't even talked about the basement, where there's a heated pool, a gymnasium, and a bowling alley.

BILTMORE VILLAGE

George Vanderbilt found the concept of a self-sustaining estate appealing, and he included a working farm with crops, herds of cattle, a dairy, and all the farmers and workers required for such an operation. The Asheville neighborhood known as **Biltmore Village** was part of this mountain empire.

If George Vanderbilt stepped onto his estate today, he'd be happy to find that one million people every year come to visit and that his vision of a self-sustaining estate endures. A vineyard (not open to the public) produces grapes that are processed at the estate's winery; a livestock breeding program produces fine stock; and their farm supplies more than 70 percent of seasonal and specialty vegetables to the estate's restaurants. Visitors can eat, shop, tour, explore, relax, and unwind

without leaving the grounds, and there's easily enough here to fill a weekend.

The **Biltmore Winery** in **Antler Hill Village,** part of the estate, operates in what was formerly the dairy; check out the industrial-farm rafters in the tasting room. Daily tours and tastings allow visitors to sample some award-winning wines and see how they're made. More than 500,000 people visit the tasting room annually, so expect a wait if you're here in high season.

Antler Hill Village is also home to **Cedric's,** a brewery named after a beloved family dog, as well as a small museum, a souvenir shop, and a green where you can relax. **River Bend Farm** is a beautiful compound that was once the hub of the estate's farming operation but now stands as a showpiece for traditional period crafts like woodworking and blacksmithing.

The **Equestrian Center** gives lessons and the opportunity to ride more than 80 miles of equestrian trails, many with sweeping views of the estate and glimpses of the main house that will take your breath away. Other ways to tour the estate include carriage rides, paved bike trails and mountain bike trails, canoes, kayaks, and rafts (the French Broad River bisects the estate), and on foot. You can even challenge your driving skills at the **Land Rover Experience Driving School.**

Admission cost for the Biltmore Estate varies by season and includes the house, gardens, and winery; activities such as horseback riding, rafting, and behind-the-scenes tours cost extra. Special events, like the Christmas Candlelight Tour (Nov.-early-Jan.) also have additional fees. Parking is free, and a complimentary shuttle runs to the house.

Outside Downtown

Outside Downtown is a big area, and I suppose that, technically, everything from the

1: architecture in Pack Square Park 2: the Quilt Garden at the North Carolina Arboretum 3: view from the Biltmore Estate

Outer Banks to Paris is Outside Downtown, but we're keeping the focus tight and looking at this as greater Asheville. Pockets of restaurants, boutiques, and breweries have sprung up in different places around town, from the area near the university to the extreme western part of West Asheville to the area between Asheville and Black Mountain. The Blue Ridge Parkway, Botanical Gardens, and Western North Carolina Nature Center are three highlights in this part of town.

BOTANICAL GARDENS

Adjacent to the UNC-Asheville campus, **The Botanical Gardens at Asheville** (151 W. T. Weaver Blvd., 828/252-5190, www.ashevillebotanicalgardens.org, dawn-dusk daily year-round, donation) is a 10-acre preserve for the region's increasingly threatened native plant species. Laid out in 1960 by landscape architect Doan Ogden, the gardens are an ecological haven. The many "rooms" are planted to reflect different environments of the mountains, including the Wildflower Trail, the Heath Cove, and the Fern and Moss Trail. Spring blooms peak in mid-April, but the Gardens are an absolutely lovely and visually rich place to visit any time of year. Because of its serious mission of plant preservation, neither pets nor bicycles are allowed. Admission is free, but as the gardens are entirely supported by donations, your contribution will have a real impact. On the first Saturday in May, the **Day in the Gardens** brings food and music to this normally placid park, and garden and nature enthusiasts from all around come to tour and to buy native plants for their home gardens. There is also a visitors center and gift shop (11am-3pm daily).

WESTERN NORTH CAROLINA NATURE CENTER

Asheville, and western North Carolina generally, tend to be very ecologically conscious, as reflected in the **Western North Carolina Nature Center** (75 Gashes Creek Rd., 828/259-8080, www.wildwnc.org,

10am-4:30pm daily, closed Thanksgiving Day, Dec. 24-25, and Jan. 1, $14 adults, $13 over age 64, $14 ages 13-15, $10 ages 3-12, free under age 3, discounts for locals). On the grounds of an old zoo—don't worry, it's not depressing—wild animals that are unable to survive in the wild due to injury or having been raised as pets live in wooded habitats on public display. This is the place to see some of the mountains' rarest species—those that even most lifelong mountain residents have never seen: cougars, wolves, coyotes, bobcats, and even the elusive hellbender. What's a hellbender, you ask? Come to the Nature Center to find out.

★ FOLK ART CENTER

Anyone with an interest in Appalachian handicrafts and folk or fine art should stop by the **Folk Art Center** (382 Blue Ridge Parkway, Milepost 382, 828/298-7928, www.southernhighlandguild.org, 10am-5pm daily, free). Home to the Southern Highland Craft Guild, the Folk Art Center has around 30,000 square feet of space that includes three galleries, an auditorium, a research library, a tiny Blue Ridge Parkway info booth, and the **Allanstand Craft Shop,** oldest continuously operated craft shop in the United States. It was started in 1897 by a Presbyterian missionary and carries out the same vision it had the year it was born: to help preserve traditional art forms and raise the visibility of the arts and crafts of the Appalachian Mountains. Although the folk arts are well represented in beautiful pottery, baskets, weaving, and quilts, you'll also find the work of contemporary studio artists in an array of media, including gorgeous handcrafted furniture, clothing, jewelry, and toys. Bring your holiday shopping list even if it's April. Every day, one or more members of the Southern Highlands Craft Guild is on hand to demonstrate their craft at the entrance to the Folk Art Center. They may be whittling away at a chunk of wood with their pocketknife, spinning wool into yarn, weaving, or tying brooms. No matter what they're doing, they're happy to talk to you and explain their process and the history of their craft.

SPORTS AND RECREATION

Asheville's a very active town and it's not unusual to see cars loaded with kayaks, mountain bikes, platform tents, or hauling little camper trailers as folks head off for adventures. With the Blue Ridge Parkway ringing the city to the south and east, with Great Smoky Mountains National Park a short drive away, and with the huge Pisgah National Forest and all its waterfalls and hiking-biking trails, it's no wonder folks use Asheville as a basecamp. But there's plenty to do in town too. The French Broad River is home to kayakers and packs of people floating on tubes. On the Biltmore Estate there are more than 40 miles of hiking and biking trails. And there are tours to take that will lead you to an afternoon of superb food and beer, get you out into lovely parts of town, and give you a better perspective on Asheville and on yourself.

For visitors to Asheville, this city looks like a perfect mountain playground: plenty of hiking and waterfalls and scenery to take in, too many restaurants to visit in a week, art galleries and boutiques and something wonderful to discover everywhere you look. But things haven't always been so rosy, especially not for all of Asheville. One of the most eye-opening and impactful looks I've had at Asheville and its history came courtesy of DeWayne Barton and his **Hood Huggers Tour** (828/275-5305, www.hoodhuggers.com, $25 adults, $15 ages 4-15). Hood Huggers tells the unvarnished story of Black Asheville, from the triumphs and points of pride to the darkest moments and ongoing moves toward equality and Black opportunity. Barton leads three tours, one starting on the Block, the former heart of Black entrepreneurship and enterprise in Asheville (meet at the Foundry Hotel); another on Burton Street, the center of one of the city's oldest Black communities; and the Southside Walking tour focused on Black Commerce. Tours take a couple of hours and lead you to locations where Barton, through stories and photographs, makes the place come alive, tying contemporary issues (like the Black Lives Matter movement) to historic ones (like redlining) to environmental issues (the ways bad policies impact minority communities) and what we can do today to ensure lasting change comes on our watch.

★ Hiking

Ready for mountain air? Join **Blue Ridge Hiking Co.** (70 College St., 828/713-5451, http://blueridgehikingco.com) for a hike. Founder Jennifer Pharr Davis has hiked more than 11,000 miles of long-distance trails and was the first woman to become the overall record holder for fastest through-hike of the Appalachian Trail, hiking all 2,181 miles in 46.5 days. You're not expected to have this kind of trail mobility or backpacking savvy, but Blue Ridge Hiking Co. is there to help you learn to love a hike, long or short. Join them on a private day hike or sunset hike ($190 for 1-3 hikers, $35 per additional hiker), a group half-day hike ($80), a private full-day hike ($290 for 1-3 hikers, $50 per additional hiker), the Brew + Brew hike ($400 for 1-3 hikers, $60 per additional hiker), led by Jennifer's husband, Brew, and ending at some Asheville breweries, or an overnight hike ($300-930). The overnight hikes are often themed—women only, 50- or 60-plus, low intensity, orienteering workshops, high peaks—so pick one from their current calendar or work with the team to create a private overnight trip perfect for you and your group. One of the places the team at Blue Ridge Hiking Co. goes is the little town of Hot Springs north of Asheville. It's easy to access the Appalachian Trail here and to find hikes good for beginners or to challenge trail pros, so they've set up the **Appalachian Trail-er Bunkhouse,** a mobile home turned bunkhouse serving AT hikers, and they have a hiking shuttle (828/622-3319).

Asheville Hiking Tours (828/818-9103, www.ashevillehikingtours.com, $55-119) leads waterfall and Blue Ridge Parkway tours and wildflower and birding walks along trails in the Roan Highlands and other wild places nearby, as well as private guided hikes. In typical years, backpacking trips are also available (starting around $350) and are built around themes like fall color and destination-specific hikes. Their guides are experts in a number of fields—zoology, forest ecology, primitive skills—and are naturalists, storytellers, and experienced backpackers.

Hiking on the **Biltmore Estate** can mean anything from walking the 2.5 miles of mulched paths in the manicured gardens to exploring the hills, meadows, streams, and riverbank on more than 22 miles of trails. None are rugged, so you don't need any special equipment: just water, your camera, and maybe a walking stick. The Outdoor Adventure Center in Antler Hill Village has maps and can help you identify the right hike, or you can join a guided hike ($20 over age 8, free under age 9) along the French Broad River or through Westover Woods.

TOP EXPERIENCE

Zip-Lining

For a different perspective on the Asheville area, head north for 30 minutes along I-26 west and spend the day at **Navitat** (242 Poverty Branch Rd., Barnardsville, 855/628-4828 or 828/626-3700, www.navitat.com, 8am-6pm daily). You can streak through the forest canopy on a pair of zip-line courses like an overgrown flying squirrel. The **Mountaintop Tour** ($110) has the tallest zip line here; it's an incredible 350 feet high—they say "Don't look down," but do; it's amazing. The longest is more than 3,600 feet. Two rappels, a pair of sky bridges, and three short hikes provide interludes from all the zipping and flying, and there are plenty of opportunities for photos and action-camera videos. A smaller course, the **Treetop Tour** ($99) has six ziplines, rope descents, sky bridges, and timber stair climbs. Or you can **combine the two courses** ($190) into one giant day of

adventure. Not down with strapping yourself to a steel cable and hurtling through space? The **Guided RTV Shadow Tour** (from $50) lets you take in the scenery and follow the zippers from the ground, safe and secure in your RTV.

If you're tempted to zip-line but want something a little less heart-pounding, consider **The Adventure Center of Asheville** (85 Expo Dr., 877/247-5539, www.ashevilletreetopsadventurepark.com, check for times). The Adventure Center has a number of high-flying adventures to try. The **Treetops Adventure Park** ($55-76) has 60 challenges (read: rope swings, sky bridges, cargo nets, short zip lines, leaps from tall platforms) spread over five different adventure trails, allowing you to face the trail that presents you with the best challenges. The **Zip Line Canopy Tours** ($69-89) has 11 zips, three sky bridges, and so many great views you'll forget about the zip lines. **Kid Zip** ($55) is a zip-line course designed for children ages 4-10. There's also the **KOLO Mountain Bike Park** ($5-21 if you bring the bike, $20-69 with rental bike and gear), where you can build up your skills before you head out on some of the single-track trails south of town.

Biking

Take a tour of Asheville by bicycle. If you're thinking: "It's too hilly; I'll never be able to climb that," **The Flying Bike** (meeting point 225 Coxe Ave., 828/338-8484, www.flyingbiketours.com, from $59) can provide you with pedal-assisted electric bikes that make the hills easier and the flats seem like nothing at all. You'll still have to work, but not as hard as these ingenious bikes use their power to make pedaling easier. You'll start with the hill to the Grove Park Inn (which will demonstrate how well the pedal-assist system works), the first stop on a three-hour tour around Asheville's historic and cultural sites.

There are more than 20 miles of **bicycle trails** on the Biltmore Estate, and you can bring your bike or rent one in Antler Hill Village from the **Bike Barn** (828/225-1425,

2-hour rentals $20 regular bike, $30 electronic bike, half-day rentals $30 regular bike, $50 electronic bike adults, $20 regular bike under age 13) and lead your own trip. You can also join Biltmore guides for a guided ride on the **Farm Trail** ($35 over age 9, $10 under age 10), on the **West Range Loop** ($100 over age 15), or an **Intro to Mountain Biking** ($75, over age 11 only).

TOP EXPERIENCE

Water Sports

Wai Mauna Asheville SUP Tours (192 Riverside Dr., 828/808-9038, www.waimaunaashevillesuptours.com, rentals from $49, tours $85-99) is a natural fit for Asheville (*wai mauna* is Hawaiian for "mountain waters"). While most SUP outfitters ignore the two most beautiful parts of the day—dawn and dusk—these folks embrace it, with four tours daily at sunrise and sunset, as well as mid-morning and midday. As rave-worthy as sunsets are, there's something about the Dawn Patrol tour. At that time of day, the river is often shrouded in fog, the birds are waking up, and the river is as still as it will ever be; it's a perfect time to paddle. Most tours go through the River Arts District, but you can do a seven-mile trip through the Biltmore Estate, an interesting way to see the estate from a different angle.

Tubing isn't a sport, inasmuch as you simply recline in an inner tube and float from point A to point B, but it's a lot of fun. If you want to go tubing in Asheville, do it with **Zen Tubing** (855/936-8823, www.zentubing.com, trips 10am-3pm, $30). The French Broad is a calm river, especially on the sections where Zen sends their tubers (what else would you call one who rides a tube?). If you pick up a six-pack of your favorite canned (or plastic-bottled) beverage, you'll want the cooler carrier tube so you can keep any snacks and beverages close at hand. Tube trips take a while, but you'll have plenty of company, as the river is mobbed by tube enthusiasts. If you've got a crowd, check out their private

three-hour tour (don't worry, it won't end up like *Gilligan's Island*) aboard the Rasta Turtle (groups of 6-12, $55 pp), a river raft-picnic table hybrid that comes with snacks and a river guide who'll paddle you toward your destination. They have two locations, one in the **River Arts District** (608 Riverside Dr.) and one in **South Asheville** (1648 Brevard Rd.), so check the website or call ahead to see which one will be the best to visit.

French Broad Outfitters (704 Riverside Dr., 828/505-7371, www.frenchbroadoutfitters.com, 10am-6pm daily) rents gear and leads trips along the French Broad River. You can get active and go for a paddle on a 6-mile ($45) or 12-mile ($65) trip that can take you past the Biltmore Estate or the Biltmore and River Arts District (on the longer version); stand-up paddleboards available on some trips. You can paddle all manner of craft ($45-175) through the River Arts District on a 6-mile trip. Or you can just get lazy and float down the river in a tube ($25 over age 12, $12.50 ages 6-12); just don't forget the tube for the beer cooler ($5). You can also rent tubes (from $20), kayaks (from $35), paddleboards (from $45), and canoes (from $50), arrange for storage for you watercraft if you're in town for a while ($1 per day), rent bikes and pedal the greenway (from $30 adults, from $15 children), or rent the camping equipment you need for day trip into the woods or an overnighter (from $10).

Asheville Outdoor Center (521 Amboy Rd., 828/232-1970, www.ashevilleoutdoorcenter.com) rents kayaks ($50 over age 12, $40 ages 8-12, $45 military), tandem kayaks ($100), canoes ($100 for 2 paddlers), rafts ($180 for 4 paddlers, $45 per additional paddler), stand-up paddleboards ($70) and tubes ($20 half-day, $425 full day) to get you out on the water for a seven-mile self-guided tour. They also offer shuttle services ($20 per boat) and parking ($5, river access $5 per boat) if you plan on heading out for a long paddle.

Golf

Play a round at the 18-hole par-70 **Grove Park**

Inn Golf Club (828/252-2711 or 800/438-5800, reserve tee times at www.groveparkinn.com, greens fees $70-140 Mon.-Thurs., $70-155 Fri.-Sun. Apr.-Nov. 15, $77-87 Nov. 16-Mar., discounted rates for junior golfers, rental clubs $55 for 9 holes, $80 for 18 holes), where President Obama played during his 2010 stay. *Golf Digest* named this course one of the top 10 courses that are at least 100 years old, and it plays beautifully. This is a must-play course for serious golfers, not just because the views are spectacular but also because the course contains so much history.

Other Outdoor Activities

The Biltmore is an Orvis-endorsed **fly-fishing school,** and it's an excellent place to learn or hone your technique. Outings include introductory lessons ($125), half-day lessons ($225), a kid's fishing outings ($125), a fly-tying class ($100), and full-day guided fishing trips on the French Broad River ($500); no fishing license is required.

For a loud, blood-pumping good time, try **clay target shooting** ($100-750). If you've never handled a shotgun before or have never shot clay targets, the introductory sporting clays lesson will have you on target in no time. For more experienced shooters, two-hour advanced lessons, a sporting clay course, and even full-day shotgun sports clinics will challenge your skills and help you refine them. If you'd still like to shoot at some targets but would rather not shoot a firearm, try archery ($45) and get a little coaching on your stance, pull, and release to see how you do with a bow in your hands. All equipment is provided for activities on the Biltmore Estate, except your hiking shoes. Stop in at the **Outdoor Adventure Center** (828/225-1425) in Antler Hill Village for the full scoop.

1: zipping on the heart-pounding Blue Ridge Experience at Navitat **2:** floating down the French Broad River with Zen Tubing

ENTERTAINMENT AND EVENTS
Nightlife
★ LIVE MUSIC

Great live music is the rule rather than the exception in Asheville, in the form of national touring acts as well as regional and local bands that give them stiff competition for audiences on any given night. It seems that everywhere you turn in this town, you'll find live musicians—buskers playing on street corners, solo guitarists in cafés, or a bluegrass trio set up on a restaurant deck. Follow the sound of drums to **Pritchard Park** (Patton Ave. at Haywood St. and College St.), where a huge drum circle forms every Friday night. There are also formal music venues where you can hear rock, jam bands, bluegrass, funk, blues, country, rockabilly, alt-country, mountain swing, old-time music, and electronica.

A favorite spot for live music is the **Orange Peel Social Aid and Pleasure Club** (101 Biltmore Ave., 828/398-1837, www.theorangepeel.net, noon-midnight or later daily). The Orange Peel is a cool concert hall with a big dance floor, great sound, and great history. It's billed as "the nation's premier live music hall and concert venue," and can back that up with some powerful acts taking the stage, including Bob Dylan, Smashing Pumpkins, Shovels and Rope, Ministry, Lettuce, The Wood Brothers, Girl in Red, Joe Russo's Almost Dead, Beach House, Bon Iver, and My Morning Jacket.

Asheville has another super cool music venue: **Rabbit Rabbit** (75 Coxe Ave., 828/255-4077, www.rabbitrabbitavl.com) Acts like Trey Anastasio Band, King Gizzard & the Lizard Wizard, Band of Horses, Bright Eyes, Sylvan Esso, and stand-up comedy shows frequent this spot, as do food trucks. On nights when there's not a big act in town, you'll find trivia, silent cinema, and silent discos (where attendees wear headphones), and of course the house kitchen dishing up tacos, burritos, and the like ($3-9).

Because you can't have too many places to see live music, there's also the **Salvage Station** (468 Riverside Dr., 828/707-8902, www.salvagestation.com), a salvage yard turned music venue. A big outdoor stage and lawn and a smaller indoor stage and setup give you plenty of space to spread out for a show. They've got a restaurant on-site, **Root Down Kitchen** (www.salvagestation.com, open during shows, $3-13), selling New Orleans-inspired food-truck grub with vegetarian, vegan, and gluten free options; several full bars, featuring loads of Asheville beers, keep the libations flowing. Acts include The String Cheese Incident, Doom Flamingo, and Goose as well as the **Brewgrass Music Festival** (www.brewgrassfestival.com) in fall.

WINE AND COCKTAILS

Asheville has a growing reputation as a craft-cocktail destination to match its food renown, and one big contributor to that movement is **Sovereign Remedies** (29 N. Market St., 828/919-9518, www.sovereignremedies.com, 5pm-10pm Wed.-Sun.). The minute it opened its doors, it became a go-to for Asheville's cocktail lovers and those hankering for de-licious food ($9-35). It serves dinner most nights, brunch on weekends, and light bites in between. Between the bartenders and some local foragers, Sovereign Remedies stays stocked with wild herbs, berries, fruits, and roots, used to infuse or macerate various li-quors and craft bitters and to create drink-ing vinegars. If it's not busy, have a seat and chat with the bartenders, and challenge them to create tasty drinks for you based around a certain spirit.

Taste natural wines and ciders at **Botanist & Barrel** (32 Broadway St., Suite 110, 828/338-9516, www.botanistandbarrelasheville.com, 1pm-8pm Mon.-Fri., 11am-8pm Sat.-Sun., $2-50) where they keep more than two dozen on hand to taste and another 300 or so bottles from across the state and the South. Natural wine or cider, which you'll sometimes see marked *pét-nat,* is a light sparkling drink that gets the fizz from the bottling process (they bottle it before the first fermentation is finished, so the natural carbon dioxide re-leased as fermentation is trapped in the bottle,

giving it the bubbles), and here they have a great selection if you're already keen on this type of wine or if you need or order a flight and learn the ropes. So order up a flight and some snacks to go with it—bowls of olives or chips, platters of dairy or vegan cheese, sand-wiches, even tinned seafood or a tinned sea-food tower, and you can add caviar ($75) if you're feeling fancy.

Over at **The Barksdale** (42 Banks Ave., 828/424-7449, 3:30pm-2am daily, $3-6), Asheville's, well, Asheville side, is on display. Quirky, friendly, weird, and certainly in full grasp of its own personality, The Barksdale is one of those places you were going to end up anyway, so why not start the evening here? They serve hot dogs named after former pro wrestlers and topped with odd toppings (fried pickle and ranch seasoned popcorn, kimchi chowchow and white Korean barbecue sauce, a dusting of blue and red Takis tortilla chips) and that, if anything, is a good indication of what's happening here.

Grab a cocktail—classic or modern—at **Top of the Monk** (92 Patton Ave., 828/254-5470, www.thirsty-monk-brewery.square.site, 4pm-10pm Sun.-Mon., 4pm-11pm Wed.-Sat.), where they've got a massive library of whis-key (this may be the biggest whiskey library in Asheville, and if it's not the biggest, it's in the top three) and some amazing views of downtown and the mountains in the distance. Cocktails are great, the view is excellent, and the people have always been awesome. This place is trying to keep it small and intimate, so if you're in a big group—more than seven people—know they discourage large parties after 7pm on weekends; oh, and as they say on the website, "no hootin' n' hollerin'!" If you're more in the mood for beer, head downstairs to the original **Thirsty Monk & Delirium Bar** (4pm-10pm Thurs., noon-midnight Fri.-Sat., 2pm-9pm Sun.), a two-story bar where the first floor focuses on domestic and local beers, and the downstairs Delirium Bar that has a Belgian focus.

Asheville has North Carolina's old-est gay bar, **o.henry's** (237 Haywood St.,

828/254-1891, www.ohenrysofasheville. com, 4pm-2am daily). A landmark unto itself, o.henry's hosts drag shows on Saturday, throws a potluck on the first Sunday of the month, and does Karaoke on Wednesday. They also have **The Underground,** an industrial dance bar known for its "Total Gold Dance Your Ass Off" parties held the first Friday of the month. If you want more drag shows to attend, **Scandals Nightclub** (11 Grove St., 828/505-1612, www.scandals-nightclub.com, 10pm-2:30am Fri.-Sat.) has your back. Drag shows with known queens and up-and-comers plus DJ-led dance parties make it a raucous spot all weekend.

Travel writers get all sorts of tips from friends and readers, and I found **The Crow & Quill** (106 N. Lexington Ave., 828/505-2866, www.thecrowandquill.com, 5pm-midnight Tues.-Sun.) through just such a recommendation—and am I ever glad I listened. It stocks nearly 1,000 spirits, and the wizards behind the bar know how to use every one of them. The cocktails are superb, the space is lively (you might catch some live music here), and everywhere you look there's some interesting bit of art. Note that at least one member of your party will have to become a member of The Crow & Quill, and pay a small membership fee ($10)—North Carolina has some rigid laws regarding spirits, and technically only private clubs are permitted serve them. Buy a drink for whoever ponies up.

BREWERIES

Asheville earned the title Beer City USA for several years running and has been a contender for the title in subsequent years. It seems there's a brewery on every corner, or one planning to open there next month, and brewers are getting experimental, introducing new styles, funky ingredients, and any little twist they can to get people talking. And they do; loyal locals and pint hounds from all over frequent the bars, breweries, and pubs here.

Hi-Wire Brewing (www.hiwirebrewing.com) came into Asheville with one location on the **South Slope** (197 Hilliard Ave.,

828/738-2452, 3pm-10pm Mon.-Thurs., 3pm-midnight Fri., noon-midnight Sat., noon-10pm Sun.), called the **Big Top** (2 Huntsman Place, 3pm-10pm Mon.-Fri., noon-midnight Sat., noon-9pm Sun.) near Biltmore Village, and a third, the **RAD Beer Garden** (284 Lyman St., 828/738-2454, 3pm-10pm Mon.-Fri., noon-10pm Sat., noon-9pm Sun.), in the River Arts District. They focus on lagers, pale ales, and IPAs, and I quite like their American Lager, the Bed of Nails brown ale, and the Lo-Pitch IPA.

Burial Beer Co. (40 Collier Ave., 828/475-2739, www.burialbeer.com, noon-11pm daily) is a favorite biergarten spaces in Asheville, and they have an Instagram-worthy mural of Sloth from *The Goonies* and Magnum P.I. on one wall of the brewery. And then their beers. Start with the names—The Fortress of Immaculate Thought, A Portal Into Infinite Nonexistence, Mythologies of Realism—they're improbably weird but perfectly fit the brews. Now, for what's in the glass; Burial isn't afraid of any style or flavor, so you'll find s'mores-inspired barrel aged imperial stouts; rich double IPAs infused with wine grapes or peaches and mangoes; IPAs with orange or pineapple sage; and coffee saisons.

Colorado's **New Belgium Brewing Company** (21 Craven St., 828/333-6900, www.newbelgium.com, noon-8pm Thurs.-Mon., tours every hour on the half hour11:30am-4:30pm Thurs.-Mon.) found an East Coast home in Asheville. It sits across the French Broad from the River Arts District and has great views. It is bikeable and very bike-friendly, and their brews on offer go beyond Fat Tire and the other cans you find in stores. They show off their top-notch barrel-aging program with a slate of ever-changing and always-delicious brews like their Carnie Blood Golden Sour, Transalantique Kriek, and La Folie Sour Flanders Ale.

DSSOLVR (63 N. Lexington Ave., Asheville, 4pm-10pm Mon.-Thurs., 1pm-11pm Fri., 11am-11pm Sat., 11am-9pm Sun.) says they're more than just a brewery, they're a beverage company, and given what you find on their tap list, they're making good on that promise. A kölsch and schwarzbier share menu space with a foraged fruit-laden wild cider, a double dry-hopped hazy IPA, funky aged IPAs, fruited sours, and more. They've got a cellar dedicated to funky and wild brews, a tiny brewhouse where they can experiment, and their regular production brewhouse. It all makes for a wildly delicious stop on your beer tour. With a heated patio, they're a great visit anytime you're in town.

In West Asheville (conveniently across the street from one of my favorite restaurants, The Admiral), **Cellarest Beer Project** (395 Haywood Rd., www.cellarestbeer.com, 5pm-9pm Mon.-Thurs., noon-10pm Fri.-Sat., noon-8pm Sun.) serves barrel-rested beer imbued with and inspired by local ingredients. They capture wild yeast to pitch into their farmhouse-inspired beers and serve everything from tart and tasty wild ales to Vienna lagers to golden farmhouse ales, IPAs, and some delightful blended farmhouse brews. Their outdoor space is spacious and hip, and if you're hungry, **West Asheville Lounge and Kitchen** (401 Haywood Rd., 828/505-7929, 11:30am-10pm Mon.-Thurs., 11:30am-11pm Fri.-Sat., 10:30am-10pm Sun., $3-15) is right next door and serves plenty of food to Cellarest customers, so you can pick up some chips and salsa, wings, chicken tendies, *queso* fries, or a big sandwich and wash it down with a beer or two.

Also in Mills River is **Burning Blush Brewery** (4891 Boylston Hwy., Mills River, 828/595-9859, www.burningblush.com, noon-9pm Mon.-Thurs., noon-10pm Fri.-Sat., noon-8pm Sun.), a spot recommended to me by a brewer friend and one I've come to love. Their beers are on point in terms of style and flavor, so whether you're going for their Helles, a rice and corn American lager, their Belgian Amber Strong, or something like a juicy or double IPA, you'll find an exemplary beer in your glass.

Asheville's oldest brewery, **Highland Brewing** (12 Old Charlotte Hwy., Suite 200, 828/299-3370, www.highlandbrewing.com,

2pm-9pm Mon.-Thurs., noon-10pm Fri.-Sat., noon-7pm Sun.) poured their first pint back in 1994, beginning to build a reputation that's made them one of the best and most consistent breweries in North Carolina in addition to being one of the first crop of breweries to spring up in the state. Visiting their taproom is an experience. They have a large meadow with a stage and bar where you can catch a show or have a picnic (or both), and there are volleyball courts, a hiking trail, and a disc golf course. The taproom pours all the flagship (the Gaelic Ale was Asheville's first beer, but I'm partial to the pilsner and High Pines Imperial IPA) and seasonal brews (October's Clawhammer Marzen is a favorite) as well as a frequently rotating list of experimental brews. They have an additional taproom downtown in **S&W Market** (56 Patton Ave., 3pm-8:30pm Tues.-Thurs., 11:30am-9pm Fri.-Sat., 3pm-7pm Sun.), with a small bar downstairs and a larger, showier bar upstairs where you'll find more taps and more room to spread out and enjoy yourself.

One of my favorite ways to get to know a city's food or beer scene is to join a tour. Asheville, naturally, has several to choose from, the best being **Asheville Brewery Tours** (828/233-5006, www.ashevillebrewerytours.com, Wed.-Sun.). Asheville Brewery Tours offers three ways to see the city: their Downtown "Brew & Chew" Walking tour ($89, $49 nondrinker) to eight places, including four breweries; the Downtown 3-Brewery Walking Tour ($69, $29 nondrinker), which is exactly what it sounds like; and the Mobile Brewery Tour (inquire for prices), where they drive you around for an afternoon of beer tasting. They also book private three-brewery ($79 pp) and four-brewery ($89 pp) tours. They visit a lot of the breweries I've already mentioned on their tours, along with **Archetype Brewing** (www.archetypebrewing.com, 174 Broadway St., 828/505-8305, 5pm-9pm Mon.-Wed., 5pm-10pm Thurs., 4pm-8pm Sun; 265 Haywood Rd., West Asheville, 828/505-4177, 3pm-9pm Mon.-Thurs., 1pm-10pm Fri., 11am-10pm Sat., 11am-8pm Sun.), **Oyster House**

Brewing Company (625 Haywood Rd., West Asheville, 828/575-9370, www.oysterhouse-beers.com, 3pm-11pm Mon.-Fri., 11am-11pm Sat.-Sun.), and others.

Beer lovers should absolutely pick up some bottles and cans while they're at the brewery, but the bottle shop to check out is **Appalachian Vintner** (745 Biltmore Ave., 828/505-7500, www.appalachianvintner.com, 11am-7pm Mon.-Sat.). Their selection of beer ranges from hard-to-find European bottles (like Vichtenaar, my favorite beer ever) to the best of craft beer from across the United States, and that means plenty of representation from Asheville and from North Carolina. Not sure what you want? Strike up a conversation with the folks in the shop and let them lead you to a tasty discovery or two.

Comedy

Around Asheville you may notice a giant purple bus zipping through the streets, laughter and bubbles (yes, bubbles) coming from the windows. That's the **LaZoom Comedy Tour** (76 Biltmore Ave., 828/225-6932, www.lazoomtours.com, $39, minimum age 13), delivering tours big in history and hilarity. The tour guides are outrageous—they're some of Asheville's weirdest (in a good way) people—and I guarantee you'll learn a thing or two: some history, a joke you may or may not want to tell your mom. They also offer Ghosted: Haunted Comedy Tour ($37), which adds in a supernatural note and tales of some of Asheville's spectral denizens, and the Fender Bender: Band & Beer Bus Tour ($49) visits a trio of area breweries for samples and some live music from local performers. In 2022 they added the Li'l Boogers: Kids Comedy Tour ($27) a hilarious all-ages tour, perfect for the funny kids, the ones who get caught in a fit of giggles, the performers, and the silly.

Performing Arts

As an artsy town, Asheville has a lively theater and dance community. **Terpsicorps Theatre of Dance** (www.terpsicorps.org), a professional dance company and school, puts on a number of shows a year, as does **Asheville Ballet** (www.ashevilleballet.com), which puts on The Nutcracker every year. **NC Stage Company** (828/239-0263, www.ncstage.org) performs many times throughout the year, staging contemporary, classic, and holiday performances, and **Asheville Community Theatre** (www.ashevilletheatre.org) draws on the deep well of talent in town to put on performances like Avenue Q, Footloose, Alice in Wonderland, and other surprising shows.

Festivals

In mid-October, the Southern Highland Craft Guild hosts the **Craft Fair of the Southern Highlands** (Harrah's Cherokee Center, 87 Haywood St., 828/298-7928, www.southern-highlandguild.org, 10am-6pm Thurs.-Sat., 10am-5pm Sun., $10 adults, free under age 12). Since 1948 this event has brought much-deserved attention to the guild's more than 900 members, who live and work throughout the Appalachian Mountains. Hundreds of craftspeople participate in the event, selling all sorts of handmade items. This event used to happen twice a year, with an additional in-person event in late July, but with pandemic-related precautions in place, it has been scaled back, and the July event has moved online, though there are plans to return to the pair of in-person events soon.

Probably the biggest of Asheville's festivals and fairs, or at least the most anticipated, is the annual **Warren Haynes Christmas Jam** (www.xmasjam.com). Warren Haynes, longtime guitarist for the Allman Brothers Band, founding member of Government Mule, and Asheville native, invites a who's who of musical acts to come perform a benefit concert for Habitat for Humanity. The acts are generally biggies in the rock-jam world and bands on the rise.

Asheville's **Restaurant Week** (www.ashevillerestaurantweek.com) generally takes place in late January. Given the city's food scene, it's a great opportunity to score some delicious meals at a bit of a discount; usually restaurants offer a prix fixe menu for $15-30.

George Vanderbilt's Great Outdoors

The thing that drew George Vanderbilt to Asheville was the mountain air and glories of nature that surround this place. The Biltmore Estate was once a huge estate of some 125,000 acres, almost every bit of it untamed. Frederick Law Olmsted worked to groom the forest around the house, the same forest you see when you drive onto the estate, but the rest was left to be a sort of natural playground. Today visitors can play in the forests, fields, trails, and waters of the Biltmore Estate and try their hand at sports and activities from the familiar (bicycling) to the exotic (the Land Rover Experience Driving School). The Adventure Center (828/225-1425) in Antler Hill Village can make reservations and point you in the right direction for any number of outdoor activities.

The 22 miles of hiking and biking trails take you all across the estate, from Antler Hill Village to the house and gardens and back. Paved and wooded trails allow all experience levels to get out and ride, run, or hike. You're free to explore the hiking trails at no cost, but you can join guided hikes ($20 over age 8, free under age 9) of the Westover Woods and a stroll along the French Broad River. Rent a bike (from $10 per hour) or bring your own and explore the 20-plus miles of bike trails on the estate. Guided rides along the Farm Trail ($35 over age 9, $10 under age 10) and the West Range Loop ($100 over age 15), and an Intro to Mountain Biking class ($75 over age 11) are great ways to spend some time in the saddle and see a new side of the Biltmore.

Equine enthusiasts can saddle up for an hour-long guided ride ($75), a two-hour private trail ride ($195), or a private trail ride and picnic lunch ($230). If you'd rather sit back and ride, there are carriage rides ($350 up to 4 people) and wagon rides (from $35) too.

If you'd rather spend the day on the water, you can. Guided raft trips ($30) and self-guided kayak trips ($30) on the French Broad give you a rare view of the estate, while a day on the water fly-fishing gives you a different experience altogether. Novice anglers may want a lesson (from $125, children's lessons available), but experienced anglers will opt for a day-long wade trip or drift boat trip ($500).

For something really adventurous, try learning to shoot sporting clays. If you've never handled a firearm, don't worry; they've got lessons ($100-247), and they'll have you knocking clay pigeons out of the sky in no time. There's also a Sporting Clay course ($100) and a full-day shotgun sports clinic ($750). Then there's the Land Rover Driving Experience. Get behind the wheel of a Land Rover and get a lesson ($275 for 1 hour, $425 for 2 hours) on off-road driving. After your lessons, go out for a full day ($1,200) and master those off-road skills while exploring a seldom-seen side of the estate property.

The one-day Beer City Festival (www.beercityfestival.com) in late-May or early-June makes for a great way to celebrate the start of summer and hear some live music while sampling some brews from across the region.

See the gardens and grounds at Biltmore when they're in truly show-stopping form at Biltmore Blooms (www.biltmore.com, Apr.-May). One look at the gardens and you'll think there are billions of bulbs and bushes blooming, and you're probably not far off. Tulips, orchids, azaleas, and hundreds of roses, vines, locals, and exotics are at their showiest, making it a perfect time to visit the estate. Biltmore has events throughout the year, the biggest of which is Christmas at Biltmore and the Candlelight Christmas Evenings (early-Nov.-early-Jan.), which sees the home decorated for an 1895 Christmas complete with carolers and performers, candlelight tours, and more.

Asheville's home to Chow Chow (www.chowchowasheville.com, tickets $15-150), a food festival celebrating the flavors of Southern Appalachia. The city's biggest chefs and culinary personalities were joined by noted guest chefs Jose Andreas, Vivian Howard, Ashley Christensen and others for demos, tastings, charity dinners, and swank soirees. It's a great opportunity to taste outstanding dishes and meet some culinary legends. The festival takes place June-September with a calendar chock-full of events small and large. Check them out, pick a time packed with things to do, get your tickets, and go.

Hi-Wire Brewing's **NC Small Batch Festival** (www.hiwirebrewing.com, $10) brings a couple dozen North Carolina breweries to Hi-Wire's Big Top location in mid-March for a delightfully odd one-day beer fest. Breweries can only bring a small one-off batch to sample—no flagships, nothing you can get in the taproom, nothing folks outside the brewhouse have tasted. You'll be in for some interesting samples from some of the state's most progressive breweries.

In June, **GRINDfest** (www.blackwallstreetavl.com), a three-day festival celebrating Juneteenth, brings Black entrepreneurs and artists together for a community-wide event featuring a poetry slam, a lip-synch battle, food vendors, artists and craftspeople, and folks there to get the folks excited about and engaged. September sees some 20,000 people celebrating at the **Blue Ridge Pride Festival** (www.blueridgepride.org), where there's a parade, a street fair, a gender identity-inclusive pageant, and all sorts of mixers, storytelling events, gatherings, and performances built around championing the diversity and accomplishments of western North Carolina's LGBTQ+ community.

Combine your love for beer and bluegrass music at the Salvage Station's **Brewgrass Music Festival** (www.brewgrassfestival.com) in early October, when Asheville is stunning thanks to the autumn leaf show. It's a full day of music with indoor and outdoor stages and plenty of room to spread out, sample some suds, and start tapping your toes to that high, lonesome sound of banjos, fiddles, and flat-picked guitars.

The **Mountain Dance and Folk Festival** (828/258-6101, ext. 345, www.folkheritage.org, $25 adults, $5 students and under age 12) is the nation's longest-running folk festival, an event founded in the 1920s by musician and folklorist Bascom Lamar Lunsford

to celebrate the heritage of his native Carolina mountains. Musicians and dancers from western North Carolina perform at the UNC Asheville Lipinsky Hall for three nights each August. Also downtown, many of the same artists can be heard on Saturday evening at the city's **Shindig on the Green** concert series (Pack Square Park, 80 Court Plaza), a music bonanza that's been going on since 1967.

SHOPPING
Antiques
For lovers of vintage, retro and aged things, the **Antique Tobacco Barn** (75 Swannanoa River Rd., 828/252-7291, www.atbarn.com, 10am-6pm daily) has more than 77,000 square feet of goodies to plunder. This perpetual winner of the *Mountain XPress* "Best Antiques Store in Western North Carolina" category has toys, art, tools, furniture, radios, sporting equipment, folk art, farm relics, oddball bric-a-brac, mid-century furniture, and all those great weird things you can only find in a collection this large. It takes a while to explore this humongous shop, so carve out some time.

Sweeten Creek Antiques and Collectables (115 Sweeten Creek Rd., 828/277-6100, 10:30am-5:30pm Mon.-Sat., noon-5:30pm Sun.) and **Screen Door** (115 Fairview Rd., 828/277-3667, www.screendoorasheville.com, 10am-5pm Mon.-Sat., noon-5pm Sun.) offer a wide selection as their vendors and pickers number in the hundreds. Somewhere in the 36,000 square feet of repurposed and rediscovered treasures in **The Regeneration Station** (26 Glendale Ave., 828/505-1108, www.regenerationstation.com, 10am-6pm Mon.-Sat., 10am-5pm Sun.), you'll find the thing you're looking for whether it's a hip light fixture, a cool industrial relic that'll be perfect on your bookshelf, signage, or some piece of esoterica. The Regeneration Station was born from the useful excess one of the owners found in their other business, a junk removal company; storing up the best of his finds, it wasn't long before crafty and like-minded folks joined in and began to breathe new life into these old pieces and this excellent spot was born.

Along Swannanoa River Rd., you'll find yourself in the **Biltmore Antiques District** (120 Swannanoa Rd.), a small shopping district that's packed with an intriguing group of antiques shops. Some specialize in imports, others in lamps, European furniture, or fine jewelry. Exploring here is always a good time because you never know what you'll find or where you'll find it.

Galleries

One of Asheville's shopping highlights is the 1929 **Grove Arcade** (1 Page Ave., 828/252-7799, www.grovearcade.com), a beautiful and storied piece of architecture that is now a chic shopping and dining destination in the heart of downtown. The expansive Tudor Revival building, ornately filigreed inside and out in ivory-glazed terra-cotta, was initially planned as the base of a 14-story building, a skyscraper by that day's standard. There are some fantastic galleries and boutiques, including **Mountain Made** (828/350-0307, www.mtnmade.com, 10am-6pm Mon.-Sat., noon-5pm Sun.), a gallery celebrating contemporary art created in and inspired by the mountains around Asheville. Another favorite is **Alpaca Wawa** (828/505-0048, www.alpacawawa.com, 11am-6pm daily), a shop loaded with beautiful alpaca wool and pima cotton goods. Pick up some alpaca, llama, angora, or other yarn (most from local fiber-bearing animals) at **Asheville NC Home Crafts** (828/350-7556, www.ashevillehomecrafts.com, 10am-6pm Mon.-Sat., noon-5pm Sun.). There are more stores and restaurants to discover in Grove Arcade, so grab a little shop directory and sit down at **Battery Park Champagne Bar** (828/252-0020, 11am-9pm Mon.-Thurs., 11am-10pm Fri.-Sat., $3-25) to figure out your next move. Battery Park has two things that go great together: wine and books. And they serve food to share as well as sandwiches and salads, all in a really relaxed atmosphere. Outside the Grove Arcade is a row of shaded stalls, and it's here that you'll find many of

the best sell-it-on-the-street artisans selling things like soap, miniature topiaries you can wear as a necklace, and fine-art prints.

I own and have gifted several prints from **Horse and Hero** (14 Patton Ave., 828/505-2133, www.horseandhero.com, 11am-7pm Sun.-Thurs., 11am-9pm Fri.-Sat.), a gallery that's developed a niche in Neo-Appalachian art and crafts. Woodblock prints, lithographs, digital prints, stickers, cards, shirts, and even sculptural pieces that can only be described as contemporary riffs on traditional Appalachian art make it an intriguing place to browse and buy.

There are a number of galleries in downtown Asheville, and while most of them exhibit works from multiple artists, none can match the size of the **Woolworth Walk** (25 Haywood St., 828/254-9234, www.woolworth-walk.com, 11am-6pm Mon.-Sat., 11am-5pm Sun.), a two-story 20,000-square-foot gallery featuring more than 160 local artists. Nearly every conceivable medium is represented, including digitally designed graphic prints, oil paintings, watercolors, jewelry, and woodworking. This gallery is a favorite not just because it has a soda fountain but because the work on display is affordable and tasteful.

Working to keep the folkways, crafts, and artistic traditions of the Southern Appalachians relevant and thriving, the **Southern Highlands Crafts Guild** (www.southernhighlandguild.org) operates several galleries in the Asheville region, the most well-known of which is the **Allanstand Gift Shop** (382 Blue Ridge Pkwy., 828/298-7928, 10am-5pm daily), at the Folk Art Center on the Blue Ridge Parkway, but the gallery in **Biltmore Village** (26 Lodge St., 828/277-6222, 10am-5pm Mon.-Sat., noon-5pm Sun.) is outstanding. Housed in an old bank building, the gallery is almost as pleasing as the art and crafts inside. For sale here are quilts in traditional and new patterns; hand-woven baskets and brooms made in the traditional fashion; pens, bowls, boxes, sculptures, and vessels whittled, carved, and turned by woodworkers; plus pottery, paintings, and other works of art. Whether you're looking for a gift or a new piece for your home, you'll find gorgeous work in every case and on every wall.

Just off Pack Square, **Noir Collective** (39 S. Market St., Suite C, 828/484-2323, www.noircollectiveavlllc.business.site, 11am-4pm Wed.-Sat.) celebrates black artists and makers in their small boutique and gallery space. Asheville artists like Jenny Pickens have paintings and prints hanging here and at other galleries around town, and you'll find a selection of Afro-centric shirts, masks, jewelry, art, and goods on the walls and shelves. The space is a significant one as it sits on the Block, the onetime center for Black entrepreneurism and culture in Asheville, and it's good to see this and other Black-owned businesses returning.

Books, Toys, and Crafts

One of the social hubs of this city is **Malaprop's Bookstore and Café** (55 Haywood St., 800/441-9829, www.malaprops. com, 10am-6pm Mon.-Sat., 11am-4pm Sun.). This fun and progressive bookstore carries a deep selection of books that includes tomes by North Carolina authors and a particularly fine collection of regional authors. You'll find the requisite coffee bar and café with wireless internet access, making it a particularly good spot to hang out. It's bright and comfortable, and the staff are well versed in all sorts of literature, so they can help you find a local author you'll enjoy reading. People in all walks of Asheville life come to Malaprop's, so expect to see creative dressers, the tattooed, business types, artists, students, and grannies. They always keep signed copies on hand, and when authors like Wiley Cash, Taylor Brown, David Joy, and other North Carolina writers stop in for a reading, they leave behind a stack of autographed copies (I've been known to swoop in and sign a shelf full of books too), so look for those special signed books and check out their schedule to see if a writer you love is in town for a talk or reading while you're in Asheville.

Given that Asheville is in the middle of

some mountains loaded with semiprecious and precious gems, and that the town has a general hippie, crunchy, recharge-your-crystals-at-the-full-moon vibe, there are some excellent gem and crystal shops in town. The crystals are cool, but I'm drawn to the fossils—of fish, sea stars, plants, even teeth and claws and shells—on display and on sale. A favorite that my wife and I visit every time we're in town is **Cornerstone Minerals** (52 N. Lexington Ave., 828/225-3888, www.cornerstoneminerals.com, 11am-7pm Sun.-Mon., 11am-9pm Tues.-Thurs., 11am-9pm Fri.-Sat.) because I like to stare at their sheets of fossil-imbued stone, and my wife always finds some cool bauble here. There are huge, and breathtakingly beautiful crystals and geodes to admire and take home (if you don't mind an overweight carry-on bag) at **Points of Light Crystal and Mineral Gallery** (391 Merrimon Ave., 828/257-2626, www.pointsoflight.net, 10:30am-6pm Mon.-Sat.), just a few minutes north of downtown. The selection here is very well curated, meaning everything from their orbs, balls, bowls, and huge decorative crystals to their sculpted pieces and mineral specimens to their jewelry and crystal clusters are of the utmost quality.

The **Mast General Store** (15 Biltmore Ave., 828/232-1883, www.mastgeneralstore. com, 10am-6pm Mon.-Thurs., 10am-7pm Fri.-Sat., 11am-6pm Sun.) is an institution in western North Carolina and beyond. They call themselves a general store, but they mean it in a very contemporary way. Cast-iron cookware, penny candies, and Mast logo shirts and jackets sit alongside baskets and handmade crafts. A good selection of outdoor clothing and equipment can get you outfitted for some time in the woods, or you can fill up a bag with candy and eat it while you drive the Blue Ridge Parkway—your call.

Dancing Bear Toys (518 Kenilworth Rd., 800/659-8697, www.dancingbeartoys.com, 10am-6pm Mon.-Sat.) is located among the motels and chain restaurants out on U.S. 70 (Tunnel Rd.), but inside it has the ambience of a cozy village toy shop. Dancing Bear has toys for everyone from babies to silly grown-ups: a fabulous selection of Playmobil figures and accessories, Lego, Brio, and other favorite lines of European toys; beautiful stuffed animals of all sizes; all sorts of educational kits and games; and comical doodads.

Asheville's creative streak doesn't stop with the visual and performing arts. The culinary arts scene is the envy of the state, and that includes the sort of packaged foodstuffs made by passionate locals that allow you to take a bite of Asheville home with you. You'll find a handpicked selection of tasty culinary treats at Asheville Goods (7 Brevard Rd., 828/252-9175, www.ashevillegoods.com, 10:30am-2:20pm Tues.-Thurs., by appointment Mon.-Fri.), in West Asheville near Biscuit Head (it's convenient: eat a giant biscuit, then do a little shopping after). They also do gift baskets and boxes with preassembled options and some custom options.

Several gift shops are of the "I went there and got this cool T-shirt" variety, but being Asheville, most of the shirts and Asheville-emblazoned gear is actually good. At Instant Karma Asheville (36 N. Lexington Ave., 828/301-8187, www.instantkarmaasheville.com, 9am-7pm Sun.-Thurs., 9am-8pm Fri.-Sat.) it's a combo kitsch, hippie, college-kid souvenir shop where you can pick up a fridge magnet proclaiming some witty barb, a Grateful Dead shirt, a vegan-leather bag, and some incense. On Wall Street, Asheville Emporium (35 Wall St., 828/785-5722, www.asheville-emporium.com, 9:30am-6pm Mon.-Thurs., 10am-8:30pm Fri.-Sat., 9am-5:30pm Sun.) they have the touristy T-shirts plus handmade gifts, gourmet treats, and home goods made by local artisans. And at Madam Clutterbucket's Neurodiverse Universe (21 Battery Park Ave., Suite 101, 828/552-3013, www.madamclutterbuckets.com, 11am-7pm Sun.-Mon. and Wed.-Thurs., 11am-8pm Fri.-Sat.) you'll find some vintage goods (quirky glassware, weird ashtrays, and little decorative pieces) and weird items in a store that prides itself in employing neurodivergent individuals.

★ River Arts District

You can get your hands dirty, so to speak, in the River Arts District as some places offer hands-on art experiences. The North Carolina Glass Center (140 Roberts St., Suite C, 828/505-3552, www.ncglasscenter.org, 10am-5pm Sun.-Mon. and Wed.-Thurs., 10am-6pm Fri.-Sat.), a hot shop (that's a glass studio, so called because the place is full of furnaces and kilns) open to budding artists and the folks curious about making art out of glass. Classes range from 30-minute "make it and take it" classes ($65-80), where you might make a glass or paperweight, to half-day workshops ($200) to multi-week courses ($835) where you learn the ins and outs of the art. They also have a gallery stocked with objects made by the artists here. Odyssey Center for Ceramic Arts (236 Clingman Ave., www.odysseyclayworks.com, 10am-6pm daily, co-op gallery 11am-5pm Fri.-Sun.) is full of sculptors and teachers. Part of their mission is to promote artistic appreciation and the advancement of ceramic arts; they hold regular classes, workshops, and talks led by master ceramic artists.

Marquee (36 Foundry St., 828/989-1069, www.marqueeasheville.com, 10am-5pm Mon.-Sat., 11am-5pm Sun.) seeks to blend Asheville's vibrant creative spirit and the feel of a European street market, and though they're in a big warehouse, they manage to pull it off. Great home decor, eclectic vendors, and 50,000 square feet of booths and studios to explore make this a natural stop in the River Arts District. At the 1910 Cotton Mill Studios (122 Riverside Dr., www.cottonmillasheville.com, hours vary), several painters work alongside potters and jewelers. Riverview Station (191 Lyman St., www.riverviewstation.com, hours vary) is a circa-1896 building that houses the studios of a wonderful array of jewelers, ceramicists, furniture designers, painters, and photographers. Another favorite gallery is CURVE Studios & Gardens (3 River Arts Place, 828/388-3526, www.curvestudiosnc.com, most studios 11am-4pm Mon.-Sat.). A fun funky studio

South Slope and River Arts District

that has been around since before the River Arts District was a thing, and once a punk-rock club called Squashpile—you can't make up stuff like that—CURVE is home to encaustic painters, ceramic workers, jewelry designers, glass artists, fiber artists, and more. This is just a sampling of what's happening in the River Arts District; visit the website for detailed listings of the artists and their studios.

FOOD

No matter what you're craving, from Mediterranean to vegetarian, four-star to down-home, Asheville has eateries that both embrace the Southern traditions of its mountain home and explore well beyond its borders. This is a town that clearly loves its food, with more than 17 local tailgate farmers markets, more than 250 independent restaurants, and more breweries per capita than any other city in the United States (26 in town, 60 in the region as of this writing). Farmers work with restaurants to provide the highest-quality produce and meats, and artisanal bakers and cheese-makers supply their tasty foodstuffs to restaurants high and low.

With such a robust food scene, it can be hard to pick out where you want to go. For a sampling of the best of what Asheville has to offer the gastronome, take a walking tour with **Eating Asheville** (828/489-3266, http://eatingasheville.com, classic tour $69, high-roller tour $79, food and brewery tour $69). Tours stop in at six of Asheville's best farm-to-table restaurants for a taste of what they're cooking. Restaurants provide two drink pairings as well as a talk about their food philosophy and sometimes a chance to meet the chef. Their new Cold One tour makes five stops where you'll pair food and beer, two things Asheville's known for.

Downtown

★ **Cúrate** (13 Biltmore Ave., 828/239-2946, www.curatetapasbar.com, 4pm-10:30pm Sun. and Tues.-Thurs., 4pm-11pm Fri., 11am-11pm Sat., $5-28) is led by Chef Katie Button, a James Beard Award semifinalist who previously cooked at the legendary El Bulli restaurant in Spain. At Cúrate she serves a Spanish tapas menu, so you'll get to try a variety of flavors and textures. One of the best meals in the place is the Spanish Experience ($55, wine pairing $30), a multicourse feast that highlights the best of the menu. A number of vegan and gluten-free selections are also on the menu. The lively restaurant features a long bar that faces the kitchen, so you can watch Chef Button and her expert kitchen brigade work.

The Foundry Hotel sits in the center of Asheville's once-thriving Black neighborhood, the Block, and one restaurant pays homage to foods and flavors from Afrolachian (the portmanteau adopted by many Black Appalachians) cuisine and dishes from across the African diaspora: ★ **Benne on Eagle** (35 Eagle St., 828/552-8833, www.benneoneagle.com, $10-32). Chef John Fleer, of nearby Rhubarb, owns this spot, but he leans on his *chef de cuisine* and a team of legends in Asheville's Black culinary world to develop and execute the menu. And they do a phenomenal job. The menu changes constantly, but expect high-end execution of dishes like Haitian *griot* (pork shoulder), an East-African

veggie platter, pepper-pot stew, *fufu gnudi* and *maafe* sauce (casava-flour *gnudi* in a spicy peanut stew). The menu will be full of unfamiliar spices, ingredients, and phrases, but it's a delicious cultural and culinary exploration, and one I'm happy to tuck into any time I'm in Asheville.

Italian restaurant ★ **Cucina 24** (24 Wall St., 828/254-6170, www.cucina24restaurant.com, 5:30pm-9pm Sun.-Thurs., 5pm-10pm Fri.-Sat., $10-35), headed by Chef Brian Canipelli, is dedicated to sourcing as much as possible from local farms, ranches, and fisheries, and these ingredients are enticingly crafted into the restaurant's curated menu offerings. You can't go wrong no matter what you order, so go wild. Pizzas and veggies are roasted in a wood-fired oven, and pastas are made in-house and come with sauces to die for. Or let the chef decide for you and get the five-course chef's dinner ($60).

One of Asheville's most amazing restaurants—and that's quite the qualification given the food scene here—is **Rhubarb** (7 N. Pack Square, 828/785-1503, http://rhubarbasheville.com, 5pm-9:30pm Mon. and Thurs., 5pm-10pm Fri., 10:30am-2pm and 5pm-10pm Sat., 10:30am-2pm and 5pm-9:30pm Sun., $9-36). Chef John Fleer is a culinary magician with a kitchen full of talented cooks. The best farmed, foraged, and pasture-raised ingredients are used to create dishes like pork belly with daylily-walnut slaw, peanut-braised collard greens, and wood-roasted whole trout.

Friends first told me about **The Market Place** (20 Wall St., 828/252-4162, www.marketplace-restaurant.com, 5pm-9:30pm Mon.-Thurs., 5pm-10:30pm Fri., 10:30am-2:30pm and 5pm-10:30pm Sat., 10:30am-2:30pm and 5pm-9:30pm Sun., $6-55), but it was Chef-Owner William Dissen's appearance on National Geographic's *Gordon Ramsay: Uncharted*—when Chef Ramsay visited the Smoky Mountains near Asheville to talk traditional foods and culinary heritage—that sealed the deal. Dissen impressed Ramsay, who called him "one of the best chefs in the country," and I agree. Seasonal farm-driven dishes that aren't afraid to put a local protein, exotic spice, and foraged fruit, nut, or veggie on the plate together. It's an intriguing and delicious menu. Whether you want to share some truffle fries, kale fritters, or another small plate and pair it with a wood-grilled slab of steak or bit of yellowfin tuna, or if you just want to dive in and go for the lamb pappardelle and the wild mushroom ravioli, every bite you take will be bliss.

Early Girl Eatery (8 Wall St., 828/259-9292, ext. 1, www.earlygirleatery.com, 8am-8pm daily, $10-15) has caused a stir among area locavores and is gaining a following among visitors. More than half of the vegetables, meat, and fish used at Early Girl were raised or caught within 20 miles of the restaurant. The menu accommodates Asheville's large vegetarian and vegan contingent, but nonveg diners can feast on pan-fried trout with pecan butter, free-range chicken, or cheeseburgers made from hormone-free beef and topped with farmstead cheese, basil mayo, and all the fixings. Their breakfast, served all day, is among the best in Asheville. Their multigrain pancakes are out of this world. Wherever you are in town, you'll find an Early Girl, as they have locations in West Asheville (444 Haywood Rd., Suite 101, 828/259-9898, ext. 2) and South Asheville (1378 Hendersonville Rd., Suite A, 828/259-9292, ext. 3), as well as Downtown.

Take a good long look at the gorgeous art deco S&W Building when you stop by ★ **The S&W Market** (56 Patton Ave., 828/575-1500, www.swmarketavl.com, 11:30am-9pm Sun.-Mon. and Wed.-Thurs., 11:30am-10pm Fri.-Sat.) for a bite and a drink. Originally built to house the S&W Cafeteria, it is back to its original intentions. Several vendors occupy the space. **Highland Brewing** (www.highlandbrewing.com) has an outpost here. **Bun Intended** (www.bunintendedavl.com, $5-12) added this brick and mortar to their food truck and serves up *bao* and noodles, curry, and fried rice bowls. **Buxton Chicken Palace** (www.buxtonchickenpalace.com, $7-13), from chef and pit master Elliott Moss,

dishes up the best damn fried chicken sandwich you'll ever eat, plus a bourbon and Cheerwine slushie. **Peace Love Tacos** (www.mountainmadreavl.com, $4-6) serves up tacos with a side of positivity. **Farm Dogs** (www.farmdogsavl.com, $5-8) is a concept from the folks at Farmburger (around the corner) and has sausages and hot dogs made from local grass-fed beef. **The Hop Ice Cream** (www.hopicecreamnc.com, $3-6) has traditional and vegan ice cream options available, as well as coffee and other treats. And **The Times Bar** (828/774-5028, www.thetimesbarasheville.com, 4:30am-11pm Mon.-Tues., 10am-11pm Wed. and Sun., 10am-midnight Thurs., 10am-1am Fri.-Sat.) shakes up classic and inventive cocktails for your sipping enjoyment and offers a full coffee bar (Wed.-Sun.) to help wake you up or clear your foggy head.

Bouchon (62 N. Lexington Ave., 828/350-1140, www.ashevillebouchon.com, 5pm-9pm Sun.-Thurs., 5pm-10pm Fri.-Sat., $3.50-35) is a green restaurant. I don't mean they're cannabis-friendly (you'll have to wait a few years on that; North Carolina is still in the dark ages with respect to cannabis), I mean they're eco-friendly and they recycle or compost everything they can, so you can dine on some decadent French cuisine guilt-free. They serve small plates and entrée-size dishes, so whether you're there to share some fries and steak tartare, or if you're hungry for *moules frites,* or if boeuf bourguignon is the only thing that'll satisfy, make this hometown favorite your stop for dinner.

Local favorite **Chai Pani** (22 Battery Park Ave., 828/254-4003, www.chaipaniasheville.com, 11:30am-3:30pm Tues.-Sun., 5pm-9pm Tues.-Thurs., 5:30pm-9:30pm Fri.-Sun., $8-14) continues to win fans with its great food and cool atmosphere. Don't go expecting your typical Indian fare; it's inspired by Indian street food vendors and serves casual and affordable specialties from all over India, including lamb burgers, paneer and chicken and fish rolls, and more. The restaurant's name means "tea and water," a phrase that refers to a snack or a small gift, and, honestly, everything is so well

put together and so tastefully made, every bite is like a gift.

Mela (70 Lexington Ave., 828/225-8880, www.melaasheville.com, 11:30am-2:30pm and 5:30pm-9:30pm daily, $10-19) is one of the best Indian restaurants in North Carolina. The elaborate menu offers dozens of choices, combining cuisines of both northern and southern India with great meat, seafood, and vegetable dishes. The restaurant is dark and elegant, but the prices are surprisingly low; you can put together a great patchwork meal of appetizers, which start at $3, along with soup and roti. Don't miss the samosas.

A longtime late-night spot, **Rosetta's Kitchen** (116 N. Lexington Ave., 828/232-0738, www.rosettaskitchen.com, noon-9pm Tues.-Sun., $6-12) has been satisfying the hungry since 2002. There's so much to recommend about this place: The food is very good, it's all vegetarian and mostly vegan, and it's made with local produce in season. They compost everything that makes its way back to the kitchen, recycle all their trash, and make sure their used vegetable oil goes to power biodiesel cars—it's Asheville's signature countercultural reinterpretation of the South, and it's one of the best vegetarian places in town. Downstairs is **The Buchi Bar,** where they serve Buchi *kombucha* and *kombucha*-based cocktails, as well as beer, wine, cocktails, and all-natural sodas.

White Duck Taco Shop (12 Biltmore Ave., 828/232-9191, www.whiteducktacoshop.com, 11:30am-9pm Thurs.-Tues., $4-6) serves tacos that intrigue and delight. I know that sounds trite or overhyped, but White Duck lives up to every word. You can get jerk chicken, fried chicken, Korean beef *bulgogi* with kimchi, duck confit with mole and cranberry salsa, even a *bánh mì* tofu taco that tastes like the awesome Vietnamese sandwich. Priced so you can scarf down two or three without breaking the bank, they're just about perfect, but if you're a taco fan (who isn't?) and someone who

likes to try things that are a little left of center, this is your place. You'll find White Duck in a couple of other cities across the state, and at two other places in Asheville: the River Arts District (388 Riverside Dr., 828/254-1398) and south of Asheville in Arden (16 Miami Circle, Arden, 828/676-1859).

The vegetarian platter at **Jerusalem Garden Café** (78 Patton Ave., 828/254-0255, www.jerusalemgardencafe.com, 11am-8pm Tues.-Thurs., 11am-9pm Fri., 10am-9pm Sat., 10am-8pm Sun., $8-24) has become a favorite when my wife and I visit Asheville. Loaded with hummus, baba ghanoush, dolmas, tahini salad, and tabbouleh, it's a filling, sharable meal (as long as we add an order of pita), and honestly it's so good I've barely ventured beyond it on the menu. The falafel wrap is a great one, as is the chicken gyro, and every time I see the lamb shawarma or Jordanian chicken arrive on a neighboring table, I have a moment of regret, but that's quickly wiped away by another delicious bite.

Blue Dream Curry House (81 Patton Ave., 828/258-2500, www.bluedreamcurry.com, 11:30am-9pm Mon.-Thurs., 11:30am-10pm Fri., noon-10pm Sat., $7-12) is one I hope becomes an Asheville staple. They have a taco served on naan; they serve pickled peanuts in a spicy, curried, briny sauce; their curries are Japanese, Indian, Thai, and Peruvian; and they aren't afraid to offer up a couple of meat options on a veggie- and vegan-centered menu.

Just across the way from Blue Dream is **Red Ginger Dimsum & Tapas** (82 Patton Ave., 828/505-8688, www.redgingerasheville.com, 11:30am-3pm and 5pm-9pm Mon.-Thurs., 11:30am-3pm and 5pm-9:30pm Fri., 11:30am-9:30pm Sat., 11:30am-9pm Sun., $6-26), and if you're a fan of dumplings, it's a must-dine. The crystal shrimp dumplings, *gua bao* (Chinese pancake with pork belly), scallion pancake, and pan-fried vegetable dumplings are spectacular dishes to share.

You might think **Crave Dessert Bar** (41 N. Lexington Ave., Suite 100, 828/254-1974, www.cravedessertbar.com, 5pm-midnight

1: S&W Cafeteria **2:** Buxton Hall Barbecue **3:** Wall Street in downtown Asheville **4:** West Asheville's Cellarest Beer Project

Wed.-Sun., $2-32) is all sweets, all the time, but that's not the case; they just happen to have an absolute smorgasbord of sweets—boozy tiramisu, decadent chocolate mousse, a s'mores platter, churros, hot doughnuts, cheesecakes galore, a caramel pineapple upside-down cake with gold leaf, and cupcakes—to go with a menu of savory dishes—empanadas, poutine, barbecued jackfruit sliders, sharable flatbreads—so you can have a well-rounded meal. Their selection of dessert wines and *digestivos*, as well as reds, whites, bubbles, and beer, makes for the perfect compliment.

French Broad Chocolates (10 S. Pack Square, 828/252-4181, http://frenchbroadchocolates.com, 11am-10pm daily) describes itself as "a sacred space for chocophiles," and with its prominent location in Pack Square, hordes of chocophiles are getting in line to find out why this particular chocolatier has been the talk of the town for a decade. French Broad offers chocolate truffles, brownies, pastries, sipping chocolates, floats, bars, beans, and a laundry list of chocolate products nearly as long as the line here on a Friday night (and trust me, it's long). This is a true "bean-to-bar" chocolatier, as they roast their own cacao in a rooftop solar roaster at their nearby factory (821 Riverside Dr., 828/504-4996, tours noon and 2pm Mon.-Tues., noon, 2pm, and 4pm Wed.-Sat., chocolate tasting noon and 2pm Sun.), and it's getting closer to being a "farm-to-bar" chocolatier, as the owners also happen to own a cacao farm in Costa Rica that they hope to harvest any season now.

The Gourmet Chip Company (43½ Broadway St., 828/254-3335, www.gourmetchipcompany.com, 11am-5pm Thurs.-Tues., $7-12) has made me love potato chips again. They make chips fresh all day (and have a huge stack of potato sacks to prove it) and top them with some lovely and intriguing ingredients: goat cheese and sea salt, dehydrated apple cider vinegar and a balsamic reduction, dark chocolate and applewood smoked bacon, buffalo sauce and bleu cheese, honey and lavender. Served up in a paper cone, they're attractive and fun to eat. The only downside is that they're so good you'll want to eat them fast, and that means using both hands, which means you can't walk down the street gobbling these delicious chips. But you should sit over them for a while and savor them anyway.

South Slope and River Arts District

What's a trip to North Carolina without barbecue? ★ **Buxton Hall Barbecue** (32 Banks Ave., 828/232-7216, www.buxtonhall.com, 11:30am-3pm and 5:30pm-9pm Sun.-Thurs., 11:30am-3pm and 5:30pm-10pm Fri.-Sat., $15-20) is old-school barbecue at its best but with some modern takes on classic sides. In researching the menu, the Buxton crew crossed the Carolinas, dining in dozens of barbecue joints and testing countless recipes to create barbecue nirvana. Chicken bog (chicken, rice, sausage) from the South Carolina Lowcountry is on the menu along with South Carolina barbecue hash and eastern North Carolina wholehog barbecue. Also on the menu are smoked sausages, fried catfish, and smoked chicken. Meals are accompanied by an excellent selection of classic barbecue sides. I used to rave about their fried chicken sandwich, a truly exceptional meal, an I'd alternate between it and barbecue when I'd visit, but the opening of a sister restaurant, **Buxton Chicken Palace** (inside S&W Market, 56 Patton Ave., www.buxtonchickenpalace.com, 11:30am-9:30pm Tues.-Thurs., 11:30am-9pm Fri.-Sat., 11:30am-7pm Sun., $7-13), a spot dedicated to chicken sammies and chicken tendies as well as those bourbon and Cheerwine slushies, I can tuck into a plate of barbecue on every visit and save my chicken fix for another meal. Whatever you do, don't leave Asheville without eating at one of these places.

If you're in the mood for a killer hot dog, burger like no other, or a Cuban sandwich that will make you think about proposing marriage to the guy or gal operating the grill, or even a bologna sandwich (seriously), head to **Foothills Food Truck** (2 Huntsman Place, at Hi-Wire's Big Top, 828/606-9372, www.foothillslocalmeats.com, 4pm-8pm Mon.-Thurs.,

Craft Brews in Beer City

Asheville is regarded as the epicenter of North Carolina's beer and culinary scenes, and it's well deserved. Asheville itself is packed with award winning restaurants and breweries, and every time a new one opens, it makes the news. Winner of the title "Beer City USA" and perpetually at the top of any beer geek's list of cities to visit, Asheville's brewery scene is exemplary in terms of variety, innovation, and sheer volume. When you're in town you'll have no problem finding a brewery to visit, but this list will give you a head start on your search for the perfect brew.

- **Hi-Wire Brewing** (www.hiwirebrewing.com) has a trio of locations: on the **South Slope** (197 Hilliard Ave., 828/738-2452), where you'll find experimental quaffs to try; the **Big Top** (2A Huntsman Place, 828/738-2451), with their flagship brews and a great food truck; and the **River Arts District Beer Garden** (284 Lyman St., 828/738-2454), a fantastic beer garden.

- **Zillicoah Beer Company** (870 Riverside Dr., Woodfin, 828/424-7929, www.zillicoahbeer. com) is new to the scene but strong with beer aged in French oak, collaboration brews with local breweries, and an exceptional kölsch.

- **Bhramari Brewing Co.** (101 S. Lexington Ave., 828/214-7981, www.bhramaribrewing. com) delivers the unexpected: black gose with orange blossom, sour pale ales, dry hopped berlinerweisse, a sour beer that tastes like fruit punch, even a *foeder*-aged honey-infused beer.

- **Burial Beer Co.** (40 Collier Ave., 828/475-2739, www.burialbeer.com) makes intriguing brews with intriguing names. Their taproom, with its indoor and outdoor spaces, excellent food truck, and funky mural, make it a great place to stop and enjoy one of the double IPAs.

- **Highland Brewing Company** (12 Old Charlotte Hwy., Suite 200, 828/299-3370, www. highlandbrewing.com) has the honor of being the first microbrewery in Asheville, and it's a fine one. They continue to keep their flagship brews relevant by tweaking the recipes, but they also continue to innovate, releasing an impressive set of single-hop brews.

- **New Belgium Brewing Company** (21 Craven St., 828/333-6900, www.newbelgium. com) is one of the biggest in the area, and their tour is exceptional. Most craft beer fans know Fat Tire and their other brews, but the taproom here carries specialties and barrel-aged beers not available elsewhere.

- **Archetype Brewing** (www.archetypebrewing.com) has locations downtown (174 Broadway St., 828/505-8305) and in West Asheville (265 Haywood Rd., 828/505-4177) where you'll find their interpretations of Belgian beers like a saison, witbier, strong ale, and more.

- **Green Man Brewery** (27 Buxton Ave., 828/252-5502, www.greenmanbrewery.com) has lagers, fruity IPAs, even tart berlinerweisses, but their monster Rainmaker Double IPA is a hit, as are their barrel-aged and sour beers like Bootsy and Snozzberry.

- **DSSOLVR** (63 N. Lexington Ave., 828/515-4473, www.dssolvr.com) serves familiar styles with surprising twists from bourbon barrel aging to foraged ingredients to blending fermented grapes into old-world brews.

- **Black Mountain Brewing** (131 Broadway Ave., Black Mountain, 828/357-5010, www.black-mountainbrewing.com) pairs their spins on familiar styles with a tasty barbecue food truck.

- **Sierra Nevada Brewery** (100 Sierra Nevada Way, Mills River, 828/708-6176, www.sierranevada.com) was described to me as "the Taj Mahal of Beer" and "like Willy Wonka's factory, but with beer," and it lives up to that hype. There's a good restaurant on-site, a great tour, an impressive facility, and a *long* tap list that goes beyond what you expect from Sierra Nevada.

- **Oskar Blues Brewery** (342 Mountain Industrial Dr., Brevard, 828/883-2337, www.oskar-blues.com) is the East Coast outpost for this Colorado staple. Old Chub Scotch Ale, Mama's Little Yella Pils, and their Pinner IPA are made fresh here.

4pm-9pm Fri., noon-9pm Sat., noon-8pm Sun., $8-14). I love this place and it has become one of my go-tos in Asheville. We meet friends at Hi-Wire's Big Top, grab a couple of orders of poutine and a sandwich (their cheeseburger is crave-worthy), then enjoy the beer and food and company.

In the River Arts District, **The Bull and Beggar** (37 Paynes Way, 828/575-9443, www.thebullandbeggar.com, 5pm-9pm Sun.-Mon. and Thurs., 5pm-10pm Fri.-Sat., $10-80) has become the dinner spot of choice for those in the know. With a menu that runs from the raw bar to the $80 bone-in rib-eye for two, they serve rich, filling, French-inspired entrées along with a killer charcuterie platter and a list of sides ($4-8) that are meal-worthy in themselves. On Monday night they offer a $9.99 burger. When I once asked a friend if we should go, she was rendered temporarily speechless by her memory of the previous week's burger.

When President Obama was in Asheville (he stayed at the Grove Park, incidentally), he and the First Lady wanted barbecue, and the ribs from **12 Bones Smokehouse** (5 Foundry St., Suite 10, 828/253-4499, www.12bones.com, 11:30am-4:30pm Mon.-Fri., $8-32) were the only thing to satisfy their craving for 'cue (the Secret Service, I'm told, feasted on Luella's). You can get a full rack (that's 12 bones, hence the name), a half rack, or even a little baby-size three-bone sampler that'll whet your appetite for more. More includes pulled pork, smoked turkey, and smoked BLT sandwiches, plus platters and all those excellent sides. Another location is in Arden, south of Asheville (2350 Hendersonville Rd., Arden, 828/687-1395, 11:30am-4pm Tues.-Sat., takeout 11:30am-7:30pm Tues.-Sat.), where, like most things in Asheville, they have a **brewery** (828/214-9827, www.12bonesbrewing.com, noon-9pm Tues.-Sat., noon-7pm Sun.); the Stay Golden Light Lager is an ideal accompaniment to a rack of ribs, by the way.

In the River Arts District, **Vivian** (348 Depot St., 828/225-3497, www.vivianavl.

com, 5pm-9pm Thurs.-Sat., 10:30am-1:30pm Sun., $14-42) delights diners with impeccable French techniques and exceptional local ingredients. Think of seared duck, pork terrine, and scallop quenelle as well as venison osso buco, smoked oysters, and fried chicken. Stop by for brunch and you'll be delighted by their fried-chicken biscuit, the smoked lamb benedict, and the usual run of eggs, quiche, and smoked fish.

West Asheville

★ **The Admiral** (400 Haywood Rd., 828/252-2541, www.theadmiralasheville.com, 5pm-10pm Thurs.-Mon., $16-45) has been West Asheville's prime food destination since it opened in a humble cinderblock building in 2007. The kitchen is driven by talent and culinary curiosity. On the menu you'll find an ever-evolving collection of New American dishes, like a rib-eye with roasted potato and cabbage or half-chicken with Carolina Gold rice and pole beans. The Admiral also has a great cocktail program. The cozy spot is divey yet chic.

West Asheville's ★ **Jargon** (715 Haywood Rd., 828/785-1761, www.jargonrestaurant.com, 5pm-9pm Sun.-Thurs., 5pm-10pm Fri.-Sat., $12-45) is out to do one thing, and it does it very well: delight diners with technique, ingredients, and the final dish. Strong relationships with farmers and food folk make the kitchen's job a little easier, as everything they serve is perfection or right next door. Grilled peaches take center stage in a summer salad, yuca gets a salt and vinegar treatment, and whether you get a vegetarian or meat-centered main, it's going to look and smell so good, you'll forget to take a picture before you dig in.

Nearby is **Hole Doughnuts** (168 Haywood Rd., 828/774-5667, www.hole-doughnuts.com, 8am-1pm Wed.-Sun., $2-3) one of my worldwide top-three doughnuts (I eat a lot of doughnuts; don't judge). Yeasted dough cooked to order, they're always hot, always fresh, and always interesting. My favorite from here had a sugared sumac glaze, making that yeasty little doughnut that much more tart.

Sunny Point Café (626 Haywood Rd., 828/252-0055, www.sunnypointcafe.com, 8:30am-2pm Sun.-Mon., 8:30am-8:30pm Tues.-Sat., $10-17) serves three meals most days but is so famous for its brunch that a line sometimes forms out the door. The breakfast menu is popular and served any time of day, although the lunch and dinner menus are also well worth a trip. This is a great bet for vegetarians—the meatless options are imaginative and beautifully created. Whatever you get, you must order one of their angel biscuits; those things are tall, airy, and so good.

Another excellent breakfast option, if you don't mind a little wait, is **Biscuit Head** (733 Haywood Rd., 828/333-5145, 8am-2pm daily, $3-12) in West Asheville, near Mission Hospital (417 Biltmore Ave., Suite 4F, 828/505-3449), and in South Asheville (1994 Hendersonville Rd., 828/585-2055). They specialize in an Appalachian delicacy: cathead biscuits. These things are huge, and as the name implies, as big as a tomcat's head. And they're so good. Get one plain and go load it up at the topping bar (where things like nut butters, fresh jams and jellies, and concoctions like sriracha-laced honey await you and your biscuit); go for a pulled pork, fried green tomato, or country ham biscuit; or go sweet with something like the biscuit french toast or the Nutella Elvis: banana, bacon, and Nutella on a monster biscuit.

★ **Gan Shan West** (285 Haywood Rd., Suite 20, 828/417-7402, www.ganshangroup. com, 4pm-9pm Mon.-Sat., $9-16) takes a broad look at Asian cuisine and serves up rice dishes, ramen, and an assortment of Asian-inspired plates in a small menu that's as intriguing as it is tasty. *Gai lon,* a broccoli-like Chinese green, gets a spicy treatment; steam buns come served in a pair and are filled with your choice of a meat or veggie filling; and dishes like ramen and *mapo doufu* will help some diners push into new territory with this cuisine.

Biltmore Estate and Village

There are no fewer than nine places to eat (plus snacks, ice cream, and coffee) on the

Biltmore Estate (1 Lodge St., 800/411-3812, www.biltmore.com, estate admission required to visit restaurants). For Biltmore lodging guests only, **The Dining Room** (7am-11am, 11:30am-4pm, and 5pm-9pm daily, reservations required, breakfast $56-20, buffet $13-22, 3-course tasting menu $65, 5-course tasting menu $95) is an elegant restaurant featuring estate-raised Angus beef, mountain trout, Biltmore wines, and vegetables grown on estate gardens. The food is spectacular, and tables with a mountain view make the meal all that much better. Evening dress and reservations are recommended.

The **Biltmore Bistro** (noon-9pm Sun.-Fri., 11:30am-9pm Sat., lunch $8-21, prix-fixe lunch $29, dinner $19-44, prix-fixe dinner $52) in Antler Hill Village, adjacent to the winery, has a well-rounded gourmet menu sourced from the Biltmore's own kitchen garden, locally raised heirloom crops, meat and seafood delicacies, and artisanal cheeses and breads. Lunch and dinner are dramatically different (pizza at lunch, braised veal cheeks at dinner), but each menu features something from the wood-fired oven.

The dining room of the **Deerpark Restaurant** (11am-2pm Fri.-Sat., 10am-2pm Sun., Fri.-Sat. buffet $20, free under age 10, Sun. buffet $35, free under age 10) is a former barn designed by architect Richard Morris Hunt, now renovated to airy splendor with walls of windows. Expect hearty and homey meals based on Appalachian cuisine. Like the Deerpark, the **Stable Café** (lunch 11am-4pm and 5pm-9pm daily, $14-35) was once livestock housing, and guests can sit in booths that were once horse stalls. This is a meat eater's paradise, where you can order estate-raised Angus beef and pork barbecue with the house special sauce, among others.

In the stable area near the house, both the **Bake Shop** (9:30am-10pm daily) and the **Biltmore Dairy Bar** (11am-6pm Mon.-Wed., 11am-10pm Thurs.-Sun.) serve fresh treats, and **The Courtyard Market** (11am-4pm daily, weather dependent) has hot dogs, salads, and snacks. The **Creamery** (11am-9pm daily) is the place for sandwiches and hand-dipped ice cream in Antler Hill Village, and **The Conservatory Café** (from 11:30am daily), adjacent to the gardens, will keep you fed after a day admiring the roses. If you have a hankering for barbecue, a quick sandwich, some snacks, or a cold drink, the **Smokehouse Food Truck** (noon-8pm daily) in Antler Hill Village serves just what you need.

While you're in Antler Hill Village, check out **Cedric's Tavern** (11:30am-4pm Sun.-Mon., 11:30am-9pm Tues.-Sat., $13-46). Named for George Vanderbilt's beloved Saint Bernard (you can see his huge collar on display at the entrance), Cedric's pays homage to pubs and taverns found in Britain, with a Southern twist. The fish-and-chips and scotch egg are both delicious. You can also grab a pint of Cedric's Pale or Brown Ale, both brewed by the Biltmore Brewing Company. Also in Antler Hill Village is the new Village Hotel on the Biltmore Estate and its restaurant, **Village Social** (828/257-5968, 7am-11am and noon-9pm Fri.-Mon., 7am-11am and noon-4pm Tues.-Thurs., $6-36). With a menu focused on small plates and tasting menus—all of which are seafood-centric—this is a place to make a meal as light or as filling as you'd like.

Burial Beer has their business offices in Biltmore Village at a former Civilian Conservation Corps location called **Forestry Camp** (10 Shady Oak Dr., 828/505-4452, www.burialbeer.com, 5pm-10pm Mon. and Wed.-Fri., noon-10pm Sat.-Sun.). This is where workers lived during the early stages of construction on the Blue Ridge Parkway, so it's got history tied to Asheville. And it's a really cool spot. They serve the whole of Burial's beer lineup here, but the kitchen puts our food that's far beyond what you'd expect to find in a brewery, which is to say this ain't your run-of-the-mill pub grub; it's real, good food.

Well-Bred Bakery & Café (6 Boston Way, 825/774-5307, www.wellbredbakery. com, 9am-4pm Sun.-Thurs., 9am-5pm Fri.-Sat., $3-15), which started north of Asheville in Weaverville, has a location in Biltmore Village. Sandwiches, salads, quiche, and

breakfast burritos share menu space with pastries, ice cream sandwiches, coffee, and specialty drinks. Stop in for a bite before wandering around Biltmore Village—which was constructed as a village for workers on the massive Biltmore Estate project—for a little sightseeing or window shopping.

Outside Downtown

There are several notable vegetarian and vegan restaurants in Asheville, and among the best is the vegan spot, **Plant** (165 Merrimon Ave., 828/258-7500, www.plantisfood.com, 5pm-9pm Wed.-Thurs. and Sun., 5pm-10pm Fri.-Sat., $10-22), where they make "vegan fare without borders." I'm an admitted omnivore, but Plant is exceptional. From the applewood smoked mushroom (served with their V2 black currant steak sauce), their seasonal spin on ramen (you won't be able to tell the difference in the broth), tempeh chili con queso, and the raw "lasagna" crudo, every bite is a delight, and you won't leave with that heavy, "I'm too full" feeling even if you stuff yourself.

One restaurant folks have been clamoring about is the Caribbean-inspired **Nine Mile** (233 Montford Ave., 828/505-3121, www.nin-emileasheville.com, 4pm-9pm daily, $8-23). With its Caribbean inspiration and heavily Jamaican bent, you'll find bold flavors and a selection of seafood, vegetarian, and vegan options here. Jerk tofu with mushrooms, green onions and cavatappi; dairy-free basil pesto with garden veggies, and mahimahi with mango salsa in a ginger-coconut sauce are just a few of the dishes on offer. They have two other locations, one in West Asheville (751 Haywood Rd., 828/575-9903, 4pm-9pm daily), and one on the south side of town (33 Town Square Blvd., 828/676-1807, 4pm-9pm daily), so if you're hungry, they've got you covered no matter what part of town you're in.

It makes sense that in a food city this close to Tennessee (Great Smoky Mountains National Park and the Tennessee border are 90 minutes away) we'd get some great flavors from the Volunteer State, and **Rocky's Hot Chicken Shack** (1455 Patton Ave.,

828/575-2260, www.rockyshotchickenshack. com, 11am-9pm Sun.-Thurs., 11am-10pm Fri.-Sat., $9-23) in West Asheville delivers. Their fried chicken starts out plain, then you tell them how hot you want it, or how much you'd like to suffer with each bite, depends on how you view hot food. Seriously, though, the hot is real hot, and the mild is delicious even if you think ice water is spicy. And if you're out here needing to feed a crowd (or just have a nostalgia for a cold fried-chicken picnic), they have platters that'll feed a family (8-16 people), with wings, dark and white meat platters, and an order that's a little bit of everything ($38-90). There's a second location just south of Asheville in Arden (3749 Sweeten Creek Rd., Arden, 828/676-3222, 11am-9pm Sun.-Thurs., 11am-10pm Fri.-Sat.).

You'll feel at home in **Avenue M** (791 Merrimon Ave., 828/350-8181, www.avenue-mavl.com, 5pm-9pm Tues.-Sat., $15-30), a place that offers free Wi-Fi for the kids' devices and some fresh water for your faithful furry friend alongside a menu of creative dishes and excellent wines. A half-dozen pastas, a great mix of veggie-friendly and omnivorous entrées, a burger and its Impossible cousin, and a legion of sharable, snackable appetizers ensure you're well fed, but also make it easy to linger here for a while.

Seafood lovers take note: **Jettie Rae's** (143 Charlotte St., 828/505-4499, www.jettieraes. com, 4:30pm-9pm Wed.-Thurs., 4:30pm-10pm Fri.-Sun., $8-60) has what you want for dinner, whether it's a pile of clam strips, caviar service, or something between. A raw bar and a menu packed with oysters, crabs, clams, fish-and-chips, and a lobster roll will have your stomach growling before you even get to the restaurant.

At **Luella's Bar-B-Que** (501 Merrimon Ave., 828/505-7427, www.luellasbbq.com, 11am-8pm Sun.-Thurs., 11am-9pm Fri.-Sat., $7-15) you can try the range of styles and sauces that make North Carolina 'cue distinct. Ribs, chopped pork, brisket, smoked wings, and sides like mac-and-cheese, fried okra, collard greens, and hush puppies are staples here, but there's a surprising item on the menu: barbecued tempeh. I'm a barbecue judge (really, I'm certified!), so trust me when I say it's good. As is everything here, from the grub to the vibe to the impressive array of local beer on draft. Pay a visit to their spot in South Asheville (33 Town Square Blvd., Biltmore Park, 828/676-3855) if you're hungry and down that way.

Vinnie's Neighborhood Italian (641 Merrimon Ave., 828/253-1077, www.vinniesitalian.com, 5pm-9:30pm Sun.-Thurs., 5pm-10:30pm Fri.-Sat., $11-26), is an Italian eatery they say is "reminiscent of Brooklyn, the Bronx and the North End of Boston." That means pasta, pizza, heroes, and calzones are offered in abundance, along with heartier veal and chicken dishes, lasagna, and eggplant parmigiana. It also means big portions that could feed a family (incidentally, they do serve family-style portions of lasagna, and eggplant or chicken parmigiana that'll feed three for $45-49), which is exactly what this style of Italian is all about.

ACCOMMODATIONS

There are a lot of places and ways to stay in Asheville at all sorts of price points. With B&Bs and inns tucked away in the neighborhoods and hills surrounding downtown, grand resorts like the Grove Park Inn and luxe stays on the Biltmore Estate, glamping, tiny cottages, boutique hotels, and, of course, the chain hotels ubiquitous to any city, you'll find a place to rest your head that's convenient to the concert you're headed to, those dinner reservations you made, to the Blue Ridge Parkway, downtown, or whatever's brought you to the mountains. The Explore Asheville website (www.exploreasheville.com) has an exhaustive list of hotels and accommodations in the area, and at the **Asheville Bed & Breakfast Association** (www.ashevil-lebba.com), inns and B&Bs in the area band together to promote getaways, tours, and seasonal packages.

Downtown

Built in a former foundry in what was once the heart of Asheville's Black neighborhood, ★ **The Foundry Hotel** (51 S. Market St., 828/552-8545, www.foundryasheville.com, $260-1,712) pays homage to the building's past, while the restaurant attached to the hotel, **Benne on Eagle** (35 Eagle St., 828/552-8833, www.benneoneagle.com, $10-32), offers a hat-tip to Black and Appalachian cuisine. Only a block off Biltmore Avenue, the Foundry is walkable but still gives you separation from Asheville's bustling downtown. Exposed brick on the walls and quirky art—wallpaper and framed pieces with details, newspaper clippings, and photos from the foundry's operating years—give the hotel a bohemian touch. The bedding, lounge, gym, and other hotel amenities are decidedly upscale. Relax and grab a drink in the **Workshop Lounge** before you head out for the evening.

In recent years the face of downtown Asheville has changed with the arrival of several hotels. AC Hotel (a Marriott chain) made a splash when it arrived, as did **Kimpton Hotel Arras** (7 Patton Ave., 828/255-0303, www.hotelarras.com, $280-595). Asheville's tallest building, on Pack Square, was reduced to a skeleton and rebuilt, and the result is this stunning Kimpton that hosts works by local artists. Grab drinks and dinner at **District 42** (828/774-5564, www.district42avl.com, 5pm-10pm Sun.-Wed., 5pm-11pm Thurs., 5pm-midnight Fri.-Sat., pizza bar 4pm-10pm Mon.-Wed., 4pm-11pm Thurs., 4pm-midnight Fri., 2pm-midnight Sat., 2pm-10pm Sun., $10-37) or sit for a more upscale dinner or brunch at **Bargello** (828/774-5564, www.bargelloavl.com, breakfast 7am-11am Mon.-Fri., 7am-10am Sat.-Sun., dinner 5pm-10pm Sun. and Wed.-Thurs., 5pm-11pm Fri.-Sat., brunch 10am-3pm Sat.-Sun., $9-64), plating up Mediterranean-inspired dishes using local ingredients.

AC Hotel by Marriott Downtown Asheville (10 Broadway St., 828/258-2522, www.marriott.com, from $340, winter rates as low as $175) is one of my favorites for the spacious rooms, generally excellent views, and a great rooftop bar, **Capella on 9** (828/771-5156, 7am-11am and 3pm-11pm Mon.-Thurs., 7am-11am and 3pm-midnight Fri.-Sat., 7am-11am and 3pm-10pm Sun., $11-30), with cocktails, wine, beer, and a tasty tapas menu—olives, charcuterie and cheese boards, *patatas bravas,* even pan-fried trout—while you take in the views.

In keeping with Asheville's mountain hippie vibe, there's a hostel in downtown. **Sweet Pea's Hostel** (23 Rankin Ave., 828/285-8488, www.sweetpeashostel.com) has loads of ways to stay. They've got a 16 coed bunks ($32), each with a power outlet and reading light; 24 pods ($40), reminiscent of a train-car sleeper with a locker, shelves, outlets, and an acoustic curtain; a pair of small private rooms ($75) with sinks and locking doors; and a studio room ($105) with a private bath. There's free Wi-Fi throughout the property. Feel free to cook up a meal in the kitchen (just clean up after yourself), hang out for some TV or a movie in the living room, or venture out into town to see what's happening. Stay here and you're on the same block as a coffee shop, brewery, a couple of restaurants, and a cocktail lounge, and you're only a short walk from everything downtown.

South Slope and River Arts District

With so many neo-hippie types, college kids, dirtbags (it's not an insult; it's what rock climbers often call themselves), kayakers, hikers, and bikers coming through, it's no surprise to find a nice hostel nestled in among the hotels and bed-and-breakfasts. At the **Asheville Hostel & Guest House** (16 Ravenscroft Dr., 828/423-0256, www.avlhostel.com, $100-112, tiny house with private bath $175) you'll find only private guest rooms and even a private tiny house. Reservations are available up to a year in advance, so it's easy to get a room if you know when you're traveling. At the hostel you'll find free waffles, coffee, and tea at make-your-own stations; free Wi-Fi; free parking; and, since you're on the South Slope, there's a lot to eat and drink nearby, and downtown is within walking distance.

Biltmore Estate and Village

If you've spent the day touring the Biltmore Estate, viewing the incredible splendor in which a robber baron of the Gilded Age basked, it may be jarring to return to real life (unless you're a billionaire). You can soften the transition with a stay at **The Inn on Biltmore Estate** (866/336-1245, www.biltmore.com, $379-2,700). It's everything you'd wish for from a hotel in this location. The rooms and suites are beautifully furnished and luxurious, the views are magnificent, and the lobby, dining room, and library have the deluxe coziness of a turn-of-the-20th-century lodge. In the off-season, it's possible to find rooms from around $200. **Village Hotel on Biltmore Estate** (from $288) in Antler Hill Village has 209 rooms and is a testament to the ongoing and growing popularity of the Biltmore. You can find specials for as low as $144.

Outside Downtown

The **Grove Park Inn** (290 Macon Ave., 828/252-2711 or 800/438-5800, www.omnihotels.com, $439-1,999, spa and golf packages available) is the sort of place Asheville residents bring their out-of-town houseguests when giving them a grand tour of the city, simply to walk into the lobby to ooh and aah. The massive stone building—constructed by a crew of 400 who had only mule teams and a single steam shovel to aid them—was erected in 1912-1913. Eight U.S. presidents have stayed here, as has a glittering parade of early-20th-century big shots, among them Henry Ford, Thomas Edison, Eleanor Roosevelt, Harry Houdini, and F. Scott Fitzgerald.

Even if you're not staying here, it's worth a visit just to see the lobby and enormous fireplaces, and take in the atmosphere while having a cocktail or dinner at one of the many on-site establishments: **Vue 1913** (5pm-10pm Wed.-Sun., $34-60) has French and American dishes and a few premium options like a Wagyu filet ($98) and an elk tenderloin ($75) if you're treating yourself; **Edison Craft Ales + Kitchen** (11am-10pm Sun.-Thurs.,11am-11pm Fri.-Sat., brunch noon-2:30pm Sun., $12-48) serves some high-quality bar food and craft beer; and **Blue Ridge** (7am-10:30am daily, 5pm-9pm Fri.-Sat., noon-2:30pm Sun., $29-48 adults, $17-23 ages 6-12) is a farm-to-table artisanal buffet. The hotel's **Sunset Terrace** (11am-3pm and 4:30pm-10pm daily, reservations required, $13-50) has phenomenal views, allowing you to enjoy dinner and the sunset.

Being a guest at the Grove Park Inn is quite an experience. In addition to the spectacle of the lodge and its multiple restaurants, cafés, bars, and shops, for an additional charge guests have access to its world-famous **spa** (daily, day pass $244). The pass gives access to the lounges, pools, steam room, inhalation room, and outdoor whirlpool tub. The indoor pool is a fantastic place, a subterranean stone room with vaulted skylights and tropical plants. For extra fees ($180-540, most $200-300), guests can choose from a long menu of spa treatments: massages, facials, manicures, aromatherapy, and body wraps.

There's also an exceptional Donald Ross-designed 18-hole par-70 **golf course** (828/252-2711 or 800/438-5800, reserve tee times online at www.groveparkinn.com, greens fees $70-140 Mon.-Thurs., $70-155 Fri.-Sun. Apr.-mid-Nov., $77-87 mid-Nov.-Mar., 9 holes $55 Apr.-mid-Nov., $45 mid-Nov.-Mar., rental clubs $55 for 9 holes, $80 for 18 holes). The 6,400-yard course is where President Obama played when he stayed at the Grove Park Inn; one look around at the mountains and views from the elevated tee boxes and you know he was impressed.

Asheville has a history in hospitality, and one of the longest continuously operated bed-and-breakfasts in town is a real charmer. ★ **Applewood Manor** (62 Cumberland Circle, 828/254-2244, www.applewoodmanor. com, $275-310) has six gorgeous rooms (each named for a type of apple) and a great farm-to-table breakfast. The owners—a husband-and-wife team—share their interests with guests via road cycling and culinary programs. They'll set you up with a bike rental and point you toward a place to ride, or you can join them for a guided ride with a former national road race champion. If that's not your speed, you can get in the kitchen for some baking or a cooking class. If you're headed to Asheville or the Smokies with a group, look into renting the whole place ($1,900) and making it your home away from home.

Just a mile from downtown in the lovely and walkable Montford Historic District, ★ **Abbington Green Bed & Breakfast Inn and Spa** (46 Cumberland Circle, 828/251-2454 or 822/251-2454, www.abbingtongreen. com, $239-469) will charm you from the moment you lay eyes on this Colonial Revival-style home. Completed in 1908, this home was designed by Biltmore Estate's on-site supervising architect, Robert Sharpe Smith, and has received a number of accolades, including one from the Preservation Society, for excellence in historic preservation, so it retains every bit of the magic it was imbued with more than a century ago. It's a AAA Four Diamond property, a rating that doesn't come easily, but with king beds, a gourmet breakfast, a cozy but well-appointed spa (services from $100), and gorgeous English-style gardens, AAA might need to make this one a six-star property. Eight rooms, including three suites in the Carriage House, give guests plenty of privacy without sacrificing the intimate homey feel of the property. There are dog-friendly rooms available if you're traveling with your four-legged friend.

Nestled in the Kenilworth neighborhood, a truly lovely bed-and-breakfast is **Sweet Biscuit Inn** (77 Kenilworth Rd., 828/250-0170, www.sweetbiscuitinn.com, $160-275). I have to admit, I was drawn here by the name, but the place, the host, and the three-course breakfast conspired to make me like it even more. The seven bedrooms and carriage house are accented by tiger-oak wood floors and high ceilings. Queen or king beds are comfy, and breakfast is excellent, especially the biscuits.

In the days before budget hotels became the norm, the motor court or cottage court was the stay-over of choice for middle-class travelers. Today these motor courts and cottage courts are relics of the past, and few remain, but the mountains of North Carolina contain a handful of fine examples. In the Asheville area, at least two are still operating, providing travelers with throwback accommodations. **Asheville Log Cabin Motor Court** (330 Weaverville Hwy., 828/645-6546, www. theashevillecabins.com, $95-305, 2-night minimum stay weekends, pets allowed for a fee), 6.2 miles north of downtown Asheville, has cable TV and Wi-Fi but no phones. Some rooms are air-conditioned, but that's not usually a necessity at this elevation. Another great cabin court is the **Pines Cottages** (346 Weaverville Hwy., 828/645-9661, www. thepinescottages.com, $109-330, up to 2 pets allowed, $15 per pet), only 6.3 miles north of Asheville. How could you resist staying at a place billed as "A nice place for nice people"?

Want to stay in a tree house? How about a retro camper with a hot tub? Or a dome with skylight windows so you can watch the stars? Or a yurt? If this sounds good, you need **Asheville Glamping** (address provided on booking, 828/450-9745, www.ashevilleglamping.com, $140-600). They have a trio of properties with a host of quirky but refined places and ways to stay, from safari-style tents to tree houses to yurts and more. When you book they'll send you the address of the property; it's a slight inconvenience but a way to keep their immensely Instagrammable campgrounds and properties a haven to their guests and free of lookers and lurkers.

At **The Beaucatcher** (60 Tunnel Rd., 825/254-0805, www.thebeaucatcher.com, $75-155), you're only a three-minute drive to downtown, and just a little longer to I-240 or the Blue Ridge Parkway. New owners took over this property back in 2016 and they've been steadily making improvements since. The rooms are comfortable, and there's plenty of space to spread out your gear if you're here for a hiking or outdoorsy adventure. In summer, the courtyard can get lively with a pair of fire pits and a beer from the stock of local brews in the lobby.

INFORMATION AND SERVICES

The **Asheville Visitors Center** (36 Montford Ave., near I-240 exit 4C, 828/258-6129, www. exploreasheville.com, 8:30am-5pm Mon.-Fri., 9am-5pm Sat.-Sun.) can set you up with all the maps, brochures, and recommendations you could need. Other sources are **Explore Asheville** (www.exploreasheville. com) and the **Asheville Area Chamber of Commerce** (www.ashevillechamber.org). **Mission Hospital** (509 Biltmore Ave.; 428 Biltmore Ave., 828/213-1111, www.mission-health.org) in Asheville has two campuses and two emergency departments.

Listen to public radio at **WCQS** (88.1 FM) and **WNCW** (88.7 FM); music stations are **WTMT** (105.9 FM) and **WOXL** (96.5 FM).

As Asheville is the best gateway city when venturing into the Smoky Mountains, know you'll find some information on planning a trip to the Smokies at **Explore Asheville** (www.exploreasheville.com). The website of **Great Smoky Mountain National Park** (www.nps.gov/gsmnp) has trip planning tools useful for day trips or overnight excursions into the park.

GETTING THERE AND AROUND

Asheville is spread around the junction of I-40, North Carolina's primary east-west highway, and I-26, a roughly north-south artery through the southern highlands. U.S. 19 runs at a diagonal, deep into the Smokies in one direction and into the northern Blue Ridge in the other. Asheville has an extensive public bus system called **ART** (www.ashevil-lenc.gov, 5:55am-midnight Mon.-Sat., 7:55am-6:30pm Sun., limited hours holidays, hours vary by route, $1, $0.50 seniors), connecting most major points in the metropolitan area, including the airport, with downtown. See the website for routes and schedules. **Asheville Regional Airport** (AVL, 61 Terminal Dr., Fletcher, 828/684-2226, www.flyavl.com) is a 20-minute drive on I-26 south of the city in Fletcher. Several airlines run flights to Atlanta, Charlotte, and other U.S. cities.

From Asheville it's easy to get to Great Smoky Mountains National Park (GSMNP). In just over an hour you can be in Cataloochee, at the north end of the park, to camp, hike, and watch for elk in a serene mountain cove; to get here, take I-40 west to exit 20 and follow the signs. You can also take I-40 west into Tennessee, follow the Foothills Parkway to U.S. 321, and skirt the edge of GSMNP to Gatlinburg, Tennessee, and the entrance to the park, a trip of about 90 minutes. From Gatlinburg, you can make a loop back to Asheville by taking Newfound Gap Road across GSMNP to Cherokee, North Carolina (about 2.5 hours), and then back to Asheville via U.S. 441 to U.S. 19 to I-40, a total loop of about 3.5 hours and some 175 miles.

You can also head straight to Cherokee from Asheville and enter GSMNP via Newfound Gap Road. It's an hour's drive following I-40 west to exit 27, then taking U.S. 19 south to U.S. 441, which runs right into Cherokee. Alternately you can take the more scenic, but much longer, route and get to Cherokee via the Blue Ridge Parkway. This route is only 83 miles, but it takes 2-2.5 hours. If you want to go this way, head south out of Asheville along U.S. 25 and pick up the Blue Ridge Parkway about 5.5 miles out of town; turn south on the parkway and drive until you reach Cherokee and GSMNP. And, of course, you can reverse the course if you're making that grand loop and return to Asheville via the Blue Ridge Parkway by picking it up in Cherokee and driving north.

Around Asheville

Throughout the mountains around Asheville you'll come across towns official and unincorporated—some collections of houses at a wide spot on a mountain road, others established towns with deep histories and more than a little creative juice flowing in their collective blood. Whatever the reason for visiting, these towns have personalities, histories, cultures, and environments distinct enough to allow the truly curious to discover a small town (or two) full of surprises.

BLACK MOUNTAIN

Named for a onetime train depot, the town of Black Mountain sits 15 miles west of Asheville and is one of several bedroom communities for the city. At one time, Black Mountain's claim to fame was the experimental Black Mountain College and its intellectual and artistic legacy. The school is long gone, and the Black Mountain College Museum and Arts Center is located in Asheville, but some of the artistic residue is still around in the form of the Lake Eden Arts Festival, or LEAF, which takes place on the former college campus.

Sights

Step into the **Swannanoa Valley Museum** (223 W. State St., 828/669-9566, www.swannanoavalleymuseum.org, 10am-5pm Thurs.-Sat. Mar.-Dec., 10am-5pm Sat. Feb., $5, free students and under age 18) to learn about the history of this area, including settlement by the Cherokee people, early industrialization, and the shutdown of the Beacon Blanket Factory. The museum offers something a little different: hikes, and not just short ones. The current iterations of the **Swannanoa Rim Explorer Series** (series of 11 hikes, $500 members) and **Valley History Explorer Hiking Series** (series of 8 hikes, $280 members) take museum members on a series of hikes that reveal the history, geography, and rugged beauty of the Swannanoa Valley; in the

recent past these hikes were open to guests and sold as packages and individual guided hikes, and there's hope to renew that program in 2023 (prices were around $50 for nonmembers; expect a little increase). Some of these hikes are difficult—steep, long, exposed in places—and others are geared toward beginners; check with the museum to register and for questions on difficulty and schedules.

The **Black Mountain Center for the Arts** (225 W. State St., 828/669-0930, http://blackmountainarts.org, 10am-5pm Mon.-Fri.) is a gallery and performance space in the heart of town. Once the town hall, the Center for the Arts now houses art classes and summer camps for kids and adults, workshops and talks, performances of all sorts (concerts, dance, poetry, storytelling, live theater), and gallery openings.

Shopping

If I said **Sassafras on Sutton** (108 Sutton Ave., 828/419-0677, www.sassafrasonsutton.com, 10am-6pm Mon.-Sat.) has it all, you might think I was exaggerating, but this bookstore, gift shop, and espresso café delivers. Well, as long as you're looking for a curated selection of fiction and local books, hand-poured candles, and a gift for yourself or someone else, they've got it all.

There are several galleries in Black Mountain, so you'll have your choice of where to browse and where to buy. Stop in at **Mountain Nest** (133 Cherry St., 828/669-0314, www.mtnnest.com, 10am-6pm Mon.-Sat., 11am-5pm Sun.), a gallery of art and handcrafted pieces; you'll find work from many North Carolinians for sale here, as well as pieces from fine artists from around the world. Styles and skill levels vary from artist to artist, but there's solid and reasonably priced work. **Seven Sisters Craft Gallery** (119 Broadway Ave., 828/669-5107, www.sevensistersgallery.com, 10am-6pm Mon.-Sat., noon-5pm Sun.) has been around for more than 30 years and carries large-scale photos, oil paintings by local and regional artists, and other art in a host of styles, media, and price points.

Entertainment and Events

In May and October, Black Mountain is the scene of the **Lake Eden Arts Festival** (377 Lake Eden Rd., 828/686-8742, www.theleaf. org), better known as LEAF. Based around roots music, LEAF is also a festival of visual arts, poetry, food, and even the healing arts. It's an amazing scene, and it takes place, appropriately, at Camp Rockmont, once the campus of Black Mountain College, the short-lived but historically important avant-garde institution that was home to a number of influential American artists and writers.

NIGHTLIFE

Pisgah Brewing Company (2948 U.S. 70, 828/669-0190, www.pisgahbrewing.com, 4pm-9pm Mon.-Wed., 2pm-11pm Thurs.-Fri., noon-11pm Sat., 1pm-10pm Sun., open late for concerts, cash only) is both a brewpub and a music venue, featuring an eclectic mix of bands from roots music to rock. Pisgah was the Southeast's first certified organic brewery, and several beers are on tap all year, including their pale ale, porter, and stout; a long list of seasonal brews rotates through the year, and a growing list of specialty brews, like their sour brown ale, is gaining a loyal following. Tour the brewery (2pm and 3pm Sat.), but stop in a try a beer anytime they're open.

You'll find a stellar mural of Roberta Flack and a tap list of great beer at **Black Mountain Brewing** (131 Broadway Ave., 828/357-5010, www.blackmountainbrewing.com, 3pm-9pm Mon.-Thurs., noon-10pm Fri.-Sat., noon-9pm Sun.). Creative spins on sour beer, some big double dry-hopped IPAs, and seasonal styles appear on the draft list, but they also carry hard cider and ginger beer from friendly fermentation specialists nearby. Their food truck, **Smoke Black Mountain** (4pm-7:30 Mon.-Thurs., noon-8pm Fri.-Sat., noon-7pm

Sun., $12-24), serves pulled pork poutine, smoked lobster rolls, brisket sandwiches, and a few other delectable bites on-site.

Black Mountain Cider + Mead (104 Eastside Dr., Suite 307, 828/419-0089, www. blackmountainciderworks.com, 2pm-7pm Thurs.-Fri., 1pm-7pm Sat.-Sun.) is one of several spots across the state making cider and one of only a select few to make mead (a fermented honey beverage that should make you think of Vikings and Beowulf). Their ciders aren't cloyingly sweet or closer to carbonated apple juice than an alcoholic beverage; rather, they're on the dry side and tend to be complex in flavor. At any time they're pouring a half-dozen of their ciders and meads, and many are blended to make some interesting concoctions. In summer, they'll throw basil into a mix of mead and cider, or blend apple cider and cherry mead, or try something completely different by adding blueberry and cardamom, fresh ginger, lavender, quince, or rose.

Food

You'll enjoy munching breakfast at **Blue Ridge Biscuit Company** (601 W. State St., 828/357-8501, www.blueridgebiscuitcompany.com, 8am-2pm Wed.-Sun., $3-12), where they serve up cathead biscuits (if you're not familiar, they contain no felines, but are big biscuits, the size of a tomcat's head) plain, buttered, sweet, with egg and cheese, and with sausage or shiitake gravy. Their twisted biscuits are quirky biscuit sandwiches and benedicts; the Grey Beard (fried chicken, fried green tomatoes, honey mustard, arugula) might just have you dancin' in the streets, but if it doesn't, the Smoky Mountain Brook (smoked trout spread, poached egg, tomato jam) will definitely have you bouncing around the room with joy.

Stop in at **Dripolator Coffeehouse** (221 W. State St., 828/699-0999, 6:45am-6pm daily, $2-6) for coffee, pastries, and the like. This cute little shop keeps winning "Best of WNC" (western North Carolina) from *Mountain Xpress* (a free magazine found nearby), and folks keep coming, not because of the awards but for the best coffee in the North Carolina mountains.

Berliner Kindl German Restaurant (121 Broadway St., 828/669-5255, http://berlinerkindl.homestead.com, 11am-8pm Mon.-Sat., $9-28) serves traditional German food like schnitzel, a variety of sausages, and the sides you'd expect: fried potatoes, German potato salad, sauerkraut, and red cabbage. They make their own sauerkraut in-house.

When you're ready for dinner, try **Black Mountain Bistro** (203 E. State Rd., 828/669-5041, www.blackmountainbistro.com, 11am-8pm Mon.-Thurs., 11am-9pm Fri.-Sat., $12-28). They keep a couple of tasty steaks on the menu, and their work with salmon and local trout is awesome, but check out the pork chop with blackberry barbecue sauce, the backyard garden pasta (loaded with seasonal veggies), and their lunchtime sandwich menu (the Up North Reuben is excellent).

Accommodations

The 45-room **Monte Vista Hotel** (308 W. State St., Black Mountain, 828/669-8870, www.mvhotel.com, $169-269) has been serving visitors to the North Carolina mountains since 1937 when the original portion of the hotel was built, but it's the second Monte Vista here; the first was a school building turned hotel back in 1919, giving this place a long history of hospitality. Rooms are more spacious than you'd think a place built in 1937 would offer, but the styling blends a modern and turn-of-the-20th-century feel. The on-site restaurant, **Milton's** (5pm-9pm Wed.-Sun., $18-32), has a good assortment of cocktails and a menu of dishes that are as comforting as they are delicious. Honey roasted pork tenderloin, chicken and dumplings with a bit of fried sage, shrimp and grits, locally raised trout, and a great hanger steak with chimichurri are some of what you'll find here.

The **Inn around the Corner** (109 Church St., 828/669-6005, www.innaroundthecorner.com, $155-245) is a classic bed-and-breakfast in a lovely 1915 home with a huge front porch.

Just about every room has a great view, but the best is from the porch bed, where you'll fall asleep under the gaze of the mountains and wake when the birds start their day.

Arbor House of Black Mountain (207 Rhododendron Ave., 828/357-8525, www.arborhousenc.com, $175-290), a four-room bed-and-breakfast, hosts travelers year-round, but like at most places in the area, peak season coincides with the turning of the leaves every fall. Views from the inn are wide and beautiful, especially when the leaves are out, but book early for leaf season.

Information and Services

The **Black Mountain and Swannanoa Chamber of Commerce** (www.exploreblackmountain.com) maintains a list of member businesses and has a small bit of visitor information on its site, but the best visitor information for Black Mountain is going to be at **Explore Asheville** (www.exploreasheville.com).

Getting There and Around

On I-40, take exit 70 or exit 64 to get to Black Mountain. From Asheville, Black Mountain is about 15 minutes east.

WEAVERVILLE

Weaverville, just 10 minutes north of Asheville, served as a vacation town for wealthy city and Piedmont dwellers in the late 1800s, though it had been settled by a handful of families since the 1780s. At one time, a pair of grand hotels—the Dula Springs Hotel and Blackberry Lodge—welcomed well-heeled and notable visitors like author O. Henry when they escaped to the mountains. The town never grew to be much more than a bucolic getaway, and today, with a population hovering around 2,500, Weaverville holds onto its former identity even as it grows into a bedroom community for Asheville. The **Weaverville Business Association** (www.visitweaverville.com) lists all the town's amenities.

Sights

At the **Dry Ridge Museum** (41 N. Main St., 828/407-3701, www.dryridgemuseum.org, 11am-5pm Wed.-Sat. Apr.-Oct., 11am-5pm Thurs.-Sat. Dec.-Mar., free) you'll find a collection of artifacts, letters, and photos telling the history of Weaverville. It's small and has odd hours but may be of interest to local history buffs.

A few miles down the road is the birthplace of North Carolina's Civil War governor, Zebulon T. Vance (if ever there was a Civil War governor's name, that's it). The **Vance Birthplace** (911 Reems Creek Rd., 828/645-6706, www.nchistoricsites.org, 9am-5pm Tues.-Sat.) has a reconstructed log house as well as a tool house, smokehouse, spring house, cabin where enslaved people lived, and a few more recreated structures. Tours of the home are available at the bottom of the hour. Vance and his legacy are notably tarnished due to his speech and actions supporting the traitorous Confederate States of America, but his support for the attempted turncoat nation and the despicable institution of slavery aren't reasons to erase him or this place from our collective history. Instead it's an opportunity to learn about the times, people, and conditions of that stain on the history of the United States. As with many other historic sites across North Carolina and the South, the Vance Birthplace is slowly rolling out the stories and biographies of enslaved people here and in the whole of Reems Creek, helping to paint a more accurate and factual portrait of this place and its people.

Recreation

Curtis Wright Outfitters (24 N. Main St., 828/645-8700, www.curtiswrightoutfitters.com, 9am-6pm Mon.-Sat.) keeps a store stocked with fly-fishing gear, clothing, tackle, and supplies. They offer a range of guided fishing trips (1 angler $200 half-day wading, $300 full-day wading, $350 half-day float trip, $75 per additional person) on area streams and rivers. You can also shoot some sporting clays (shooting $125, beginner instruction $195, advanced instruction $250), or take part in one of their fly fishing schools ($175) or classes ($75) to hone your technique or learn to tie flies. They also offer falconry ($125, $50 to observe) where you'll be able to handle the birds after some instruction and under careful guidance.

Shopping

There are a lot of great potters in western North Carolina, but Rob and Beth Mangum of **Mangum Pottery** (16 N. Main St., 828/645-4929, www.mangumpottery.com, 9am-5pm Mon.-Fri., 10am-4pm Sat.) are two of the most innovative. They make beautiful earthy-colored dinnerware and mugs to satisfy the practical side of life, and they also build the most unexpected things out of pottery—ceramic clocks, ceramic furniture, ceramic musical instruments that really play—all in Seussian shapes and colors.

Maggie B's Wine & Specialty Store (10-C S. Main St., 828/645-1111, www.maggiebswine.com, 11am-6pm Tues.-Sat.) is Weaverville's first wine and specialty food shop opened by a husband and wife who know what tastes good. Maggie B's has an excellent selection of wine and beer and an assortment of meats, cheeses, and snacks to make for a perfect picnic. If you're here and you're hungry, they do have a menu of sandwiches and salads ($5-11), and they sell wine and beer by the glass.

The artwork at **MIYA Gallery** (20 N. Main St., 828/658-9655, www.miyagallery.com, 10am-5pm Mon.-Sat.) includes fine art, jewelry, furniture, and sculpture. More than 90 area artists and craftspeople have their work on display here. Pick something up, or just admire the leather books, exquisite and experimental wooden vessels, and fine photo prints of mountain scenes.

Food

If you're in Weaverville and you have a hankering for pizza, **Blue Mountain Pizza** (55 N. Main St., 828/658-8778, www.bluemountainpizza.com, 11am-9pm Wed.-Sun., $9-25) is your spot. Blue Mountain Pizza serves specialty pizzas, calzones, stromboli, subs, and salads. Their Henny Penny Pizza is a barbecued chicken pizza with red onion and bacon, and the Marge is simply olive oil, Roma tomatoes, fresh mozzarella, and basil. Grab a specialty pie, make your personal favorite, or even pick up a take-and-bake pizza or just the dough and play pizza parlor back at your place.

A few doors down from Mangum Pottery you'll find **Well-Bred Bakery & Café** (26 N. Main St., 828/645-9300, www.wellbredbakery. com, 9am-4pm daily, $2-8), which sells soups, sandwiches, quiche, and salads as well as a dazzling array of artisanal breads and elaborate desserts. They promise "karma-free coffee" (I think that means fair-trade) and even sell the *New York Times,* so you don't have to go into crossword-puzzle withdrawal on your trip.

Mediterranean fare is the go-to at **Twisted Laurel Weaverville** (10-A S. Main St., 828/645-2700, www.twistedlaurel.com, 11am-9pm Sun.-Thurs., 11am-10pm Fri.-Sat., $9-17) and that means plenty of Greek- and Italian-inspired dishes to choose from. An Italian sub or a gyro, Greek-style meatballs, the classic chicken parm, even pizza pies that play on house favorites (like the Fat Jake's, with chicken, bacon, onions, and ranch) and veggie- or meat-loaded options. Their draft beer selection is great, and considering they have a sister restaurant in Asheville, it'd better be.

At the moment there's one brewery in Weaverville, **Eluvium Brewing Company** (11 Florida Ave., 828/484-1799, www.eluviumbrewing.com, 2pm-9pm Mon.-Thurs., 11:30am-10pm Fri.-Sat., noon-9pm Sun.), and since downtown Weaverville is so small, it's easy to find. They keep more than a dozen beers on draft, with a few guest taps mingling with the house brews. For house brews, they take a broad approach to style, making hazy IPAs, farmhouse ales, cream ales, a sour lager, porters, stouts, and more.

Also in Weaverville, **Glass Onion** (18 N. Main St., 828/645-8866, www.glassonionasheville.com, 5pm-8pm Wed.-Sun., $22-38) serves a fantastic dinner. Dishes are mostly Italian, but a few French influences sneak in, and everything on the menu uses foraged and locally sourced ingredients. House-made ravioli are stuffed with wild mushrooms. Rigatoni comes served with wild-boar bolognese (you must try it). The black Angus rib-eye au poivre (see, told you some French slipped in) comes from Brasstown, a spot in the far southwestern corner of the state, but not too far from Weaverville.

Accommodations

Dry Ridge Inn Bed and Breakfast (26 Brown St., 828/658-3899, www.dryridgeinn. com, $159-199) has eight guest rooms in a former parsonage built in 1849. Rooms feature king or queen beds, a gas fireplace, and reliable Wi-Fi. A fridge stocked with complimentary beverages is on the main floor. Breakfast is served either in the dining room or on the patio. Weather permitting, have breakfast outside and feel that fresh mountain air that made this town a vacation spot for generations.

The Inn on Main (88 S. Main St., 828/645-4935 or 877/873-6074, www.innonmain.com, $119-219) offers an eco-friendly place to rest your head. They use no cleaning chemicals or deodorizers in the inn, all bath products are natural, and they cook their vegetarian meals using as many organic ingredients as possible. There are three rooms, a pair of one-bedroom mini suites, and a two-bedroom apartment that can sleep five. Each of the accommodations is comfy and cozy; on top of that, the owners, who still live on-site, know the area and are quick with a recommendation.

Information and Services

The **Weaverville Business Association** (www.visitweaverville.com) provides visitor information. You can also find visitor information at **Explore Asheville** (www. exploreasheville.com).

Getting There

Weaverville is just 10 minutes north of Asheville along a very easy drive. Simply follow U.S. 70 west, U.S. 19 north, and U.S. 23 north, then turn right on Weaver Boulevard.

MADISON COUNTY

North of Asheville, Madison County is a world unto itself. Just 30 minutes north of Asheville, the wild mountain terrain is spotted with hot springs and towns no bigger than ink blots on a map, but still this county, which shares a border with an equally wild corner of Tennessee, draws visitors. Some come for the solitude, others the hot springs, others the rafting and to explore the great outdoors; still others come for the music. As is true all along the Appalachian Range and especially in the Blue Ridge Mountains, music plays an important role in the identity of the place. In most towns you'll find a stage, porch, coffee shop, or gas station where bluegrass musicians will gather to play, carrying on the long-held traditions of the people here.

Sports and Recreation

On a 4,700-foot mountaintop above Mars Hill, the **Wolf Ridge Ski Resort** (578 Valley View Circle, 828/689-4111 or 800/817-4111, www.skiwolfridgenc.com, 9am-4:30pm and 6pm-10pm Mon.-Sat., 9am-4:30pm Sun. Dec.-Mar., $28-82 adults, $23-66 students and ages 5-18, free over age 64 and under age 4, rentals $28-36) has more than 80 acres of prime skiing and snowboarding slopes. It is also the home of the Snow Sports School, which offers private and group lessons for all ages of beginning and intermediate winter sports enthusiasts. There are multiple lifts, two lodges to relax in, and multiple hearty dining options. The attached **Scenic Wolf Resort** offers year-round cabin accommodations ($300-550 in season), a huge indoor heated pool, and numerous recreational activities.

Sandy Bottom Trail Rides (1459 Caney Fork Rd., Marshall, 828/649-3464 or 800/959-3513, www.sandybottomtrailrides.net, 8am-5pm daily, 1 hour $65, 2 hours $95, 3 hours

$130, $10 discount for cash), based at a 100-year-old family farm, leads horseback treks deep into the forest to an early-19th-century garnet mine. You can take private riding lessons (additional $20 per hour) with an experience guide, and there's a gem mine ($50 pp full day, $25 pp half day, one gallon limit) on the property you can visit. The mine itself is closed, but you can root through the tailings (that's the stuff that's left over from the commercial mining) and find some gorgeous and possibly precious stones. Bring your own tools and buckets, and feel free to ride here as part of your equestrian experience, or drive: the road will get you close, but you'll have a short hike in, so be prepared.

There are plenty of white-water rafting opportunities in the area, with several guide companies to choose from. **Hot Springs Rafting Co.** (81 Bridge St., 843/319-4586, www.hotspringsraftingco.com, rafting $50-85, funyak $50 per day, river tubing float trips $30) keeps you on the river right around Hot Springs. Their guided rafting trips are quite the thrill, but the unguided trips and "funyaks" (think white-water raft meets inflatable kayak) can give you a satisfying day on the water. **French Broad Adventures** (12 Good Adventures Lane, Marshall, 828/649-0486 or 800/570-7238, www.frenchbroadrafting.com, white-water rafting $55-88, flat-water rafting $40-53, zip-lining $95, canyoneering $130) can get you equipped and ready for a guided or unguided rafting trip on the French Broad River, which has both white-water and calm sections. Or get your adrenaline rush in the trees on a course that mixes zip lines, rappels, and short hikes to make a unique mountain experience.

Entertainment and Events

Mars Hill, a tiny college town, is a center of mountain culture thanks to Mars Hill College. The **Bascom Lamar Lunsford "Minstrel of the Appalachians" Festival** (828/689-1115, www.blueridgemusicnc.com, early fall, free) is a nearly 50-year-old annual gathering of some of the best mountain musicians, dancers, and craftspeople from this hot bed of folk traditions. Mars Hill College is also the home of the Southern Appalachian Repertory Theatre (Owen Theater, 44 College St., 828/689-1232, http://sartplays.com), a highly regarded ensemble presenting a range of contemporary drama, musicals, and family productions. SART's stage is in the Owen Theater, a great-looking old Baptist Church on the Mars Hill College campus.

Many other venues in Madison County towns feature live bluegrass and old-time music. Zuma Coffee (7 N. Main St., Marshall, 828/649-1617, www.zumascoffee.com, 8am-4pm Mon.-Fri., 8am-3pm Sat., under $10) has a free weekly bluegrass jam session (7pm Thurs.) and serves up a good cup of coffee. The Depot (282 S. Main St., Marshall, 828/206-2332), a former railroad depot building, has free concerts (6:30pm Fri.). And the Madison County Arts Council (90 S. Main St., Marshall, 828/649-1301, www.madisoncountyarts.com) wouldn't be worth their salt if they didn't host a few concerts, but lucky for you, they have plenty. The Arts Council puts on shows at their headquarters on Main Street and at the Ebbs Chapel Performing Arts Center (271 Laurel Valley Rd., Mars Hill, 828/689-3465, www.ebbschapelauditorium.com); check the schedule for shows, times, and prices.

Food

The Smoky Mountain Diner (70 Lance Ave., Hot Springs, 828/622-7571, www.hotspringsnc.org, 6am-2pm Mon.-Wed., 6am-7pm Thurs.-Sat., $2-17) is one part diner, one part your granny's kitchen table. Country staples like cornbread, pinto beans, chicken livers, and pork chops are on the menu, as are biscuits, pancakes, French toast, omelets, and even pizza. If you're so inclined, they have all-you-can-eat pinto beans for $5.

Big Pillow Brewing (26 Andrews Ave. N., Hot Springs, 828/539-1939, www.bigpillowbrewing.com, noon-8pm Tues.-Thurs., noon-9pm Fri.-Sat.), Hot Spring's first brewery, has arrived, and it brought with it the Grey Eagle Taqueria ($5-15). They have a very cool space with a biergarten feel and a stage where there's live music every Wednesday night. Their beer—they keep 9 or 10 on draft—runs the gamut from IPAs to kettle sours to porters and pale ales, and to go with that, the Grey Eagle Taqueria serves up tacos, burritos, bowls and more, so grab a light lager and some tacos and chow down.

You can grab a bite to eat or pick up some gourmet groceries (anyone fancy a fancy picnic?) at Vast Rivière Provisions (158 Bridge St., Hot Springs, 828/777-9379, www.vasteriviere.com, 11am-7pm daily, $10-24). Options are on the healthy side, so go with a quiche and mixed greens, a ramen or rice bowl, or a salad; or you can head to the store for grab-and-go and ready-to-eat meals along with goods for a charcuterie tray or stocking up a pantry.

When you head over to Dave's 209 (13075 Hwy. 209, Hot Springs, 828/622-0001, www.daves209.com, 11:30am-7:30pm Mon.-Tues. and Thurs.-Sat., 11:30am-5pm Sun., $2-11.50), be ready for a craveable burger and a milk shake you'll adore. This motorcycle-friendly spot is frequented by visitors on two wheels, four wheels, and more, and it's because of those burgers and the secret seasoning—Mountain Dust—they put on their fries. One taste and you'll get it.

Accommodations

Defying that worn-out stereotype of mountain isolation, Madison County has for centuries been a destination for vacationers because of its natural hot springs. Going back at least to the mid-18th century—and, according to tradition, long before the first European settlers arrived—the springs have had a reputation for curative powers. A succession of grand hotels operated at Hot Springs, all long since burned down. In one of the area's odder historical moments, the resort served as an internment camp for German prisoners during World War I, mainly commercial sailors and members of an orchestra who had the misfortune of being in the United States when the war broke out.

Modern visitors can still take a dip in the mineral springs. **Hot Springs Resort and Spa** (315 Bridge St., Hot Springs, 828/622-7676, www.nchotsprings.com, suites $120-225, cabins $75-250, camping $45-60, RV sites $65-75) is a much simpler affair than the old hotels; it's not a luxury destination but a place where you can lodge or camp for the night and soak in the famous 100°F water. Spa services run $50-130, and there's a series of outdoor mineral baths (1:30pm-9:45pm Mon.-Thurs., 9am-9:45pm Fri.-Sun., premium mineral bath $25-55 pp); come early as rates increase after 6pm.

There's an abundance of **rental homes** in Hot Springs, many of which you'll find under the Lodgings tab at www.hotspringsnc.org, but if you want to keep it simple, go with **Springbrook Cottages** (94 Andrews Ave. S., Hot Springs, 828/622-7385, www.springbrookcottages.com, $85-100). They have seven one-bedroom cottages overlooking Spring Creek and each cottage has a balcony where you can soak up that view in private. Three of the cottages have kitchens, so if you're planning on using Hot Springs as a base camp and you want to make a meal or two, be sure to request a cottage with something more than a microwave and a fridge.

Appalachian Trail hikers, and those who like to play hard and live cheap, should take notice of **Laughing Heart Lodge** (289 NW U.S. 25/70, Hot Springs, 828/622-0165, www.laughingheartlodge.com). Here you'll find several types of accommodations. First, the hostel ($30 bunk room, $40 single private room, $55 double private room, tent with full hostel facilities use $15), which was built in 1974 but still offers a modicum of comfort and privacy; then the lodge ($100-170), which has seven rooms, each with a private bath.

Information and Services

You'll find visitor information through the **Madison County Tourism Administration** at www.visitmadison-county.com. This site covers all the towns in the county and is therefore comprehensive. If you'd like to get more specific, try www.hotspringsnc.org from the **Hot Springs Tourism Association** for details on the town of Hot Springs and www.townofmarshall.org, for information that's more municipal than touristy on the town of Marshall. **Mars Hill**'s website—www.townofmarshill.org—is also geared more toward municipal information than tourist interests, but there is some that visitors may find of interest.

Getting There

To get to Madison County and the towns of Marshall and Hot Springs, you'll want to head north out of Asheville along U.S. 25/70. Take exit 19A for Weaverville-Woodfin, but continue on U.S. 25/70. You'll reach Marshall first, a 20-mile drive from Asheville; Hot Springs is another 16 miles north. Mars Hill is a 20-minute drive north from Asheville via U.S. 23/19. Follow U.S. 25/70 out of Asheville and stay on this route past Weaverville, where it will turn into U.S. 23/19; take exit 11 onto Highway 213 to get to Mars Hill.

Southern Blue Ridge and Foothills

The mountains of Polk, Rutherford, and Henderson Counties, south of Asheville, have an air of enchantment to them—meaning that the area gives the impalpable sense of having had a spell cast on it. No doubt a parapsychologist could assign a name to this atmosphere; it has a weird energy where it seems as likely that you'll encounter a fairy or an alien as a postal worker. There are some quantifiable symptoms of this peculiarity. For one, Polk County has its own climate; called the Thermal Belt, the meteorological pocket formed on this sheltered slope of the Blue Ridge has distinctly milder summers and winters than the surrounding areas. In the 19th century it became a favorite summering spot for the Southern elite. Some old houses and inns remain as vestiges of this genteel past.

In early 1874, Bald Mountain, north of Chimney Rock, began to rumble; it grew louder until, by the spring of that year, the mountain shook with such force that windows and crockery in valley homes shattered. A smoking, hissing crack opened in the side of the mountain, causing residents to fear a volcanic eruption. Many moved away or found religion. The shaking and rumbling eventually settled down. A crew of spelunkers a generation later concluded that the mountain was hollow and that enormous boulders sometimes became dislodged inside, showering into the caves below and causing the enormous booms. At least that's one theory.

Chimney Rock itself was the scene of bizarre phenomena in the first decade of the 1800s. Locals and visitors began to report witnessing spectral gatherings, crowds of people gathered on top of the rock and rising together into the sky. In the fall of 1811 multiple witnesses saw, on different occasions, two armed cavalries mounted on winged horses battling in the air over Chimney Rock, their gleaming swords clashing audibly. Whichever phantom cavalry triumphed in that battle, the rock is now maintained by the state of North Carolina and climbed daily by hundreds of visitors, none of whom have reported sightings of any spectral cavalry, horse droppings, or flashing sabers.

BREVARD

Brevard is the pleasant seat of the improbably named Transylvania County (unlike in vampire stories, it's not creepy, but beautiful in a Gothic forest way) only 48 minutes southwest of Asheville. As you might expect, Halloween is a big deal in this town. Brevard is also known for sheltering a population of rather startling and odd-looking white squirrels. The local legend about their origins is that their ancestors escaped from an overturned circus truck in Florida in 1940 and made their way to Brevard as pets. More likely, say researchers, they came from an exotic pet breeder in Florida and were acquired by a Brevard area family. In any case, the white squirrels escaped into the wild of Transylvania County, and you'll probably see their descendants in the area when you visit.

Sports and Recreation

About 10 miles south of Brevard, **DuPont State Recreational Forest** (U.S. 276, 828/877-6527, www.dupontstaterecreationalforest.com) has more than 90 miles of hiking trails on 10,000 acres. Some of Transylvania County's beautiful waterfalls are located within the forest and accessible on foot via moderate or strenuous forest trails, or, for people with disabilities only, with special permits and advance reservation, by vehicle. Visitors should use caution, wear brightly colored clothing, and leave that bearskin cape at home September-December, when hikers share the woods with hunters. The **Aleen Steinberg Visitor Center** (89 Buck Forest Rd., Cedar Mountain, 9am-5pm daily mid-Mar.-Dec., 10am-4pm Sat.-Sun.

Southern Blue Ridge and Foothills

© MOON.COM

TENNESSEE

NORTH CAROLINA

SOUTH CAROLINA

GEORGIA

Great Smoky Mountains National Park

Pisgah National Forest

Mt Mitchell State Park

Pisgah National Forest

Pisgah National Forest

10 mi
10 km

Marion
Little Switzerland
Black Mountain
Weaverville
Mars Hill
WOLF
Marshall
ZIP LINE WITH NAVITAT
FOLK ART CENTER
★ WESTERN NORTH CAROLINA NATURE CENTER
★ BILTMORE ESTATE
Asheville
DOWNTOWN ARCHITECTURE; LIVE MUSIC; RIVER ARTS DISTRICT
Canton
NORTH CAROLINA ARBORETUM
Mt Pisgah
Blue Ridge Pkwy
Waynesville
Richland Balsam
Pisgah National Forest
CRADLE OF FORESTRY
PISGAH RANGER DISTRICT
Sliding Rock
Looking Glass Falls
Brevard
French Broad River
Lake Toxaway
Sapphire
Whitewater Falls
Cashiers
Highlands
Sylva
Dillsboro
Gneiss
Cherokee
END OF THE BLUE RIDGE PARKWAY
Waterville
Maggie Valley
Dry Falls
Bridal Veil Falls
Bryson City
Franklin
Lake Lure
Lake Lure
Chimney Rock
Chimney Rock
Rutherfordton
Columbus
Tryon
Saluda
Hendersonville
Flat Rock
CARL SANDBURG HOME NATIONAL HISTORIC SITE
Pisgah National Forest

Jan.-mid-Mar.) has restrooms and trash cans and is staffed by volunteers who are happy to help with trail recommendations. The visitors center is near the trailhead to Hooker Falls.

Many of the hiking and mountain biking trails are true rugged forest paths; others, like those that lead to a trio of waterfalls—Hooker, Triple, and High Falls—are wide maintained avenues through the woods. The hike, or hikes, as you'll follow several trails, to Triple and High Falls can be hot, sweaty affairs in spring and summer, so bring water. But the views are more than worth it, and in fall it's a phenomenal hike. After you make this longer hike, make the shorter one to the lower Hooker Falls and go for a swim in the crisp mountain water. Already cool, it will feel downright cold—and quite refreshing—on a hot day. If you hike the three falls, you're looking at a 2-mile loop for High Falls, a 0.4-mile trail to Triple Falls, and another 0.4-mile trail to Hooker, for a total of 2.8 miles. Downloadable maps and more information are available through Friends of DuPont Forest (www.dupontforest.com).

★ WATERFALL TOURING

Local Guide Craig Miller helps visitors discover some of the more beautiful and remote waterfalls in Transylvania County through his Land of Waterfalls Tours (828/884-8982, www.tourwaterfalls.com, $75 for 2 people, $10 per additional person). When you're ready to chase some waterfalls, Miller will meet you at your hotel, B&B, or another convenient spot to start your tour. Most tours hit 6-7 waterfalls, and all within an easy walk of the parking area (which makes this great for kids or folks with mobility difficulties), but you can customize your tour to fit your ability level and interests (as you can imagine, Craig leads a lot of photographers to the falls around here).

You'll find maps for sale—and possibly some for free—showing the area's waterfalls in the outdoor shops and visitors center. And there are specific books—full sized guides like this, as well as little pocket-size trail-friendly write-ups and maps. I've used all of these and

then some, but I always end up looking at the waterfalls page on www.explorebrevard.com, so save yourself a few minutes and start there.

Entertainment and Events

The Brevard Music Center (349 Andante Lane, 828/862-2100, www.brevardmusic.org) has attracted the highest-caliber young musicians for more than 70 years for intensive summer-long classical music instruction. Throughout the summer, Brevard Music Center students, as well as visiting soloists of international fame, put on world-class concerts, performing works that have included Tchaikovsky as well as Gilbert and Sullivan.

Brevard Brewing Company (63 E. Main St., 282/885-2101, www.brevard-brewing.com, 2pm-10pm daily) was the first brewery in the county, and it always keeps six taps flowing with its own brews, including a Bohemian pilsner, a Munich-style dunkel, a lager, an IPA, and an American red ale. Ecusta Brewing (43 Pisgah Hwy., Suite 3, Pisgah Forest, 828/966-2337, www.ecustabrewing.com, 1pm-9pm Mon.-Thurs., noon-9pm Fri.-Sat., noon-8pm Sun.) is a few miles north of town but worth the short drive. Its range of styles will please everyone from hop-heads (IPAs, pale ales) to sour fans (sours incorporating ginger and mint, blood orange, and wild yeasts).

An import from Colorado but no less welcome is Oskar Blues Brewery (342 Mountain Industrial Dr., 828/883-2337, www.oskarblues.com, noon-8pm Sun.-Thurs., noon-9pm Fri.-Sat.), which serves popular beers that include Mama's Little Yella Pils (a Czech pilsner) and Old Chub Scotch Ale as well as hard seltzer and the thirst-quenching Margarita Gose. If you're hungry, the Oskar Blues Chubwagon ($4.50-12) serves burgers, fries, hot dogs, and a mean chicken-tender sandwich.

The Hub and Pisgah Tavern (11 Mama's Place, Pisgah Forest, 828/884-8670, www.

1: Brevard's small-town charm 2: waterfall in Transylvania County 3: covered bridge above High Falls in Dupont State Recreational Forest 4: Sliding Rock waterfall

thehubpisgah.com, 10am-6pm Mon.-Fri., 9am-6pm Sat., 10am-5pm Sun.) is a kind of all-in-one taproom, bike shop, gear depot, and food-truck stop that sits right at the edge of the Pisgah National Forest. The tavern serves cold brews on tap as well as in cans and bottles. Beer choices span the country, but you'll always find a good selection of local beers. While you work on your pint, shop for a new bike or some new gear, or step outside and see which food truck is serving; if there's a line of locals waiting to order, that's a good sign.

Brevard's new **Lumber Arts District** (100-300 blocks of King St., Brevard) has a number of things going on in an area once home to Brevard Lumber and other building-supply houses. Live music at **185 King Street** (185 King St., Brevard, 828/877-1850, www.185kingst.com, 4pm-9pm Tues., 4pm-11pm Wed.-Fri., noon-11pm Sat., noon-10pm Sun.), where you'll also find a **kitchen** (4pm-8pm Tues., 4pm-9pm Wed.-Fri., noon-9pm Sat., noon-8pm Sun., $4-14) serving snacks, along with **Noblebraü Brewing** (4pm-9pm Tues., 4pm-11pm Wed.-Fri., noon-11pm Sat., noon-10pm Sun.) with a half-dozen brews on draft. Nearby **UpCountry Brewing Company** (212 King St., Suite B, Brevard, 828/885-7538, www.upcountrybrewing.com, 4pm-9pm Mon., 2pm-9pm Wed.-Thurs., 2pm-10pm Fri.-Sat., 2pm-9pm Sun.) has spirits from their distillery in Asheville as well as beers in cans and on draft; style-wise they're wide-ranging, and you'll find sours, stouts, several spins on IPAs, and a great maibock.

Shopping

Brevard calls to a number of fine and folk artists, and some of the best local work is represented at **Number 7 Fine Arts and Crafts Cooperative** (2 W. Main St., 828/883-2294, www.number7arts.org, 11am-5pm Mon.-Sat., noon-4pm Sun.). This gallery has featured works by a diverse group of around 25 Transylvania County artists for more than 15 years. Ask about the photography, textiles, oils and watercolors, sculptures, and pottery on display—the artists themselves work the

register and can help you find a piece you love.

Named for Brevard's famed creatures, the **White Squirrel Shoppe** (6 W. Main St., 828/877-3530, www.whitesquirrelshoppe.com, 10:30am-5:30pm Mon.-Thurs., 10am-6pm Fri.-Sat., 11:30am-5pm Sun.) is where to go for souvenirs. The shop's got a bit of everything, so drop in and pick up a memento or two.

Over in the Lumber Arts District, **The Underground Salvage Co.** (22 W. French Broad St., Brevard, 828/885-2744, 10am-5pm Thurs.-Sat.) is a wonderland for the curious and crafty. These folks salvage old barns, houses, and buildings of all sorts and have a warehouse full of stuff to show for it. Live-edge wood slabs and reclaimed lumber, antique doors, fireplace fixtures, tin ceilings, and all sorts of stuff is on hand for you to buy, or you can take home something they made in the shop around back. They also have furniture and fixtures (door knobs, hinges, and the like) and all sorts of stuff to dig through.

Outdoor gear and a solid selection of T-shirts, plus some North Carolina beer on tap—which you can sip while you shop—makes **D. D. Bullwinkel's Outdoors** (60 E. Main St., 828/862-4700, www.ddbullwinkels.com, 10am-6pm Mon.-Thurs., 10am-7pm Fri.-Sat., noon-6pm Sun.) a must-stop. You'll find whatever you forgot or just realized you need on a trip along the parkway, including backpacks, hiking poles, boots and socks, water bottles, and technical clothing. The staff are outdoors devotees, so ask any of your gear questions or for suggestions on where to hike, picnic, or skinny dip.

Food

Located in Brevard's Lumber Arts District, ★ **Vescovo** (175 King St., Brevard, 828/885-7630, www.vescovobrevard.com, 5pm-9pm Tues.-Sat., $17-45) has become a favorite spot in town. Everything here—the dry-aged steaks, the crazy-fresh seafood, and the Italian dishes—is beautiful on the plate and terrific on the fork. Start off with the Filet Meatballs or the Beets by Trey (he's the chef-owner), move on to the Cacio e Pepe or the veggie-loaded Spaghettini Verdura, then your choice of mains—scallops, sea bass, steak, a monster pork chop—and cap it off with an after-dinner espresso or drink.

★ **Marco Trattoria** (204 W. Main St., 828/883-4841, www.marcotrattoria.com, 11am-3pm daily, 5pm-9pm Mon.-Sat., $9-24) is from the former owners of Hobnob, one of Brevard's top restaurants for years. Following a little break to find some inspiration, chef Marc Dambax is back with an Italian-inspired restaurant that's quickly become known as one of the best restaurants in town. Pizzas fly out of the wood-fired oven, and the menu is full of Italian classics and Dambax's Italianate spin on things through dishes like North Carolina mountain trout *piccata* and pancetta-wrapped monkfish served over seasonal veggies.

The Blind Mule at Toxaway Station (14 S. Gaston St., 828/553-8978, www.blindmulerestaurant.com, 5pm-9pm Wed.-Sun., reservations required, $10-35) serves a menu rich in tapas and small sharable plates, but they don't forget the entrées, with 3-4 on offer at any given time. Fresh seasonal ingredients inspire the menu, which changes weekly, and whether you're ordering a salad, some poutine, a burger, an Indian-spiced lamb pot pie, or an entrée (their treatment of trout—often served with some great grits—is a winner), you'll leave happy you stopped by for a meal.

For an old-school shake or a quick bite, head to **Rocky's Grill & Soda Shop** (50 S. Broad St., 828/877-5375, 11am-6pm Thurs.-Mon., $5-12). This must-stop has been around since 1942, and the nostalgic counter with its line of chrome stools will transport you back to the heyday of soda fountains. Grab a malt, a milk shake, an ice cream soda, a root beer float, or an egg cream, which are especially rewarding after a morning hike or bike ride.

When the weather's right, dining on the patio at **Jordan Street Café** (48 W. Jordan St., 828/883-2558, www.thejordanstreetcafe.com, 4pm-9pm Thurs., 4pm-10pm Fri.-Sat., 11am-2pm and 4pm-9pm Sun., dinner $10-28, brunch $14-20) is the way to go. They serve a little bit of everything—fish-and-chips, blackened chicken sandwiches, burgers, salads, daily flatbread pizza and quesadilla specials—but the menu is simple enough to keep it focused.

If you want a picnic lunch you can always head to the store and pick up a few things for your meal alfresco, or you can pay a visit to **Smoke On Drive-Thru BBQ** (585 S. Caldwell St., Brevard, 828/552-4584, www.eatsmokeonbbq.com, 11am-8pm Mon.-Sat., $12-25). Pick up a pulled pork, pimento cheese, brisket or jackfruit sandwich or taco plate; grab a hearty platter piled with ribs, smoked chicken, pulled pork, or brisket; and don't forget the sides, then head out to a park downtown, a picnic table in the Pisgah National Forest, or an overlook on the Blue Ridge Parkway for a memorable meal.

PISGAH RANGER DISTRICT

Just north of Brevard in the town of Pisgah Forest is the main entrance to the **Pisgah Ranger District** (1600 Pisgah Hwy., Pisgah Forest, 828/877-3265, www.fs.usda.gov, 9am-4:30pm daily Nov.-Mar., 9am-5pm daily Apr.-Oct.) of the Pisgah National Forest. The forest covers 500,000 acres, which is a large swath of western North Carolina, but this 157,000-acre ranger district has many of the forest's favorite attractions. A good topographic map is available from National Geographic (www.natgeomaps.com). You'll find miles of U.S. Forest Service roads to explore, plenty of backcountry camping, and some amazing mountain bike riding, including some excellent single-track runs. In the ranger district are more than 275 miles of hiking trails and several campgrounds; the most easily accessible is **Davidson River Campground** (1 Davidson River Circle, Pisgah Forest, campground 828/384-6666, reservations 800/444-6777, www.recreation.gov, year-round, $28-56), which is 1.5 miles from the Brevard entrance. It has showers and toilets.

The **Shining Rock Wilderness** and the **Middle Prong Wilderness,** which adjoins Shining Rock to the southwest, are a rugged terrain that rises from 3,200 feet at its lowest point, along the West Pigeon River, to a towering 6,400 feet at Richmond Balsam. **Cold Mountain,** made famous by the book and movie of the same name, is a real peak located within the Shining Rock Wilderness, and seeing it helps make the struggles of the fictional characters more real. These mountains are steep and the forests dense, and what trails there are have no signage. This is a popular area among experienced backwoods trekkers, but it is not recommended for casual visitors because it is exceedingly easy to get lost. At a minimum, hikers should be adept at using both a compass and a topographic map before venturing into these wilderness areas.

Not to be confused with Shining Rock, **Sliding Rock** is an easily accessible waterfall and swimming spot with a parking lot ($4), bathhouse, and lifeguards (10am-6pm daily late May-early Sept.). You can actually ride down the 60-foot waterfall, a smooth rock face (not so smooth that you shouldn't wear sturdy britches), over which 11,000 gallons of water rush every minute into the chilly swimming hole below.

If you have kids with you, make sure you stop at the **Cradle of Forestry** (11250 Pisgah Hwy., Pisgah Forest, 828/877-3130, www.cradleofforestry.com, 10am-5pm Wed.-Mon. mid-Apr.-early Nov., $6 adults, $3 ages 5-12). This museum and activity complex commemorates the rise of the forestry profession in the United States, which originated here at a turn-of-the-20th-century training school in the forests once owned by George Washington Vanderbilt, master of the Biltmore Estate. Plow days and living history days throughout the year give an interesting glimpse into this region's old-time methods of farming and frontier living. Self-guided trails lead through the woods to many interesting locations of this campus of America's first school of forestry. Most of what's here is geared toward little ones.

Accommodations

Slip back in time at the ★ **Sunset Motel** (523 S. Broad St., 828/884-9106, www.thesunsetmotel.com, $115-160), a kitschy throwback to the days of the classic roadside motel: It's cheap, comfortable, and has chairs right outside your door so you can visit with your neighbors. It also has the best modern convenience—free Wi-Fi. The staff is super friendly and ready to help with suggestions for places to eat and things to do. You can add on tickets to the Brevard Music Center, waterfall tours, and more when you book your room.

Built in 1885 and listed on the National Register of Historic Places, **The Inn at Brevard** (315 E. Main St., 828/884-2105, www.theinnatbrevard.com, $195-300) is spacious, beautiful, and kid-friendly. The stately 14-room B&B was built in 1885 and makes a good picture; the rooms are well appointed, and there's a full breakfast every day. Throughout the Inn you'll find photography showing the inn through history and the owners' incredible art collection of paintings from the Renaissance to today.

One of the most lauded places to stay in North Carolina is the nearby ★ **Greystone Inn** (220 Greystone Lane, Lake Toxaway, 21 miles west of Brevard, 828/966-4700, www.greystoneinn.com, $309-429). Perched on the banks of Lake Toxaway, Greystone Inn has 30 rooms, many with balconies overlooking the lake; a spa (treatments from $90) that's the picture of tranquility; and a gorgeous lakeside restaurant serving breakfast (8am-11am daily, $12-15), lunch (noon-3pm daily, $16-20), and dinner (5pm-9pm daily, $20-51). The concierge can help you arrange activities like falconry, horseback riding, mountain biking, road cycling, fishing, and recreation on Lake Toxaway. The elite have been playing on Lake Toxaway for quite some time, and back in 1910, Lucy Armstrong, a socialite from Savannah, and her husband were vacationing here, joining the Rockefellers, Vanderbilts, Firestones, and other Gilded Age barons on their getaway, when she fell in love with the place. By 1913 she decided to build a vacation home here, and by 1915, what we know as the Greystone Inn was built. After years of use, Armstrong died and the property fell into disrepair until the mid-1980s, when the current owners discovered the place and began the long process of restoring it to its former glory and beyond.

CAMPING

Davidson River Campground (1 Davidson River Circle, Pisgah Forest, campground 828/384-6666, reservations 800/444-6777, www.recreation.gov, year-round, $28-56) is just outside Brevard in the Shining Rock Wilderness Area. There are around 160 sites here, some with river access. Each site comes equipped with a picnic table, fire ring, and grill. Hot showers and flush toilets are available. It's the most convenient campground for exploring the hiking and fishing in the area as well as checking out the waterfalls.

Just a 10-minute drive south of Brevard, on 14 mountaintop acres, is **Ash Grove Mountain Cabins and Camping** (29 Ash Grove Way, 828/885-7216, www.ash-grove. com, tent and RV sites $33-55, cabins $130-150, $10 per night for 2 pets), with some pet-friendly facilities available. This retreat is open year-round, unlike others in the area, so you can experience all four seasons in this lovely spot. The cabins are quaint and cozy, and the campsites are well maintained. Common areas feature a bonfire pit, a few lawn games, and a tiny waterfall.

The Adventure Village & Lodgings (129 Israel Rd., 828/862-5411, www.theadventure-village.com) has loads of places to stay. Across the property are 19 cabins ($89-155), 50 RV sites ($44) with 50 more expected to open by late 2022, and a whole heap of primitive tent camping sites ($22). The property is 90 acres all set up to help you have a good visit. There's a catfish pond, biking and hiking trails, a playground, and a swimming and wading pool. Add in the super-friendly folks who run the place and you've got an excellent spot to stay.

HENDERSONVILLE

An easy drive of 30 minutes south from Asheville, Hendersonville is a comfortable small city with a walkable downtown filled with boutiques and cafés. It's also the heart of North Carolina's apple industry. Hundreds of orchards cover the hillsides of Henderson County, and all along the highway, long packinghouses bustle in late summer as they process more than three million tons of apples. There are also many shops and produce stands run by members of old orchard-owning families, where you can buy apples singly or by the bushel, along with cider, preserves, and many other apple products.

Sights

One of North Carolina's cool small transportation museums is located at the Hendersonville Airport. The **Western North Carolina Air Museum** (1340 Gilbert St., 828/698-2482, www.westernnorthcarolinaairmuseum.com, noon-5pm Sat.-Sun., free) houses a collection of more than a dozen historic small aircraft, both originals and reproductions. Most are from the 1930s and 1940s, though some are even older; all are wonderfully fun contraptions to visit.

Sierra Nevada Brewery (100 Sierra Nevada Way, Mills River, information 828/681-5300, taproom 828/708-6242, www.sierranevada.com, 11am-9pm Sun.-Thurs., 11am-10pm Fri.-Sat.) is about 20 minutes from Hendersonville, midway between Hendersonville and Asheville, and it's a beer lover's playground. They have tours of the brewery (on the hour 11am-3pm Mon.-Thurs., 11am-4pm Fri.-Sat., noon-4pm Sun., free), tours showing off their sustainable practices (2:30pm Fri.-Sat., free), and a three-hour Beer Geek Tour (their name, not mine; 2:30pm Thurs., $30), as well as plenty of beer to sample. There's a fantastic little restaurant ($9-28) on-site and an indoor and outdoor space for concerts and special events.

Shopping

Hendersonville's downtown **Curb Market** (221 N. Church St., at 2nd Ave., 828/692-8012, www.curbmarket.com, 8am-2pm Thurs. and Sat. year-round, 8am-2pm Tues. Apr.-Dec.) has been in operation since 1924. Here you can buy fresh locally grown fruits, vegetables, and flowers; fresh-baked cakes, pies, and breads; jams, jellies, and pickles made in local home kitchens; and the work of local woodcarvers, weavers, and other craftspeople.

Along the curved main street cutting through downtown are plenty of shops and some adorable man-sized bear statues that shop owners and community members have painted, bedazzled, and displayed, but one shop that stands out is **Dancing Bear Toys** (418 N. Main St., 828/693-4500, www.dancingbeartoys.com, 10am-5:30pm Mon. and Wed.-Sat.). This place is lousy with games, toys, kits, models, gadgets, and accessories for kids and lighthearted adults.

Food

★ **Umi Japanese Fine Dining** (633 N. Main St., 828/698-8048, www.umisushinc. com, 11am-3pm and 4:30pm-9pm Mon.-Thurs., 11am-3pm and 4:30pm-9:30pm Fri., noon-9:30pm Sat., noon-9pm Sun., $8-28) surprised me. For starters, I didn't expect to find good sushi anywhere in the mountains except maybe Asheville, but this is some of the best I've eaten in the state. Every roll is as close to perfect as you'll get because their sushi chef and his crew of maki rollers take fish deliveries 3-4 times a week. Sure, you can get beef teriyaki or miso salmon, but why would you when the rolls are so good? They also have a nice sake menu, and they serve their own wine here.

Asheville's **White Duck Taco Shop** (500 7th Ave. E., Hendersonville, 828/595-9871, 11:30am-9pm Tues.-Sun., www.whiteducktacoshop.com, $4-7) has slowly spread across the region and now has locations here in Hendersonville as well as Charlotte and Matthews, North Carolina; Greenville, South Carolina; and two locations in Tennessee. At every spot they serve an eclectic and delicious blend of tacos like Korean beef bulgogi, duck with mole, Thai peanut chicken, buffalo chicken, a tofu *bánh mì*, and more.

There are a good many gastropub-type restaurants in Hendersonville, so a restaurant like **Postero** (401 N. Main St., Hendersonville, 828/595-9676, www.posterohvl.com, 11:30am-2:30pm Thurs.-Sat., 5pm-8:30pm Tues.-Thurs., 5pm-9:30pm Fri.-Sat., $12-30) really stands out, but let me say this place would stand out anywhere. Whether you're getting a table full of starters to share (their duck liver mousse and their locally sourced cheese and charcuterie boards are top-notch) or an entrée to fall in love with (and you will fall in love with monkfish that gets a Tuscan treatment, a massive pork chop with a comforting set of sides, or whatever's special today), pair it with a couple of crafty cocktails or local libations, and you're in for a great meal.

I find local trails are a good way to familiarize myself with an area, and the **Hendersonville Cheers! Trail** ($10) is no exception. This craft beverage trail features beer, wine, cider, and mead (an ancient wine-beer hybrid made with fermented honey) across 23 possible stops in the region. Maps are available at the **Visitor Center** (201 S. Main St., 828/693-9708, www.visithendersonvillenc.org, 9am-5pm Mon.-Fri., 10am-5pm Sat.-Sun.), and after you collect a dozen stamps, you can redeem your passport for some Cheers! Trail swag.

You can dine on some tasty grub and benefit a program devoted to aiding the survivors of violence at **Dandelion, a Local Eatery** (127 5th Ave. W., 828/595-9365, www.safelightfamily.org, 11am-2:30pm Mon.-Fri., $10). The menu stays simple, but you'll leave full and happy after a sandwich—there's a dozen on the menu—or a Southern dish like grits or Tomato Pie (it's exactly what it sounds like, and you should totally try it) or a filling salad. Their Halfski is a classic half sandwich, half soup combo, and the chicken salad sandwich is one of the best in the area.

Accommodations

At **Melange Bed & Breakfast Inn and Gardens** (1230 5th Ave. W., 828/697-5253, www.melangebb.com, from $225) is just a short walk from downtown and is the sort of place you don't want to leave. The six rooms are comfy and tastefully decorated (not over-done with thematic decorations or antiques, like too many B&Bs), and you just feel at home here. If you have special dietary needs—vegan, paleo, gluten-free—they're happy to accommodate.

Pinebrook Manor (2701 Kanuga Rd., 828/698-2707, www.pinebrookmanor.com, $195-265) has four rooms named for liter-ary figures, and I think their pricing reveals something about the owners' literary tastes. The hosts are top-notch, the whole place is lovely, and the breakfast is much better than the typical B&B quiche.

There are a number of recognizable chain hotels in and around Hendersonville and nearby Flat Rock, and if you need to boost your loyalty points, any of those will do for a night or two, but I always like local options even if it's not a B&B. In Hendersonville, the **Echo Mountain Inn** (2849 Laurel Park Hwy., Hendersonville, 828/693-9626, www.echomountaininn.com, $99-205) consists of two facilities, the 17-room Main Inn, built in 1896, and the Little Echo, a motel-style stay with 8 rooms; each facility has a distinct look and feel, but the Main Inn is the more elegant of the two. And near Flat Rock, but still only a few minutes from Hendersonville, **The Lodge at Flat Rock** (42 McMurray Rd., Flat Rock, 828/693-9910, www.mountainlodgeflat-rock.com, $99-205) has more of a traditional hotel feel in an all-suites configuration.

FLAT ROCK
Sights

Just south of Hendersonville is the historic village of Flat Rock. Founded in the early 19th century as a vacation spot for the Charleston plantation gentry, Flat Rock retains a delicate, cultured ambience created many years ago. Many artists and writers have lived in this area, most famously Carl Sandburg, whose house, Connemara, is preserved as the **Carl Sandburg Home National Historic Site** (1800 Little River Rd., Flat Rock, 828/693-4178, www.nps.gov/carl, grounds sunrise-sunset daily, house tour $8 adults, $5 over age 61, free under age 16). Sandburg and his family lived here for more than 20 years, and during that time he wrote and won the Pulitzer Prize for *Complete Poems*, no doubt observed bemusedly as his wife and daugh-ters raised champion dairy goats (a herd of goats lives on the grounds today). Half-hour tours take visitors through the house to see many of the Sandburgs' belongings. There is a bookstore in the house and more than five miles of trails through the property. As a poet whose first steps were in the mountain clay, I have a soft spot for this place, and it's easy for me to see what Sandburg found so inspiring and appealing about the quiet, the air, and the space; take a moment to sit and reflect while you're here, and try writing a couple of lines of your own.

Throughout the mountains you're in apple country. **Sky Top Orchards** (1193 Pinnacle Mountain Rd., 828/692-7930, www.skyto-porchard.com, 9am-6pm daily Aug.-Nov.) is a pick-your-own orchard with 22 varieties of apples as well as fresh cider, jams, jellies, and awesome apple cider doughnuts. Be sure to bring cash when you visit, as their card reader doesn't always work.

Entertainment and Events

Another literary landmark in the village is the **Flat Rock Playhouse** (2661 Greenville Hwy., Flat Rock, 828/693-0731, www.flat-rockplayhouse.org). Now the state theater of North Carolina, the Flat Rock Playhouse's his-tory dates to 1940, when a roving theater com-pany called the Vagabonds wandered down from New York and converted an old gristmill in the village into a stage. They returned every summer for the next few years, entertaining the locals with plays held in a succession of locations, from the old mill to a circus tent, eventually constructing a permanent theater.

They now have a 10-month season, drawing more than 90,000 patrons each year.

Shopping

You'll find quite a few nice galleries and studios in Flat Rock along a strip called Little Rainbow Row. One place that jumps out is the anchor of Little Rainbow Row, **The Wrinkled Egg** (2710 Greenville Hwy., 828/696-3998, www.thewrinkledegg.com, 10am-5pm Mon.-Sat., noon-5pm Sun.). This weird little store sells custom care packages for kids heading off to summer camp: scout camp, equestrian camp, religious camp, and whatever other summer camps kids go to these days. It's a fun place to stop to get a little something for the kids in your life.

Firefly Craft Gallery (2689-D Greenville Hwy., Flat Rock, 828/231-0764, www.fireflycraftgallery.com, 11am-5pm Tues.-Sat.) carries the work of dozens of artisans, artists, and craftspeople from western North Carolina in a wide range of media. You'll find jewelry, oil paintings, watercolors, pottery, sculpture, photography, and more in this charming spot. Just up the road a piece, **The Gallery at Flat Rock** (2702-A Greenville Hwy., Flat Rock, 828/698-7000, www.galleryflatrock.com, 11am-4pm Tues.-Sat., noon-4pm Sun., and by appointment) presents a well-curated selection of fine art from 60 or so regionally and nationally acclaimed artists as well as artist talks and workshops.

Food

Flat Rock's a pretty small town but there are a few good places to eat if you know where to look. I feel like I have to recommend a place for barbecue, and the folks at **Hubba Hubba Smokehouse** (2724 Greenville Hwy., Flat Rock, 828/694-3551, www.hubbahubbasmokehouse.com, 11am-3pm Thurs.-Sun. mid-Apr.-Oct., $10-20) make it easy because the 'cue and sauces—which encompass styles from North and South Carolina as well as Texas—deliver. Locals say you can eat any of the barbecue naked (meaning without sauce, not without pants), but I'm a sauce lover,

so you're going to have to decide for yourself. Their sister restaurant, **Campfire Grill** (2770 Greenville Hwy., Flat Rock, 828/595-9849, www.campfiregrillnc.com, 11am-3pm Tues.-Wed., 11am-8pm Thurs.-Sat., $15-32), serves smoked wings, some awesome salads (the harvest salad will do you right), burgers, sandwiches, and entrées like chicken pot pie and crab cakes for lunch and dinner; the menu lets you have a substantial meal or split a salad and sandwich for a lighter lunch. **Honey and Salt** (2730 Greenville Hwy., Flat Rock, 828/676-8322, www.honeyandsaltnc.com, 8am-2pm Wed.-Sun., $6-12) keeps breakfast and lunch simple with grit and granola bowls, egg sandwiches, biscuits, and an assortment of bakery goods.

SALUDA AND VICINITY

Just 10 minutes east and south of Hendersonville, bordering South Carolina, Polk County is home to several interesting little towns, most notably Tryon and Saluda, along with a lot of beautiful mountain country. In Saluda you'll find a tiny downtown laid out along the old Norfolk Southern Railway tracks. The tracks at Saluda are the top of the steepest standard-gauge mainline railroad grade in the United States. This county's history abounds with exciting stories of runaway trains that derailed at spots like Slaughterhouse Curve; more than two dozen railroad workers have been killed on this grade. Visitor information on Polk County is available through **First Peak of the Blue Ridge** (www.firstpeaknc.com).

Sports and Recreation

Equestrian life plays a growing role in Polk and the surrounding counties of North Carolina's southern mountains. The **Foothills Equestrian Nature Center** (3381 Hunting Country Rd., Tryon, 828/859-9021, www.fence.org), known as FENCE, occupies 380 beautiful acres along the border with South Carolina. The equestrian center has stables for 200 horses and two lighted show rings. FENCE hosts cross-country, three-day,

A-rated hunter and jumper, dressage, and many other equestrian events throughout the year, along with offering regular hikes and bird-watching excursions on its beautiful property.

The Gorge (166 Honey Bee Dr., Saluda, 828/373-2312, www.thegorgezipline.com, $125) gives you a treetop view of the mountains and Green River Gorge as you zip-line from tree to tree. There are 11 zips, three rappels, and a heart-pounding sky bridge on this course that descends 1,100 feet in total. The zip lines total well over a mile, and this is one of the best in the state; if adrenaline is your thing, you have to check it out.

Entertainment and Events
Saluda's got a lot going on throughout the year. The **Saluda Arts Festival** happens on the third Saturday in May and features 80-plus artists from the Carolinas and Tennessee in this all-day art fair. The **Saluda Tailgate Market** (4:30pm-6:30pm Fri. May-Oct.), an agriculture-only market, brings growers and ranchers into town to sell what's fresh. The **Top of the Grade Concert Series** runs June-September and brings in musicians and bands for free monthly concerts. In July, Saluda celebrates **Coon Dog Day** with a festival devoted to these baying and barking hounds that includes a parade, skills tests, a street fair, and music.

Food
We love to eat in North Carolina, and even in a tiny town like Saluda, you'll find some great bites. With a menu that's packed with flavorful dishes, **The Purple Onion** (16 E. Main St., Saluda, 828/749-1179, www.purpleonionsaluda.com, 11am-8:30pm Mon. and Thurs.-Sat., 11am-3pm Sun., $6-34) is a favorite. Pizzas—including a great wild mushroom and arugula pie—and salads take inspiration from the Mediterranean coastlines of Spain, Italy, and Greece. Entrées like the Sunburst mountain trout and the Brasstown farm rib-eye keep other inspirations and flavors local.

Wildflour Bakery (173 E. Main St., 828/749-3356, http://wildflourbakerync.com, 9am-2pm Sat.-Mon., 9am-8pm Wed., 11am-8pm Fri., $8-13, pizza night $8-26) stone-grinds wheat every morning to make absolutely delicious breads. Breakfast and lunch are served, making this a great place to fill up before a day of kayaking or hiking. Don't miss Pizza Night (Wed. and Fri.), where they serve up regular or thin-crust (and even gluten-free) pies with your choice of toppings, along with 10 specialty pizzas. You can bring your own wine or beer on pizza night, so order a pie or two, crack open a local brew, and settle in for a little while.

CHIMNEY ROCK AND LAKE LURE
Just one of the many geological beauties you'll find along the Blue Ridge Parkway corridor, **Chimney Rock State Park** (Main St., Chimney Rock, 828/625-9611, www.chimneyrockpark.com, ticket plaza 8:30am-5:30pm daily, park 10am-4:30pm daily Jan.-mid-Mar., 8:30am-5:30pm daily mid-Mar.-early-Nov., 8:30am-4:30pm daily early-Nov.-Dec., $17 adults, $8 ages 5-15, free under age 5) is about 45 minutes from Asheville, at Milepost 384.7 on U.S. 74 Alt east. The 315-foot tower of stone that is Chimney Rock stands on the side of the mountain. To get to the top of the chimney, you can take a 26-story elevator ride, or hike the **Outcroppings Trail,** a 0.25-mile trail nicknamed "The Ultimate Stairmaster." No matter how you get here, the view is spectacular.

There are number of additional dizzying views to take in and mountain-hugging trails to hike in Chimney Rock State Park. The **Needle's Eye** and **Opera Box** are two such formations. The **Hickory Nut Falls Trail** takes you to the top of the 400-foot Hickory Nut Falls via a moderately difficult 0.75-mile trail. One of the most recognizable views is on the **Skyline-Cliff Trail** loop, a strenuous two-hour hike that will take you to some places you may recognize from the 1992 film *The Last of the Mohicans*. There are also kid-friendly trails. Bring your little ones along on the 0.6-mile **Woodland Walk,** where animal sculptures and "journal entries" from Grady the Groundhog wait to be discovered. A trail map covering the entire park is available at the park's website (www.chimneyrockpark.com).

Chimney Rock is more than just hiking trails. In November, Santa rappels down the tower in a pre-Christmas display of his chimney-navigating prowess, but year-round you'll find rock climbers in the park for bouldering, top-rope, and multi-pitch climbs. Want to try but don't know the terms? **Fox Mountain Guides** (888/284-8433, www.foxmountainguides.com, 2-hour lesson $110 for 1 climber, $160 for 2 climbers, $180 for 3 climbers) will gear you up and show you the ropes.

Nearby **Rumbling Bald Mountain** (112 Mountain Blvd., Lake Lure) is part of Chimney Rock State Park, and climbers couldn't be happier. Here you'll find more than 1,500 bouldering "problems" to solve (solving it means traversing it successfully). Currently, only the south face is open to climbing, and commercial climbing guides are not allowed to operate here.

Sports and Recreation

Lake Lure, a 720-acre artificial highland lake, was created in the 1920s. Several local outfitters will set you up for a day on the lake or on area rivers. Try **Lake Lure Adventure Company** (470 Memorial Hwy., 828/625-8066, www.lakelureadventurecompany.com, 9am-8pm daily Memorial Day-Labor Day, call Sept.-Apr.) for water-ski and wakeboard trips ($205 per hour), fishing (half-day $300), or kayak and stand-up paddleboard rentals (from $20 per hour). Rent a boat (2-hour minimum, from $95 per hour) to ride around and sightsee, go fishing, or have a picnic. For a relaxed sightseeing tour on the lake, **Lake Lure Tours** (next to Lake Lure Town Marina, 877/386-4255, www.lakeluretours.com, 9am-5pm daily, tours hourly from 11am, $18 adults, $16 seniors, $8 under age 12) offers dinner and sunset cruises as well as daytime jaunts.

In nearby Mill Springs, about 15 minutes south on Highway 9, a huge equestrian center hosts competitions, horse shows, lessons, and rides year-round. **Tryon International Equestrian Center** (TIEC, 25 International Blvd., Mill Spring, 828/863-1000, www.tryon.coth.com) puts on free hunter-jumper shows and competitions, hosts concerts and events, and has everything riders, spectators, and equine enthusiasts could want. Choose from eight on-site restaurants including **Legends Grille** (828/863-1122, 5pm-9pm Tues.-Thurs., 11am-10pm Fri.-Sat., 11am-9pm Sun., $14-47), an upscale eatery serving steaks and seafood; **Roger's Diner** (828/863-1113, 7am-3pm Mon., 7am-9pm Tues.-Thurs. and Sun., 7am-10pm Fri.-Sat., $8-13), serving breakfast and traditional diner fare; and **Blue Ginger Sushi** (828/863-1121, 11am-9pm Wed.-Sun., $6-16). There's also a coffee shop, a snack bar, a pizza oven, and a sandwich-centric café.

Since riders and show enthusiasts travel from far and wide, TIEC has lodging for horses and riders. The **Stable House Inn** (828/863-1015, $125) has 50 rooms, each with two queen beds; the **Tryon River Cabins** have one- ($185), three- ($750), and five-bedroom cabins ($1,000) available, each with weekly rental discounts, along with several RV pads ($43).

There are two golf courses at **Rumbling Bald Resort** (112 Mountains Blvd., Lake Lure, www.rumblingbald.com). **Bald Mountain Golf Course** (828/694-3042, 18 holes, par 72, greens fees $56 Mon.-Fri., $61 Sat.-Sun.) makes the most of the bald rock faces that gave the course its name and gives you some beautiful views of them as they tower overhead. You may recognize the 16th hole, a picturesque par-3 where a couple of scenes from *Dirty Dancing* were shot. At **Apple Valley Golf Course** (828/694-3043, 18 holes, par 72, greens fees $63 Mon.-Fri., $68 Sat.-Sun.) you'll find a set of links that's been called one of the most beautiful mountain courses. This is especially true in fall when the hillsides surrounding the course are in full blaze.

1: Chimney Rock State Park **2:** Lake Lure

Food

In addition to the dining options at Rumbling Bald, the Lodge on Lake Lure, and TIEC, there are a few other spots worth checking out.

When you're in Lake Lure and you need a bite to eat, picnic supplies, or something to snack on back at your getaway house, stop by **Lured Market and Grill** (2655 Memorial Hwy., Lake Lure, 828/625-9192, 11am-3pm Sun.-Mon., 11am-7pm Wed.-Thurs., 11am-9pm Fri.-Sat., $5-13). Chock-full of local and regional flavors—craft beer, wine, snacks, and cheese—and stocked with everything from pantry sundries to lake-life necessities, Lured carries what you're looking for or something close, and their little grill serves a bevy of sandwiches, salads, burgers and handheld eats. Try the Trout Bites or the Not Your Routine Poutine starters, then go for a big salad and a burger or their Quirky Turkey Sandwich topped with peach habanero jam for extra quirky points.

Dining at **La Strada at Lake Lure** (2693 Memorial Hwy., Lake Lure, 828/625-1118, www.lastradaatlakelure.com, 11:30am-late daily, $13-28) is Italian American through and through, and you're bound to see plenty of rock climbers in there carbing up as they prepare for a day on the rock face. The menu is packed with pizza and pasta, with many of the classics—chicken parm, lasagna, chicken alfredo—appearing alongside daily specials that use ingredients that are a little closer to home.

I am a fool for french toast, and at **Victory Kitchen & Restaurant** (961 Buffalo Creek Rd., Lake Lure, 828/436-5023, 8am-2pm Tues.-Sat., 8am-noon Sun., 5pm-8pm Wed.-Fri., $5-15) I've found a version I look forward to getting, if I don't order the shrimp and grits, that is. This place has great breakfast; sleepyheads take note that it's served until 11am, as well as a great lunch, including a killer cheeseburger topped with a fried egg, just in case you like a little breakfast with lunch.

Accommodations

The 1927 **Lake Lure Inn and Spa** (2771 Memorial Hwy., 828/625-2525, www.lakelure. com, from $135) is a grand old hotel that was one of the fashionable Southern resorts of its day. Franklin Roosevelt and Calvin Coolidge stayed here, as did F. Scott Fitzgerald. The lobby is full of strange antiques that are the picture of obsolete opulence—a Baccarat chandelier much older than the hotel and a collection of upright disc music boxes, up to eight feet tall, that were all the rage before the invention of the phonograph. The Lake Lure Inn has been restored beautifully and equipped with two restaurants, a bar, and a spa.

Rumbling Bald Resort on Lake Lure (112 Mountains Blvd., Lake Lure, 828/694-3000 or 800/260-1040, www.rumblingbald. com) has studios ($125-165), condos ($235-415), RV facilities ($80-95), and vacation homes ($285-650) in a quiet mountain cove. On the resort's property there a few miles of hiking and biking trails as well as a variety of water activities: pontoon boats ($200 for 2 hours, $350 for 4 hours, $650 for 8 hours); kayaks, canoes, paddleboats, and stand-up paddleboards (from $22-27 per hour); and scenic cruises ($22 adults, $5 under age 4). There's also a fitness center, golf, tennis, and a spa (828/694-3017, treatments from $55).

At Rumbling Bald there's one restaurant where you can grab a bite: **Legends on the Lake** (828/694-3032, 11am-9pm Wed.-Sun., $10-25), serving pizza, salads and sandwiches, and a small selection of entrées.

HIGHLANDS AND VICINITY
Waterfalls

This part of the country is blessed with some beautiful waterfalls, some of which are easily visited. Whitewater Falls (Hwy. 281, at the Georgia state line, south of Highlands), at over 400 feet, is reported to be the highest waterfall east of the Rockies. An upper-level viewing spot is located at the end of a wheelchair-accessible paved trail, while a flight of more than 150 steps leads to the base of the falls. The falls are a fabulous sight, but remember to stay on the trails; several visitors have fallen to their deaths when they left the trail to get a different perspective.

A much smaller but still very beautiful waterfall is **Silver Run Falls** (Hwy. 107, 4 miles south of Cashiers), reached by a short trail from a roadside pullout. **Bridal Veil Falls** (U.S. 64, 2.5 miles west of Highlands) flows over a little track of road right off U.S. 64. You'll see a sign from the main road where you can turn off and actually drive behind the waterfall, or park and walk behind it. Another waterfall that you can walk through is **Dry Falls** (U.S. 64, between Highlands and Franklin, $3 per vehicle), reached by a small trail off the highway, curving right into and behind the 75-foot waterfall.

Sports and Recreation

North Carolina's newest, **Gorges State Park** (Hwy. 281, Sapphire, 828/966-9099, http://ncparks.gov, park 7am-7pm daily Dec.-Feb., 7am-9pm daily Mar.-Apr. and Oct., 7am-10pm daily May-Sept., 7pm-8pm daily Nov., picnic areas 8am-7:30pm daily, visitors center 9am-5pm daily) is a lush mountain rainforest that receives 80 inches of precipitation annually. The steep terrain rises 2,000 vertical feet in four miles, creating a series of rocky waterfalls and challenging trails. This 7,500-acre park is the only state park west of Asheville, and it's a sight, with a collection of waterfalls and a fantastic concentration of rare and unique plant and animal species; explore on a number of rugged trails for hiking, mountain biking, and horseback riding, or fish for rainbow and brown trout as well as smallmouth bass. Primitive camping (free) is allowed in designated areas.

Food and Accommodations

The 3,500-foot-high town of Cashiers ("CASH-ers") is home to the **High Hampton Resort** (124 Hwy. 107, Cashiers, 800/648-4252 or 828/547-0662, www.highhampton.com, 2-night minimum, from $250), a popular resort for generations of North Carolinians. This was originally the home of Confederate General Wade Hampton,

the dashing Charlestonian cavalryman. The lodge, a big old 1930s wooden chalet with huge cozy fireplaces in the lobby, is surrounded by 1,400 acres of lakeside woodlands, with an 18-hole golf course, a good buffet-style restaurant (dinner jacket requested in the evening), clay tennis courts, and a fitness center that features a climbing tower.

INFORMATION AND SERVICES

In addition to Asheville's **Mission Hospital** (509 Biltmore Ave., Asheville, 828/213-1111, www.missionhealth.org), there are several regional hospitals with emergency or urgent care departments. In Hendersonville, the primary hospital is **Pardee Hospital** (800 N. Justice St., Hendersonville, 828/696-1000, www.pardeehospital.org). In Brevard, the main hospital is **Transylvania Regional Hospital** (90 Hospital Dr., Brevard, 828/884-9111, www.missionhealth.org), and in Rutherfordton it is **Rutherford Regional Medical Center** (288 S. Ridgecrest St., Rutherfordton, 828/286-5000, www.myrutherfordregional.com).

Maps and guides are available at the **Hendersonville and Flat Rock Visitors Information Center** (201 S. Main St., Hendersonville, 800/828-4244 or 828/693-9708, www.visithendersonvillenc.org) and at the **Transylvania County Tourism Development Authority** (175 E. Main St., Brevard, 800/648-4523 or 828/884-8900, www.visitwaterfalls.com).

GETTING THERE AND AROUND

The Brevard-Hendersonville area is an easy drive from Asheville, with Hendersonville less than 30 minutes down I-26 and Brevard a short jog west from it on U.S. 64. To reach Tryon and Rutherfordton, follow U.S. 74 south and east from Hendersonville. **Asheville Regional Airport** (AVL, 61 Terminal Dr., 828/684-2226, www.flyavl.com), south of Asheville, is very convenient to this region; several airlines have flights to Atlanta, Charlotte, and other U.S. cities.

Great Smoky Mountains

The Smokies draw more than 12 million visitors annually. It's easy to see why: These mountains are laced with hiking trails, rivers, and waterfalls and populated with diverse wildlife—from rare salamanders to huge elk.

The diversity is second only to the sublime mystery of the area. The wild forests of the Great Smoky Mountains have historically been home to outlaws and rebels hoping to hide from the world under the cover of the fertile landscape. In fact, in 1996, the Atlanta Olympic Park bomber fled to the Smokies to evade capture. While people watching the news were scratching their heads, wondering how one man could vanish in such a relatively small geographical area, folks in these parts had their doubts he'd ever be found. After driving a little ways in the

Highlights

Look for ★ to find recommended sights, activities, dining, and lodging.

★ **Cades Cove:** The most visited spot in Great Smoky Mountains National Park is a formerly bustling mountain village that is witness to the depth of history in the Southern highlands (page 93).

★ **Clingmans Dome:** From this third-highest peak in the eastern United States, set in a dramatic alpine environment, you'll find an astounding view up to 100 miles on a clear day (page 96).

★ **Newfound Gap Road:** Bisecting the park, the 33-mile route offers plenty of long views, short hikes, and streamside driving (page 97).

★ **Museum of the Cherokee Indian:** The Cherokee people have lived in the Smoky Mountains for thousands of years. This excellent museum tells unforgettable tales of their history (page 110).

★ **Qualla Arts and Crafts Mutual:** Ancient craft traditions still thrive among Cherokee artists in western North Carolina. At the Qualla Mutual, visitors can learn about and purchase the work of today's masters (page 111).

★ **Oconaluftee Indian Village:** Demonstrations in traditional cooking, flint knapping for arrowheads and spear points, and ritual dance give visitors a glimpse into 18th-century life at this recreated Cherokee Indian Village (page 112).

★ **Great Smoky Mountains Railroad:** Depart Bryson City on a rail tour along mountain

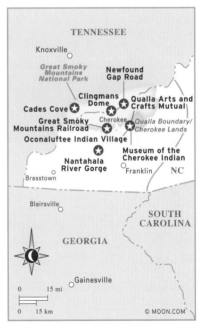

rivers and lakes; enjoy kid-centric tours or tours focused on fall color, moonshine, and craft beer (page 116).

★ **Nantahala River Gorge:** So steep that in some places the water is only brushed by sunlight at high noon, this gorge is an unbeatable place for white-water rafting (page 116).

Great Smoky Mountains

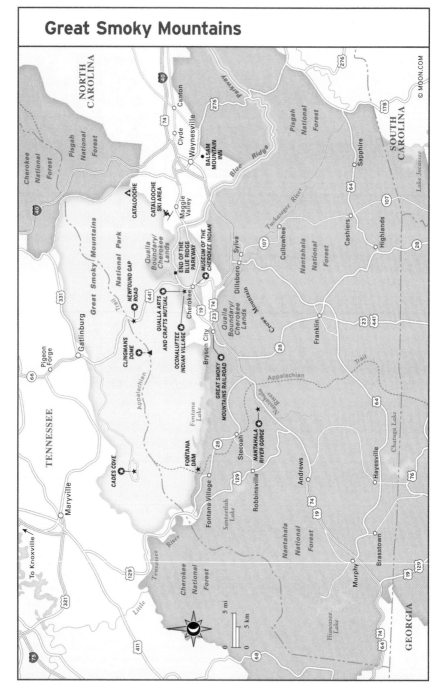

© MOON.COM

High Country southwest of Asheville, among the rugged terrain and the lush vegetation, it isn't difficult to imagine how someone could hide here unnoticed.

The 521,085-acre Great Smoky National Park straddles the North Carolina-Tennessee state line and is just about equally split between the states. The slightly larger North Carolina side of the park is wilder and less developed than the Tennessee side, and in both places you can find spots so remote they have stood undisturbed by humans for untold lengths of time. You'll also find places like Cades Cove, a wide, secluded valley that welcomed some of the first pioneers to push west into Tennessee.

In addition to pioneers traveling westward, the Smokies were also home to the Cherokee people, who have roots here going back centuries, from the early days described in their mythology, when the Ani-gituhwa-gi shared these mountains with witches, fairies, and birds the size of bears. The early 19th century and the Trail of Tears were the darkest hour for them, when they were split into two groups—those forced into exile and those forced into hiding and resistance. Today, the Cherokee Nation is still split, but the Eastern Band's seat of government is here in the land known as the Qualla Boundary.

PLANNING YOUR TIME

Many people plan visits to the Smokies around what's blooming or turning color on the mountainsides, but it's a wonderful area to visit any time of year. Spring wildflowers begin to appear in late March, peaking in late April. Azaleas, mountain laurels, and rhododendrons put on the best show during summer, blooming first at lower elevations and then creeping up the mountains. Flame azalea is an unusual plant, peaking in different areas as the microclimates dictate; they're ablaze with color April-July. Mountain laurel overlaps with blooms in May-June, and rhododendron shows its color in June-July. Fall colors appear in the opposite order, with the mountaintops the first to show autumn's arrival in early October. Colors then bleed down until late October-early November, when trees from the foot to the crest of the mountains are aflame with color. Summer heat can throw off the schedule for blooms and fall colors, as can rainfall levels. If you call the Great Smoky Mountains National Park or check with regional websites, you can find out how the season is progressing.

Bisecting the park is the Newfound Gap Road, striking northwest from Cherokee, where it meets with the southern end of the Blue Ridge Parkway, to Gatlinburg and Pigeon Forge, Tennessee. On the Tennessee side of the park, the valleys spread out a little and mountain coves form, making that the area to visit for side-road exploration and short loop roads. Cherokee is a great place to stay, as it's not as touristy as Gatlinburg, which is good to visit for a day. There are campsites available on both sides of the park if you're roughing it, or find a rustic cozy cabin for a taste of country living. While you can certainly get from Cherokee to Gatlinburg in an hour and see a sight or two in a day, the more time you can spend here, the better. This is the nation's most visited national park for a reason, so spend at least three days; a week provides enough time for a touristy day in Tennessee, a couple of days for trail and side-road exploration, a day learning about Cherokee culture in Cherokee, and time in the casino. Many campgrounds here limit stays to one week mid-May-October and two weeks November-mid-May, so plan accordingly if you're packing your tent.

Previous: the iconic Great Smoky Mountains National Park sign; elk along the Oconaluftee River; Mingus Mill.

Great Smoky Mountains National Park

Great Smoky Mountains National Park (GSMNP, 865/436-1200, www.nps.gov/grsm) is like no other, and it's very close to my heart. My family would vacation here for weekend and weeklong getaways, and I remember taking my first bite of trout here, riding my first roller coaster at Silver Dollar City in Pigeon Forge (now Dollywood), and seeing R2-D2 outside of Ripley's Believe It or Not in Gatlinburg. GSMNP comprises more than 800 square miles of cloud-ringed high peaks and rainforest. There are tens of thousands of species of plants and animals that call the park home, with 80 species of reptiles and amphibians alone, which is why the park is sometimes called the Salamander Capital of the World. More than 200 species of birds nest here, and 50-plus mammal species, from mice to mountain lions, roam these hills. The nonprofit organization Discover Life in America (www.dlia.org) has been conducting an All-Taxa Biodiversity Inventory, a census of all nonmicrobial life forms in the GSMNP; as of 2012 they had discovered over 900 species of plants and animals previously unknown to science. The deep wilderness is an awesome refuge for today's outdoor enthusiasts, and the accessibility of absolutely ravishing scenery makes it ideal for visitors of all ability levels and nearly all interests.

VISITING THE PARK
Weather Considerations

To get a sense of the variability of the weather in the GSMNP, keep in mind that the elevation ranges from below 1,000 to over 6,600 feet. Low-lying areas like the one around Gatlinburg, Tennessee, are not much cooler than Raleigh in the summer, with an average high of 88°F in July. Gatlinburg's average lows drop just a few degrees below freezing during only three months of the year (Dec.-Feb.). The opposite extreme is illustrated by Clingmans Dome, the highest elevation in the park, where the average high temperature is only 65°F in July, and only in June-August can you be sure that it won't snow. If ever there were a place for wearing layers of clothing, this is it. No matter what season the calendar tells you it is, be on the safe side and

thick fog shrouding Newfound Gap Road in early spring

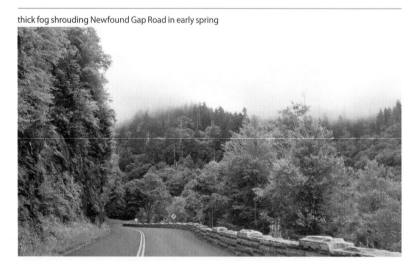

Great Smoky Mountains National Park

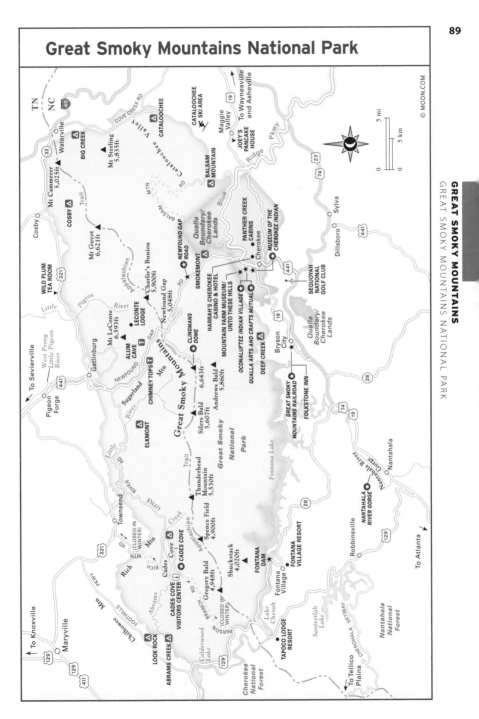

© MOON.COM

pack clothing for the other three as well. Keep these extremes in mind in terms of safety as well; a snowstorm can bring two feet of snow at high elevations, and it's not at all unusual for the weather to be balmy at the foot of the mountain and icy at the top. At times the temperature has fallen to -20°F. Roads can be closed in the winter or restricted to 4WD vehicles and those with snow chains. Drive very slowly when it's icy. Leave plenty of room between you and the next car, and shift to a lower gear when going down slippery slopes. You can find out current conditions by calling the park's weather information line (865/436-1200, ext. 630).

Seasonal Considerations

The most crowded times in the park are mid-June-mid-August and all of October. Traffic is most likely to be heavy on the Cades Cove Loop Road and Newfound Gap Road. Several roads in the park are closed in winter, but closing dates vary. Among these are Balsam Mountain, Clingmans Dome, Little Greenbrier, Rich Mountain, and Round Bottom Roads as well as the Roaring Fork Motor Nature Trail.

Safety

Sometimes even the most experienced outdoorspeople have emergencies. Whether you're going into the backcountry alone or with others, make sure that someone you trust knows where you're going, what your likely route is, and when to expect you back. The National Park Service recommends leaving their phone number (865/436-1230) with someone at home to call if you're not back when expected.

Some of the basic safety rules may seem obvious, but it's good to review them. Climbing on rocks and waterfalls is always dangerous, and crossing a deep or flooded stream can be treacherous as well. If you have to cross a stream that's more than ankle deep, it's recommended that you unbuckle the waist strap on your backpack (so you don't get pinned underwater if you fall), use

a hiking stick to steady yourself, and wear nonslippery shoes.

Cold is a concern, even in summer. Wear layers, pack additional warm duds (warmer than you think you'll need), and try to stay dry. It may be shorts-and-T-shirt weather when you set out, but even in the summer it can be very cold at night. Plan well, double-check before setting out that you have everything you could possibly need on your trek, and, says the National Park Service, "eat before you're hungry, and rest before you're tired" (it's good advice; trust me, I'm an Eagle Scout). Water from streams must be boiled or filtered to make it potable.

Wildlife can pose hazards. Despite assurances to the contrary, there are still panthers (mountain lions) in these mountains. Ignore what the officials say in this (and only this) regard; locals see and hear them throughout Appalachia. But panthers are rare and reclusive, as are coyotes, wild hogs, and other resident tough guys. It's always better to hike or camp with at least one companion. A sturdy walking stick can be a lifesaver, and bear spray, cheap and readily available in many different kinds of stores, is good for deterring more than bears.

Permits and Regulations

Permits are required for camping in the national park but are quite easy to obtain. You can register at any of the 12 visitors centers and ranger stations. This must be done in person, not online or over the phone. Fishing requires a permit as well, which can be bought at outfitters and bait shops in nearby towns. Strict rules governing fishing apply; these can be found on the park website (www.nps.gov/grsm). Other rules apply to interacting with wildlife. Don't feed animals, and make sure to seal up your foodstuffs to discourage night visitors. Firearms are forbidden in the park, as is hunting.

Your dog is welcome in the park, but only in certain areas. To prevent transmission of diseases to or from the wildlife, and to avoid disrupting or frightening the resident fauna,

One Day in GSMNP

Great Smoky Mountains National Park (GSMNP, 865/436-1200, www.nps.gov/grsm) was the first—and the largest—of three National Park Service units established in the southern Appalachians. The park was founded in 1934, followed in 1935 by the Blue Ridge Parkway and in 1936 by Shenandoah National Park. These sister facilities include some 600 miles of contiguous road and close to 800,000 acres of land, all of it acquired from private landholders and all of it standing today as a testament to the wild rugged beauty of the Appalachian Mountains and the people who helped tame these places.

MORNING

Enjoy breakfast at the **Pancake Pantry** (628 Parkway, 865/436-4724, www.pancakepantry. com, 7am-4pm daily June-Oct., 7am-3pm daily Nov.-May, $6-10) in Gatlinburg, the first pancake house in Tennessee. Head out of town toward GSMNP and stop off at the **Sugarlands Visitor Center** (1420 Old Hwy. 73 Scenic, Gatlinburg, 865/436-1200, www.nps.gov/grsm, daily, closed Christmas Day) to pick up maps, then continue on down Little River Road to **Cades Cove.** Easily the most popular auto tour in the park, Cades Cove has amazing scenery but even more amazing wildlife-watching. Get here at the right time of day (early morning or near dusk) and you'll see herds of deer grazing the fields and black bears playing, eating, and napping in the remnants of former apple orchards.

If you're in an SUV, truck, or high-clearance off-road-appropriate vehicle, leave Cades Cove via **Rich Mountain Road,** a beautiful eight-mile road that takes you up and over the mountains to Townsend (not far to the east of Gatlinburg). The views of Cades Cove are unparalleled, so have your camera ready.

AFTERNOON

Leave the park for lunch in Gatlinburg, then hit the **Roaring Fork Motor Nature Trail,** from which you can hike to four falls with relative ease. For a 2.6-mile round-trip hike, try **Grotto Falls Trail,** which leads through a lovely forest to the 25-foot Grotto Falls. You can hike behind the falls, and if you're lucky, you may see pack llamas hauling supplies to the LeConte Lodge. As you're leaving the Motor Nature Trail, stop at the **Thousand Drips Falls,** sometimes called Place of a Thousand Drips. It's just a few steps off the road and is an excellent cascade as it falls down the mossy rock face.

dogs are not permitted on hiking trails. They are allowed to accompany you at campgrounds and picnic sites.

WILDLIFE IN THE PARK

The largest animals in the park are also the most recent arrivals. In the spring of 2001, the National Park Service reintroduced **elk** to the Great Smoky Mountains, a species that used to live here but was hunted to regional extinction in the 18th century. In the years since their reintroduction, the herd has reproduced steadily, boding well for a successful future. If you hear a strange bellowing in the early autumn, it may be a male elk showing off for his beloved. One of the best places to see the elk is in the Cataloochee Valley, particularly in fields at dawn and dusk. Be sure to keep your distance; these animals can weigh up to 700 pounds, and the males have some formidable headgear.

An estimated 1,600 **black bears** live in the GSMNP—two per square mile—so it's quite possible that you'll encounter one. They are a wonder to see, but the 100-400-pound creatures pose a real risk to humans, so it's important to be aware of how we interact with them. It is illegal to come within 150 feet of a bear or elk, and those who knowingly get closer can be arrested. If you see a bear, the recommended procedure is to back away slowly. The National Park Service recommends that if the bear follows you, you should stand your ground. If it keeps coming toward you persistently and looks menacing, make yourself big and scary. Stand on a rock to look taller, or get close to anyone else present, to show the bear that it's outnumbered. Make a lot of noise (bear bells or bear whistles are handy for this) and throw rocks or sticks. Should a bear actually attack you, the National Park Service recommends that you "fight back aggressively with any available object." Don't try to run, because they're much faster than you, and don't climb a tree, as black bears are avid climbers.

The best course of action is simply to avoid them and hope that any sightings you have will be from a safe distance. When camping, lock your food in the trunk of your car, or hoist it into a tree too high off the ground for a bear to reach it and suspended far enough from the nearest branch that it can't be reached by climbing the tree. Bears may approach picnic areas. Don't feed them, no matter how sweet they look. "Habitual panhandler bears" (this is a real term, Scout's honor) die younger than those afraid of humans, as they are more likely to be hit by cars, swallow indigestible food packaging, become easy targets for hunters, or, if they are too problematic, be captured and euthanized.

Bears are not the only huge ferocious animals in the park. Believe it or not, there are hundreds of snorting tusky **wild hogs** here, descendants of a herd that escaped from a hunting preserve in Murphy in the 1910s. There are also **coyotes, wolves, bobcats,** and extremely rare **mountain lions,** often called panthers or painters in this region.

Of the many natural miracles in this park, one of the most astonishing is the light show put on for a couple of weeks each year by synchronous **fireflies.** Of the park's 14 species, only one, *Photinus carolinus*, flashes in this manner. While the average backyard's worth of fireflies twinkles like Christmas lights, synchronous fireflies, as their name implies, are capable of flashing in unison, by the hundreds or thousands. The sight is so amazing that,

during the peak flashing period in June, the park organizes nighttime expeditions to the best viewing spots.

If you go hiking in the backcountry, you may see a **snake.** It's unlikely that you'll encounter a poisonous one, as there are only two kinds of vipers here—rattlesnakes and copperheads—that pose a danger to humans. There has never been a death from snakebite in the park, and snakes are shy. But to be on the safe side, watch where you step or put your hands; you don't want to be the first on that list.

SIGHTS

Oconaluftee Visitor Center and Mountain Farm Museum

As you begin your trip along Newfound Gap Road through the park from the North Carolina side, your first stop will probably be the "Welcome to Great Smoky Mountains National Park" sign, but the second stop you'll likely make is the **Oconaluftee Visitor Center and Mountain Farm Museum** (1194 Newfound Gap Rd., Cherokee, 828/497-1904, www.nps.gov/grsm, 9am-4:30pm daily Dec.-Feb., 9am-5pm daily Mar. and Nov., 9am-6pm daily Apr.-May and Sept.-Oct., 9am-7pm daily June-Aug., closed Dec. 25, Mountain Farm dawn-dusk daily), just two miles north of Cherokee on U.S. 441 (Newfound Gap Rd.). You can pick up a park map, grab the schedule of ranger-led programs, and see exhibits on the people who called these hills home long before the park was in existence. The visitors center and adjacent comfort station are LEED Gold certified.

Next to the visitors center is **Mountain Farm Museum** (sunrise-sunset daily year-round, free), which showcases some of the finest farm buildings in the park. Most date to the early 1900s, and among them are a barn, an apple house, and the Davis House, a log home built from chestnut wood and constructed before the American chestnut blight decimated the species. This collection of structures is original to the area and dates to the turn of the 20th century. Though the

The Appalachian Trail

The 2,184-mile Appalachian Trail runs from Georgia to Maine, with 95.5 miles within North Carolina and another 200 straddling the border of North Carolina and Tennessee. It's a high climb, with many peaks over 5,000 feet and gaps brushing 4,000 feet, but the fantastic balds (natural and agricultural areas devoid of trees) along the trail here—like Cheoa Bald and Max Patch—are big draws for day hikers and segment hikers, and having vistas this beautiful this early on in the long journey helps through-hikers retain their focus and determination to reach their goal.

The Appalachian Trail cuts a path through the Nantahala Forest, regarded by many as one of the best sections of the southern portion of the trail, before crossing the rills of the southern Blue Ridge and following the crest of the Smokies along the Tennessee border. This section of the trail is rated between a 3 and a 6 on the AT's 10-point scale, which means the trail ranges from moderate elevation changes on well-graded trails to strenuous and short but steep climbs, extended climbs that last hours, and short sections with difficult footing. For through-hikers, who often have years of trail experience, the path here isn't as difficult as it may be for some day hikers or even overnight hikers.

Finding a day hike isn't hard west of Asheville, especially in the deeper mountains along Great Smoky Mountain National Park. Driving the Newfound Gap Road from the town of Cherokee into Tennessee, go about 16 miles from the Oconaluftee Visitors Center to the Newfound Gap parking lot. The trailhead is to the left of the overlook. Take the moderate four-mile hike to Charlies Bunion, a peak along the trail with a very odd name. You'll gradually gain around 1,600 feet in elevation, but if you bring a picnic lunch, you'll have a lovely dining spot.

barn is the only structure original to this site, the other buildings were moved here from inside and adjacent to the park and arranged much like a typical farm of the era. If you visit during peak times, you'll see living-history interpreters in costume, demonstrating the day-to-day chores on this farm: preparing meals, sewing, maintaining and harvesting the garden, taking care of the hogs, and the like.

★ Cades Cove

On the Tennessee side of the park, the 11-mile one-way Cades Cove Loop Road traverses Cades Cove, a historic settlement dating to the late 18th century. Originally part of the Cherokee Nation, the land was ceded to the United States in 1819. The population grew throughout the 19th century until it was a busy town of several hundred. The village is preserved today as it appeared around 1900, with homes, churches, barns, and a working gristmill, but without the people—a mountain counterpart to Cape Lookout National Seashore's Portsmouth Village. Because of the cove's scenic beauty and abundance of wildlife, this is the most popular part of the nation's most visited national park. The loop road through Cades Cove takes about an hour to drive when visitors are sparse; on crowded days—peak summer and fall seasons and most weekends—it can take several hours to cover the 11 miles.

To take this lovely-in-any-season drive, follow Little River Road west from the Sugarlands Visitor Center for 17.2 miles. The road becomes Laurel Creek Road and leads to Cades Cove in another 7.4 miles. You can also access Cades Cove by entering the park at Townsend on Highway 73, then turning right on Laurel Creek Road, following it for 16 miles to the entrance to the cove. Cades Cove is closed to vehicle traffic every Wednesday May-September, when the loop is open exclusively to bicycle and foot traffic. The rest of the year, the road is open to motor vehicles sunrise-sunset daily, as long as the weather allows.

The Cades Cove Campground (10042 Campground Dr., Townsend, TN, campground 865/448-4103, reservations 877/444-6777, www.recreation.gov, $25) is a popular spot where you'll definitely want to reserve a campsite. This campground is open year-round, and although the occupancy is a little lower in the dead of winter, you'll still find a few intrepid visitors taking refuge from the cold in one of the 159 campsites. Hikers take note: There are several backcountry campsites off the trails in Cades Cove, making it a good base for overnight trips.

Today, several historic structures remain standing along the valley floor. Among them is the most photographed structure in the park, the **Methodist Church.** From time to time, a wedding is held here, though it's more common for visitors to leave handwritten prayers on scraps of paper large and small at the altar.

The **Cable Mill Area** is the busiest section of the loop, even if the Methodist Church is the most photographed. At the Cable Mill, you can see an actual mill in operation and even buy cornmeal and flour ground on-site. In addition to the mill and Methodist church, there are two other churches, a few barns and log houses, and a number of smaller structures.

Halfway around the loop, you'll find the **Cades Cove Visitor Center** (Cades Cove Loop Rd., Townsend, Tennessee, 865/436-7318, 9am-4:30pm daily Dec.-Feb., 9am-5pm daily Mar. and Nov., 9am-6pm daily Apr.-May and Sept.-Oct., 9am-7pm daily June-Aug., closed Dec. 25), which has a good bookstore and gift shop, and, most important, one of two public restrooms you'll find on the tour (the other is at the Cades Cove Campground Store at the entrance).

Cataloochee

Nestled in the folds of the mountains and encircled by 6,000-foot peaks, the Cataloochee Valley was settled in the early 1830s. This isolated valley on the northeastern edge of GSMNP was home to two communities—Big

and Little Cataloochee—and more than 1,200 people in 1910. By the 1940s, all but a few were gone, leaving the valley, and its new status as one of the more beautiful spots in the new national park, for hills and hollows nearby. Today, the few historic structures that stand in Cataloochee Valley are all that remains of the communities, save a few memories and written stories.

Cataloochee Valley is not far from I-40, but poor signage makes it a little difficult to find. On I-40, take exit 20 onto U.S. 276. Take an immediate right onto Cove Creek Road. The condition of the road—it's alternately gravel and paved—and the narrow winding route will make you doubt you made the right turn, but you did. Zigzag up this road for about 12 miles. Suddenly it will open into the wide grassy expanse that is Cataloochee Valley. Before you begin your descent into the valley, stop at the overlook just past the intersection with Big Creek Road. From here, you can marvel at the valley sweeping away before you and the mountains rising up all around.

The valley is open to vehicle traffic 8am-sunset. Though less visited than other areas, like Cades Cove on the western side of the park, Cataloochee sees its fair share of visitors. Most arrive in the evenings shortly before sunset to see the elk grazing in the fields. If you don't plan on camping and you'd rather avoid the crowds, as small as they may be, visit in midday, take a hike, and see if you can find the elk in the woods; it's where they go to escape the heat.

The ★ **Cataloochee Campground** (campground 828/497-9270, reservations 877/444-6777, www.recreation.gov, reservations required, mid-Apr.-Oct., $25) has 27 tent and RV sites. There is a horse camp with seven sites not far up the valley; down the valley there's a group campground with three sites and room for much larger parties. This highly recommended campsite is one of the most secluded you'll find in the front country.

1: Cades Cove 2: Clingmans Dome 3: Palmer Chapel in Cataloochee 4: a hiking trail along a river

SIGHTS

There are four prominent structures still standing in Cataloochee Valley: two homes, a school, and a church. A few other structures and ruins, cemeteries, fences, and walls remain throughout the valley. The most prominent building is the **Palmer Chapel and Cemetery.** The chapel was built in 1898, but it's been some time since there's been a regular service here. Now it stands empty, its doors open to the forest, the view from its windows nothing but trees. Throughout the year there are some great opportunities to capture the chapel in all sorts of lighting, weather, and seasonal conditions. Today the chapel sees sporadic use, the most regular being the annual reunion of the descendants of some of the oldest Cataloochee families. Descendants of the Barnes, Bennett, Caldwell, Noland, and Palmer families gather here to eat, hold a short church service, and maintain the cemetery.

Across the road is the **Beech Grove School,** the last of three schools to serve the children of the valley. It's empty too, save a few artifacts. Beech Grove School operated on a very different school schedule than most were familiar with: The only regular school sessions were held November-January, sometimes February, and rarely into March.

Just up the road is the **Caldwell House.** We know from records that the owner, Hiram Caldwell, was prosperous, but you could tell that by looking at the 1906 home and comparing it to the other historic homes in the park, which are mostly log cabins. The Caldwell House is frame-built, similar to modern houses, with paneling on the interior walls.

The final structure is the **Palmer House,** located off Big Creek Road, not far from the Cataloochee Ranger Station. Once this was a log home—two, actually—connected by a covered walkway called a dog trot, but as the owners came into money in the early 1900s, they began making improvements and remodeling the home. They covered the exterior and interior with weatherboarding and began using fancy wallpaper in some rooms (scraps of the wallpaper are there today). When the son inherited the property, he began to remodel, adding rooms to the home and operating it as a boarding house. Renters were primarily anglers, there to fish in the three miles of stocked trout stream the family owned.

★ Clingmans Dome

At 6,643 feet, Clingmans Dome is the third-highest mountain in the eastern United States and the highest in the Great Smoky Mountains. A flying saucer-like observation tower at the end of a long steep walkway gives 360-degree views of the surrounding mountains, and on a clear day, the view can be as far as 100 miles. More often, though, it's misty up here in the clouds, and Clingmans Dome receives so much precipitation that its woods are actually a coniferous rainforest. The road to the summit is closed December-March, but the observation tower remains open for those willing to make the hike. To get to Clingmans Dome, turn off Newfound Gap Road 0.1 miles south of Newfound Gap, and then take Clingmans Dome Road (closed in winter), which leads seven miles to the parking lot. The peak is near the center of the park, due north from Bryson City.

Fontana Dam

At the southern edge of GSMNP lies Fontana Lake, a 10,230-acre reservoir created in the 1940s as part of the efforts of the Tennessee Valley Authority (TVA) to supply electricity to communities and industrial facilities in the region. The 480-foot-tall, 2,365-foot-wide Fontana Dam, complete with three hydroelectric generators, was completed in 1944, providing electricity to the factories churning out materials for World War II, including in Oak Ridge, Tennessee, where research leading to the atomic bomb was conducted.

To build Fontana Dam, the TVA purchased more than 1,000 tracts of land and relocated around 600 families in five communities. Those folks left behind homes, schools, churches, and barns, all of which were covered by the lake. This displacement of so many families and elimination of these small communities was part of the tradeoff that resulted in the modernization of the region, when electric power became cheap and readily available, and many jobs were required to complete the project. The dam also provides much-needed flood control to a region that receives 55-82 inches of rainfall each year. Today, the TVA can regulate the depth of the lake by releasing water as they anticipate flood events, and the water level of Fontana Lake can vary by as much as 50 feet.

Fontana Dam is the highest concrete dam east of the Mississippi, and it provides great recreational opportunities. The Appalachian Trail crosses the dam itself, and thousands of boaters and anglers take to the lake each year. There are more than 238 miles of shoreline along Fontana Lake and over 10,000 acres of water surface. If you have your own boat, you can launch it from the **Fontana Marina** (40 Fontana Dam Rd., 828/498-2017, www.fontanavillage.com), or you can rent a kayak, canoe, or paddleboard ($15-20 per hour, $60 per day) as well as a pontoon boat ($75-85 per hour, $350-400 per day) or fishing boat ($70 per hour, $300 per day); if you need a slip, rent one ($5-40 per day). Fishing guide services, shuttles to backcountry sites ($30-95 one-way, $50-190 round-trip), and seasonal tours of the lake ($30 adults, $15 ages 3-12) are also available.

The exhibits at the **Fontana Dam Visitor Center** (Fontana Dam Rd., www.tva.com, 9am-7pm daily Apr.-Aug., 9am-6pm daily Sept.-Oct., free), off Highway 28 near the state line, about 45 minutes from Bryson City, tell the story of the region and the construction of the dam. There's also a small gift shop and a viewing platform overlooking the dam. Hikers take note: They sell backcountry camping permits and have showers in the back.

★ Newfound Gap Road

While many visitors use this 32-mile road that bisects Great Smoky Mountains National Park as a mere throughway, it's actually one of the prettiest drives you'll find anywhere. This curvy road alternates between exposed and tree-enclosed, and a number of scenic overlooks provide spectacular views of the Smokies. Stop at one that has a trail (more than half of them do) and take a short walk into the woods or eat a picnic lunch on one of the mountainside overlooks. Whatever you do on this road between Cherokee and Gatlinburg, take your time and enjoy the ride.

SPORTS AND RECREATION

The Great Smoky Mountains National Park covers over 500,000 acres, and within that expanse are more than 800 miles of hiking trails, ranging from easy walks around major attractions to strenuous wilderness paths suited to the most experienced backpackers. A section of the Appalachian Trail goes through the park, crossing the Fontana Dam. There are dozens of books available about hiking in the Smokies, available at bookstores and outfitters throughout the region as well as online. The park's **Backcountry Information Office** (865/436-1297, 8am-5pm daily) has knowledgeable staff who are a good first resource when planning a hiking trip. The park website (www.nps.gov/grsm) has some downloadable maps to give you a general sense of the lay of the land. The Great Smoky Mountains Association website (www.smokiesinformation.org) has a good online bookstore.

Hiking

The Great Smoky Mountains National Park contains hundreds of miles of hiking trails, ranging from family-friendly loop trails to strenuous wilderness treks. Below are a sampling of hikes in the park. Before embarking on any of these trails, obtain a park map, and talk to a park ranger to ascertain trail conditions and gauge whether it's suited to your hiking skills.

SPRUCE-FIR TRAIL

A quick and easy foray into the woods is the **Spruce-Fir Trail,** off Clingmans Dome Road, a walk of just over 0.3 miles. Almost flat, and mostly following a wooden boardwalk, this

Best Hikes

This is a beautiful country to tour by car, but you're not doing the landscape justice if you only experience it through your windshield. Here are some fantastic chances to get out and be surrounded by nature.

ANDREWS BALD

At Clingmans Dome, a few miles off Newfound Gap Road, this **3.5-mile round-trip** trail is one of the loveliest and most rewarding hikes you'll find.

KEPHART PRONG

A perfect trail if you're new to the Smokies, this **4-mile round-trip** hike passes through a Civilian Conservation Corps camp, crosses the Oconaluftee River and Kephart Prong, and is loaded with wildflowers in spring.

DEEP CREEK LOOP TRAIL

This wide, mostly flat and easy trail takes you past Tom Branch, Indian Creek, and Juney Whank Falls in the span of **4.9-miles round-trip** on this hike near Bryson City.

HEN WALLOW FALLS TRAIL

In Cosby, a few miles northeast of Gatlinburg, you'll find this **4.4-mile round-trip** hike to a delicate waterfall some 90 feet high.

MOUNT CAMMERER TRAIL

It's a tough **11.2-mile round-trip** hike to the summit, but you're rewarded with some of the best views in the park, courtesy of a stone fire tower built in the 1930s.

LITTLE RIVER TRAIL

Keep this trail short and sweet as you follow an old logging road alongside the Little River and through the home of the synchronous fireflies, or follow all **12.3 miles** for an out-and-back day hike.

ABRAMS FALLS TRAIL

A hike suited to just about anyone that leads to a great waterfall, this **5-mile round-trip** hike is in Cades Cove, and you'll drive right by the trailhead.

RICH MOUNTAIN LOOP

This **8.5-mile round-trip** loop in Cades Cove is one of the most fabulous hikes in the park.

is an ideal trail if you simply want to stretch your legs and experience a bit of easily accessible forest atmosphere.

OCONALUFTEE RIVER TRAIL

A longer but also fairly easy walk is the **Oconaluftee River Trail,** which begins behind the Oconaluftee Visitors Center. This path, which is gravel-covered, follows the river and goes through part of the Mountain Farm Museum grounds. Unlike all the other trails in the GSMNP, dogs and bicycles are allowed. It's about three miles round-trip, popular with families, and absolutely littered with wildflowers in the spring. An added bonus is that one end is adjacent to the GSMNP "Welcome" sign, and the National Park Service has conveniently installed a post and platform to hold your camera for selfies in front of it.

QUIET WALKWAYS

At many of the pullouts deeper in the park, you'll find **Quiet Walkways.** These short, easy trails pull you into the woods just far enough off the road that the road noise is drowned out by birdsong, rustling leaves, flowing streams, and mountain breezes that build a cocoon around you. Signs at the trailhead encourage you to take your time and lose yourself in the sounds of nature, the aroma of the leaves, water, flowers, and mountain air, and the textures of the wild woodlands.

ALUM CAVE AND ARCH ROCK

At the **Alum Cave Trail** trailhead, off Newfound Gap Road, you'll find a trio of hikes ranging from easy to rugged. Hiking to **Arch Rock** is an easy 2.8-mile round-trip. Arch Rock has eroded into a giant arch. A moist, winding set of stairs goes under, up, and through the arch, and the trail continues to **Alum Cave,** another mile in, making for a 4.6-mile round-trip. Just before you get to Alum Cave is Inspiration Point, with a commanding view of the valley below, including the interesting Eye of the Needle rock formation on an adjacent ridge. Shortly after Inspiration Point you'll come to Alum Cave, where Epsom salts and saltpeter (used in the manufacture of gunpowder) were mined starting in the 1830s. To get to Alum Cave the path transitions from easy to moderate, but if you want to push on another 3.7 miles to the peak of Mount LeConte, for a hike that's a little over 10 miles round-trip, you'll be in for a much more difficult trail. For around 2 miles you'll encounter many exposed ledges, some with waterfalls to negotiate, all with a cable handhold for when the rocky path is slick. When you get to the top, you'll find yourself at the LeConte Lodge, but not at the actual summit. To reach the highest point, the summit of Mount LeConte, follow a short trail to High Top. The views from High Top are nice but not fantastic; for the best views, try Myrtle Point, a great spot to photograph the sunrise, or Cliff Top, near the lodge.

BOOGERMAN TRAIL

The **Boogerman Trail** is a loop trail off Cove Creek Road in the Cataloochee section of the park. This is a moderate 7.5-mile round-trip that takes 2-3 hours to complete. You'll pass old-growth trees, streams and cascades, and several old homesites, including that of "Boogerman" himself, an early resident named Robert Palmer.

CHIMNEY TOPS TRAIL

Another popular hike on the Newfound Gap Road is the **Chimney Tops Trail.** This four-mile round-trip starts out easy enough, but the last mile gains more than 830 vertical feet. Severe weather in 2012 turned parts of the trail into an obstacle course of rocks, roots, and mud, and at times the trail may be closed for ongoing rehabilitation. If the trail is open, the effort is worth the reward, as the views of Mount LeConte and Mount Kephart to the east and Sugarland Mountain to the west are amazing. This is one of the few mountains in the Smokies with a bare-rock top, and although the trail here is steep, it doesn't require any technical gear, just caution and the ability to scramble up steep rocks.

WATERFALLS

As if the mountains and valleys, flora and fauna, and close-enough-to-touch clouds weren't wonder enough, the GSMNP has literally hundreds of waterfalls. Several of the most popular and most beautiful are accessible from major trails. Close to Bryson City, 25-foot **Indian Creek Falls** is a moderate hike of less than two miles round-trip; it's a two-for-one deal, as the path also goes by Tom Branch Falls. Crossing Deep Creek on bridges and logs and going by old homesites, this is an especially interesting hike. The Deep Creek-Indian Creek Trailhead is at the end of Deep Creek Road in Bryson City. It gets very crowded in nice weather, particularly because this is a popular area for tubing, which makes parking quite difficult. Restrooms are available at the picnic area. Also accessible from the Indian Creek Trailhead is the path to 90-foot **Juney Whank Falls.** This hike is shorter but more difficult than to Indian Creek Falls. Since it shares the same trailhead, you can expect to find the same crowds and parking difficulties.

Mingo Falls, a beautiful 120-foot plume, is just outside the park, on the Qualla Boundary (Cherokee land). It can be seen from the Pigeon Creek Trail, which begins in the Mingo Falls Campground, off Big Cove Road south of Cherokee. The hike is very short, less than 0.5 miles round-trip, but it is fairly strenuous.

Some longer hikes on the Tennessee side of the park lead to equally beautiful falls. **Rainbow Falls** is 80 feet high and produces such a cloud of mist that when the sun hits it right, you can see a rainbow. In winter it sometimes freezes solid, which is an amazing sight. The Rainbow Falls Trail, near Gatlinburg, is a difficult 5.5 miles round-trip. It ascends about 1,500 vertical feet and is rocky most of the way, but it provides some great views of the falls and of Gatlinburg. Parking is available on Cherokee Orchard Road in Gatlinburg, but it fills up quickly, and you may need to pay to park a little farther from the trailhead.

The tallest waterfall, 100-foot **Ramsey Cascades,** is also the most difficult to reach. Those able to make a strenuous eight-mile round-trip hike are richly rewarded with a journey through old-growth hardwood forests and along fast-moving rivers. The pool at the bottom of the falls is a great place to glimpse some of the creatures that make GSMNP the Salamander Capital of the World. The parking area for the Ramsey Cascades Trail is off Greenbrier Road, a few miles southeast of Gatlinburg. The nearest portable toilets are at the picnic area on Greenbrier Road.

As tempting as it may be, don't try to climb the waterfalls; it's never a good idea. Because of its height, Ramsey Cascades is particularly dangerous. Maps and guides to the waterfalls are available at many locations in the park and at bookstores and outdoors shops nearby.

Horseback Riding

Three commercial stables in the national park offer rental horses. **Smokemont Riding Stable** (135 Smokemont Riding Stable Rd., 828/497-2373, www.smokemontridingstable. com, $40 per hour, 2.5-hour waterfall ride $100, 4-hour ride $160, wagon ride $20) is located in North Carolina near Cherokee. Two are in Tennessee: **Smoky Mountain Riding Stable** (865/436-5634, www.smokymountainridingstables.com, $27 per hour) and **Cades Cove Riding Stable** (10018 Campground Dr., Townsend, TN, 865/448-9009, http://cadescovestables.com, $40 adults, $35 ages 6-12).

In North Carolina, near Cherokee, an equestrian-friendly campground at **Round Bottom Horse Camp** (Straight Fork-Round Bottom Rd., campground 865/436-1261, reservations 877/444-6777, www.recreation.gov, mid-Apr.-late-Oct., $23) has five campsites, stalls, and bedding for horses. Its location, just inside the park and far up a narrow riverside road, makes it perfect for long rides with larger groups.

Bicycle Rentals

The **Cades Cove Store** (near Cades Cove Campground, 865/448-9034, www.cadescovetrading.com, 9am-6pm daily) rents bicycles in summer and fall ($15 per hour adults, $10 per hour under age 16, 24-hour rental $50). May-September, the park closes off the loop road through Cades Cove for the full day on Wednesday so that cyclists and hikers can enjoy the cove without having to worry about automobile traffic. It's an awesome program, and whether you get here early and rent a bike, bring your own, or just decide to hoof it around the loop, there's no better way to experience this part of the park.

Field Schools

Two Tennessee-based organizations affiliated with the GSMNP offer ways to get to know the park even better. The **Smoky Mountain**

1: bridge on the Kephart Prong trail 2: Ramsey Cascades 3: Juney Whank Falls in the Deep Creek area

Field School (865/974-0150, www.smfs.utk. edu) teaches workshops and leads excursions to educate participants in a wide array of fields related to the Smokies. One-day classes focus on the history and cultural heritage of the park, the lives of some of the park's most interesting animals, folk medicine, and cooking of the southern Appalachians. Instructors also lead one-day and overnight hikes into the heart of the park. This is a great way to discover the park far beyond what you would be able to do on your own, so check their schedule and sign up for a class that interests you.

The **Great Smoky Mountains Institute at Tremont** (9275 Tremont Rd., Townsend, TN, 865/448-6709, www.gsmit.org) teaches students of all ages about the ecology of the region, wilderness rescue and survival skills, and even nature photography. Many of the classes and guided trips are part of Road Scholar, kids camps, or teacher-training institutes; however, there are also rich opportunities for unaffiliated learners.

FOOD

Unless you're staying at the LeConte Lodge, you'll have to leave the park for meals. The easiest way is simply to drive into Bryson City or Cherokee, or in Tennessee, Gatlinburg or Pigeon Forge, which are all right on the edge of the park. In Gatlinburg, try the **Smoky Mountain Brewery** (1004 Parkway, Suite 501, Gatlinburg, 865/436-4200, www.smoky-mtn-brewery.com, 11am-midnight daily, $11-28), a popular brewpub and restaurant. The menu is about what you'd expect—burgers, wings, and cheesesteaks—but they also have some pretty good pizzas and even barbecue ribs. Their beer selection includes porters, wheat beers, red ales, and hoppy pale ales.

If there's one thing Gatlinburg has, it's pancake houses. But frankly, they all fall short of the original pancake house, the very first one to open in Tennessee: **Pancake Pantry** (628 Parkway, 865/436-4724, www.pancakepantry. com, 7am-3pm daily, $6-10). They griddle up 24 varieties of pancakes and crepes as well as waffles, omelets, and french toast. Breakfast is served all day, but if you feel like a burger or sandwich for lunch, there are a few of those too. If you're going for a hike, go easy on the pancakes—they sit a little heavy—but you can get a to-go boxed lunch made just for hikers and day-trippers into the park.

Delauder's Smoky Mountain BBQ (1875 E. Parkway, 865/325-8682, 4pm-8pm Thurs., 12:30pm-8pm Fri.-Sat., noon-8pm Sun., $5-25) will draw you in through smell alone, and once you taste the pulled pork or ribs, you won't want to leave. Other options are a Smoky Mountain Potato (a baked potato heaped with barbecue and fixings), nachos piled with barbecue goodness, and a number of sandwiches, including the Holy Bologna Sandwich, a grilled bologna behemoth topped with pulled pork, onions, pickles, sweet jalapeño mustard, barbecue sauce, and cheese.

Smith & Son Corner Kitchen (traffic light no. 8, 812 Parkway, 865/430-1978 or 865/436-8878, www.smithandsoncornerkitchen.com, 11am-9pm Sun.-Thurs., 11am-10pm Fri.-Sat., $10-25) has a prime location, loads of space, and a sizable menu that remains navigable. The salads are whoppers, and when paired with an appetizer, there's more than a meal for one. Burgers and sandwiches are fresh and filling, and the entrées—ranging from smoked chicken to meatloaf to fajitas to fried catfish—are so generous you won't mind sharing a bite or two.

While you're here, you may as well sample some 'shine. **Sugarlands Distilling Company** (805 Parkway, 865/325-1355, www. sugarlands.com, 10am-10:30pm daily, tours free) has an excellent distillery where you can see the whole operation in action, do a little sampling, and grab a quart or two to take home. With eight moonshines ranging from flavored to high-test and a pair of whiskeys to try, you'll have to pace yourself.

ACCOMMODATIONS

There is only one inn in the entire 500,000-acre park, and it's an unusual one: the ★ **LeConte Lodge** (865/429-5704, www. lecontelodge.com, late Mar.-mid-Nov., $162 adults, $89 ages 4-12, includes lodging, breakfast, and dinner). Like the summit, the Lodge is accessible only via the network of hiking trails that crisscross the park. And if the accessibility limitation isn't rustic enough for you, this collection of cabins has no running water or electricity. What the lodge does have is views for days and the seclusion of the Smoky Mountains backcountry. Oh, and a hearty breakfast and dinner come with each room.

LeConte Lodge has no hot showers, but in every cabin there is a bucket for a sponge bath (which can be surprisingly refreshing after a hot day on the trail), which you can fill with warm water from the kitchen, though you need to supply your own washcloth and towel. There are a few flush toilets in a separate building. The only lights, aside from headlamps and flashlights, are kerosene lanterns. For the most part, it's a rustic spot, harking back to the lodge's 1934 origins on the slopes of Mount LeConte. Dinner and breakfast are served at the same time every day, 6pm for dinner and 8am for breakfast, and the meals are substantial enough to fuel you for another day on the trail.

The Lodge doesn't lack for charm, but it does for comfort, so if you're the five-star-hotel breakfast-in-bed type, this may not be the place for you. Catering to hikers who are happier to have a dry place to sleep and a bed that's comfier than their sleeping bag, it's short on the luxury amenities, and guest rooms are bunk beds in small drafty cabins. But if you're a hiker or if you just love to have a completely different experience when you travel, this is a one-of-a-kind place to stay. Rooms book quickly—up to a year in advance.

For those who don't want to camp or hike to a rustic lodge, there are countless motels just outside the GSMNP. Reservations are always a good idea, especially in summer and in leaf season. There are many choices in Cherokee, Maggie Valley, Bryson City, Pigeon Forge, Gatlinburg, Sevierville, and other neighboring communities. In addition to the many chain motels, affordable mom-and-pop

motels also dot this landscape in abundance. Two good choices in Gatlinburg are **Westgate Smoky Mountain Resort & Water Park** (915 Westgate Resorts Rd., Gatlinburg, 865/430-4800, www.westgateresorts.com, from $179) and the **Riverhouse at the Park** (904 River Rd., Gatlinburg, 865/436-7821, www.riverhousemotels.com, $102-220). In Cherokee, on the North Carolina side of the park, go with a hotel like **Cherokee Grand Hotel** (196 Painttown Rd., 828/497-0050, www.cherokeegrandhotel.com, $179-219), only five minutes from the park entrance, or cabin accommodations with **Panther Creek Cabins** (Wrights Creek Rd., Cherokee, 828/497-2461, www.panthercreekresort.com, cabins $75-325, pets $49 for 1 dog, $39 2nd dog), a quiet, quaint, comfortable set of cabins just outside downtown Cherokee.

Camping

The GSMNP has many locations for camping. Campers can stay up to 14 consecutive nights at car-accessible campsites, but no more than three consecutive nights at backcountry campsites, and only nonconsecutive nights in shelters and at campsite 113. There are 10 car-accessible campgrounds, each of which has cold running water and flush toilets but no showers, power, or water hookups. Most of these sites are first come, first served, but May 15-October 15, sites at the Elkmont, Smokemont, Cades Cove, Cataloochee, and Cosby campgrounds can be reserved (877/444-6777, www.nps.gov/grsm).

The **Cataloochee Campground** (campground 865/436-1200, reservations 877/444-6777, www.recreation.gov, mid-Apr.-Oct., reservations required, $25) has 27 tent and RV sites. There is a horse camp with seven sites not far up the valley; down the valley is a group campground with three sites and room for much larger parties. This highly recommended campsite is one of the most secluded you'll find in the front country.

Cosby Campground (127 Cosby Park Rd., Cosby, TN, campground info 423/487-2683, reservations 877/444-6777, www.

recreation.gov, mid-Apr.-Oct., $17.50) has 157 sites for tents and RVs. Despite being home to the park's third-largest campground, Cosby is known as the quietest of the park's gateways. There are a number of trails that originate from the campground.

The **Elkmont Campground** (434 Elkmont Rd., Gatlinburg, 865/430-5560, reservations 877/444-6777, www.recreation.gov, $25-27, mid-Mar.-late-Nov.) has 220 campsites, 55 of them along the Little River, with front-row seats to the firefly light show, provided you're here at the right time. This is the largest of the campgrounds in GSMNP, and one of the most used. In addition to the firefly show and the attraction of Little River, this site also serves as a good base for exploring the area.

The **Cades Cove Campground** (10042 Campground Dr., Townsend, TN, information 865/448-4103, reservations 877/444-6777, www.recreation.gov, year-round, $25) is a popular spot where you'll definitely want to reserve in advance. Occupancy is a little lower in the dead of winter, but you'll still find a few intrepid visitors taking refuge from the cold at one of the 159 campsites. Hikers take note: There are several backcountry campsites off the trails in Cades Cove, making it a good base for overnight trips.

Just outside the park, **Fontana Village Resort** (300 Woods Rd., Fontana Dam, 828/498-2211 or 800/849-2258, www.fontanavillage.com, lodge $119-179, cabins $159-339, camping $15-40) offers a place to lay your head in your choice of accommodations: tent or RV camping, one- to three-bedroom cabins, and lodge rooms. There are 100 lodge rooms, 110 cabins, and 20 campsites.

Another car-accessible camping option is the **Mile High Campground** (828/269-2945, www.campmilehigh.com, mid-May-mid-Oct., tent or RV $25, primitive cabin $35) located on the Cherokee Reservation and owned by a member of the Eastern Band of the Cherokee. It is near Blue Ridge Parkway's Milepost 458; turn onto Wolf Laurel Gap, and the campground entrance is one mile along, on the left, after the "Molly's Gap Road" sign. This campground is indeed a little over a mile high in elevation and has around 50 sites in tent and RV areas along with primitive cabins. A beautiful campground near a number of hikes, the Blue Ridge Parkway, Cherokee, and the Great Smoky Mountains National Park, it's a great spot to set up for a few days. All campsites have fire rings and are fairly private. Bears and elk are common sights, so take pictures, but use caution.

Backcountry camping is abundant. It is only permitted at designated sites and shelters, and a permit is required, but the permits are free and can be obtained at any of 15 different visitors centers and campground offices throughout the park or online (https://smokiespermits.nps.gov). The Appalachian Trail runs through, hugging the ridgeline and the border between North Carolina and Tennessee, and shelters on the trail fill up fast with through-hikers and day hikers, but other shelters and campsites on side trails are ideal for out-and-back camping trips. The Kephart shelter and the shelter at Laurel Gap are on two beautiful trails, and a number of campsites—numbers 52-57—are on the Mountains-to-Sea Trail that traverses North Carolina. There are also five drive-in horse camps ($20-25) and seven group campgrounds ($35-65). A map of the available campsites can be found on the park's website (www.nps.gov/grsm). Before camping at the GSMNP, be sure to familiarize yourself with the park's backcountry regulations and etiquette, available online and at locations in the park.

INFORMATION AND SERVICES

The official website of **Great Smoky Mountains National Park** (www.nps.gov/grsm) has a good deal of the information you'll need to plan a trip. At the visitors centers in Sugarlands, Oconaluftee, Cades Cove, and Clingmans Dome you'll find additional information from helpful rangers and fellow travelers. The websites of **Smoky Mountain Host**

1: Cosby Campground 2: LeConte Lodge

(www.visitsmokies.org) and the Blue Ridge National Heritage Area (www.blueridge-heritage.com) provide additional information. Detailed touring suggestions for sites associated with Cherokee history and heritage can be found at the website on the North Carolina Folklife Institute (www.ncfolk.org) website, and in the book *Cherokee Heritage Trails.*

The nearest hospitals are LeConte Medical Center (742 Middle Creek Rd., Sevierville, TN, 865/446-7000, www.lecontemedicalcenter.com), about 25 minutes from the west park entrance; Blount Memorial Hospital (907 E. Lamar Alexander Pkwy., Maryville, TN, 865/983-7211 or 800/448-0329, www.blountmemorial.org), an hour from the west park entrance; Cherokee Indian Hospital (1 Hospital Rd., Cherokee, NC, www.cherokeehospital.org, 828/497-9163), minutes away from the Oconaluftee Visitors Center in Cherokee; and Swain Community Hospital (45 Plateau St., Bryson City, NC, 828/488-2155, www.myswaincommunity.com), a little less than 30 minutes from the eastern park entrance in Cherokee.

GETTING THERE AND AROUND

From Asheville it's easy to get to GSMNP. In just over an hour you can be in Cataloochee, at the north end of the park, to camp, hike, and watch for elk in a serene mountain cove; to get here, take I-40 west to exit 20 and follow the signs. You can also take I-40 west into Tennessee, then follow the Foothills Parkway to U.S. 321 and skirt the edge of GSMNP to Gatlinburg, Tennessee, and the entrance to the park, a trip of about 90 minutes. From Gatlinburg, you can make a loop back to Asheville by taking Newfound Gap Road across GSMNP to Cherokee (about 2.5 hours) and then back to Asheville via U.S. 441 to U.S. 19 to I-40, a total loop of about 3.5 hours and some 175 miles.

You can also head straight to Cherokee from Asheville and enter GSMNP via Newfound Gap Road. It's an hour's drive on I-40 west to exit 27, then take U.S. 19 south to U.S. 441, which leads into Cherokee. Alternately you can take the more scenic, but much longer, route and get to Cherokee via the Blue Ridge Parkway. This route is only 83 miles, but it takes 2-2.5 hours. If you want to go this way, head south out of Asheville along U.S. 25 and pick up the Blue Ridge Parkway about 5.5 miles out of town; turn south on the parkway and drive it until you reach Cherokee and GSMNP. And, of course, you can reverse the route if you're making that grand loop and return to Asheville via the Blue Ridge Parkway by picking it up in Cherokee and driving north.

Maggie Valley

Maggie Valley is a vacation town from the bygone era of long family road trips in wood-paneled station wagons. Coming down the mountain toward Maggie Valley you'll pass an overlook that, on a morning when the mountains around Soco Gap are looped with fog, is surely one of the most beautiful vistas in the state.

SIGHTS AND ENTERTAINMENT

In a state with countless attractions for automotive enthusiasts, Maggie Valley's Wheels Through Time Museum (62 Vintage Lane, 828/926-6266, www.wheelsthroughtime.com, 10am-5pm Thurs.-Mon. Apr.-late Nov., $15 adults, $12 ages over 65, $7 ages 6-14, free under age 6) stands out as one of the most fun (and it's the only one, to my knowledge, to have Jason Momoa stop by on a tour through the Smokies and Mike Wolfe from TV's *American Pickers* pay them a visit). A dazzling collection of nearly 300 vintage motorcycles and a fair number of cars are on display, including rarities like a 1908 Indian, a 1914 Harley-Davidson, military motorcycles from both world wars, and some gorgeous postwar bikes. This collection, which dates mostly to before 1950, is maintained in working order—almost every one of the bikes is revved up from time to time.

Elevated Mountain Distilling Co. (3732 Soco Rd., 828/944-0766, 10am-5pm Mon.-Wed., 10am-11pm Thurs., 10am-midnight Fri.-Sat.) is right on the main drag in Maggie Valley, but if you decide to go for more than a quick sample or two, bring a designated driver, because the moonshine—flavored or straight—is fiery. Tastings include a sample of five of the distilling company's spirits. On the fourth Saturday of each month, Elevated Mountain hosts a bluegrass jam and, in September, a small music festival.

SHOPPING

As you might expect, Maggie Valley has its fair share of touristy T-shirt shops and places where you can pick up some fudge and a refrigerator magnet. **Maggie Mountaineer Crafts** (2394 Soco Rd., 828/926-3129, www. maggiemountaineercrafts.com, 10am-5pm Sat.-Sun. Jan.-Mar., 9am-5pm daily Apr. and Nov.-Dec., 8am-6pm daily May-Oct.) and its attached sister store, **A Day in the Valley,** have all that and more. They've got plenty of fudge (and they ship; seriously, it's that good) and shirts to choose from, but they also have a pretty large selection of quilts and home decor items; knives, moccasins, and toys; and a great section of local foodstuffs like apple butter, sorghum molasses, and some seasonal treats. Throw in the deck overlooking the creek and you have yourself a charming little souvenir store.

Antiques shopping at **Sutton and Son's Antiques** (3156 Dellwood Rd., Waynesville, 828/944-1212, www.suttonandsonsantiques. com, 10am-5pm Mon.-Sat., 1pm-5pm Sun.) is an experience best summed up by their tagline: "Treasure hunting in the Smokies." The store is large and loaded with a nicely curated selection of antiques such as mountain crafts, automotive memorabilia, kitchen goods, and records.

RECREATION
Skiing and Winter Sports

Maggie Valley's **Cataloochee Ski Area** (1080 Ski Lodge Rd., off U.S. 19, 800/768-0285, snow conditions 800/768-3588, www.cataloochee. com, late Nov.-mid-Mar., lift tickets $26-76, rentals $28-33) has slopes geared to every level of skier and snowboarder. Classes and private lessons are available for all ages. At Cataloochee's sister snow-sports area, **Tube World** (4721 Soco Rd., 828/926-0285, www. cataloochee.com, late Nov.-mid-Mar., minimum 42 inches tall, $30-35), you can zip down the mountain on inner tubes.

Hiking

Near Maggie Valley, the mountains become rough. Located on the valley floor, Maggie Valley is surprisingly short on trails, and those that exist are quite strenuous. There's the 2.6-mile stroll around **Lake Junaluska,** but the majority of the trails are found at the crest of the mountains, along the Blue Ridge Parkway. To the east of Maggie Valley, the mountains are a little more forgiving. There are many trails of various intensities and lengths, but in the immediate area, you'll have to take the Heintooga Spur Road, a connector road between the parkway and Great Smoky Mountains National Park, to a mile-high campground, a picnic area with unparalleled views, and the **Flat Creek Trail.** On Heintooga Spur Road, you'll pass into Great Smoky Mountains National Park proper and be treated to no fewer than five stunning overlooks, the best of which is the Mile High Overlook, offering a glimpse of Clingmans Dome, Mount LeConte, Mount Kephart, and Mount Guyot.

The Blue Ridge Parkway is not far from Maggie Valley, which means there are a number of hiking trails to explore. Easy trails include the **Buck Springs Trail** (Milepost 407.6, Blue Ridge Pkwy.), just over 1 mile long, and the 0.25-mile **Bear Pen Gap Trail** (Milepost 427.6, Blue Ridge Pkwy.) that connects to the Mountains-to-Sea Trail; additionally, you can go for a stroll around **Lake Junaluska** in the

Maggie Valley

town of Maggie Valley. Moderate trails are longer and usually involve some elevation gain and loss; a couple of the best are **Graveyard Fields Loop Trail** (Milepost 418.8, Blue Ridge Pkwy.), a 3.2-mile loop through alpine-like meadows. Extend your hike here by following one of the spur trails that lead to some fantastic waterfalls. Another moderate option is the **Richland Balsam Trail** (Milepost 431, Blue Ridge Pkwy.), a loop through a spruce and fir forest. Tougher trails often pay off with the best views, and **Waterrock Knob Trail** (Milepost 451.2, Blue Ridge Pkwy.) does that on a 1.2-mile trail that's steep and a little rocky but manageable. It leads to a summit where views await. Another option is the **Devil's Courthouse Trail** (Milepost 422.4, Blue Ridge Pkwy.), a short but strenuous hike of just under 0.5 miles leading to another panoramic summit view.

FOOD

★ **Joey's Pancake House** (4309 Soco Rd., 828/926-0212, www.joeyspancake.com, 7am-noon Mon.-Tues. and Fri.-Sun., $2-9) has been flipping flapjacks for travelers and locals alike since 1966, and it's exactly what you picture: paper menu placemats, hot coffee, a little kitschy, and packed with regulars. Lines form on weekends for the pancakes, waffles, and

country ham—get here early. If you're taken by the pancakes, pick up some of Joey's mix to take home with you.

My favorite restaurant in Maggie Valley is **Frankie's Italian Trattoria** (1037 Soco Rd., 828/926-6216, www.frankiestrattoria.com, 2pm-9pm Tues.-Sat., $10-24). Service is great, the wine list more than adequate, and the food—pizza, linguine with clams, eggplant parm—puts it over the top.

If you're looking for a late lunch or early dinner that includes a piping hot pizza pie or a burger, then **Pavino's** (1560 Soco Rd., 828/944-0007, https://pavinos.com, 3pm-9pm Wed.-Sat., 3pm-7pm Sun., $9-23) is it. Thin crust and hand-tossed pies from personal to family-size, burgers, grinders, calzones, all piping hot and ready to put your hunger to bed.

Try the local spin on barbecue at **Pop's Butts on the Creek BBQ** (1584 Soco Rd., 828/926-7885, www.popsbuttsonthecreeknc.com, 11am-8pm Tues.-Sun., $10-29). Like a lot of places in western North Carolina, Pop's doesn't adhere to our state's unspoken rule that barbecue is pork only, and no ribs. I'm glad because they have a killer rib game, and their brisket and burnt ends are a welcome and beefy relief from all the pork. That said, the chopped pork is great (thanks to their butts-only approach), their spare rib dinner could feed two people, and those burnt ends are especially good on a sandwich.

ACCOMMODATIONS

Along Maggie Valley's main drag (Soco Rd./ U.S. 19) you'll see a lot of creek-side motels and mom-and-pop mountain inns. Among the pleasant independent motels are The Valley Inn (236 Soco Rd., 800/948-6880, www.thevalleyinn.com, from $79) and Jonathan Creek Inn and Villas (4324 Soco Rd., 800/577-7812, www.jonathancreekinn. com, from $100), which has creek-side rooms with screened porches.

High in the mountains—at 4,500 feet elevation—Smokey Shadows Lodge & Country Gourmet Dining (323 Smoky Shadows Lane, 828/926-0001, www.smok-eyshadows.com) offers up lodge rooms (from $110) and a pair of cabins (from $150) in a converted grist mill that once served the Cataloochee Valley. With a long covered porch affording some spectacular views, and a yard frequented by elk, it's a special kind of place. They also have a dining room where they serve family-style country dishes ($35)— think tomato pie, pot roast, meatloaf, and other homey dishes—or you can take your meal on the porch (call and reserve a seat on the porch; there may not be one if you wait until you get there to ask for it).

If you want to get a feel for the mountains, try one of the cabin rentals. Bear Run Log Cabins (1604 Moody Farm Rd., 828/926-7566, www.bearrunlogcabins.com, $150-180 June-Dec., $130-150 Jan.-May) has a quartet of cabins that sleep five and have Wi-Fi, a fireplace, and a small kitchen. Their decks overlook Jonathan Creek, one of the area trout streams. Cozy, comfy, and cabin-y, they're exactly what you picture when you think of a mountain cabin getaway.

Stay in a cabin at Twinbrook Resort (20 Twinbrook Lane, 828/962-1388, www.

twinbrookresort.com, cabins $249-499, RV site $59) or bring your RV; either way, you're staying in a beautiful place. Here you're within easy striking distance of the park and the parkway, only 30 minutes' drive to the Oconaluftee Visitors Center, a little longer if you take the scenic route on the Blue Ridge Parkway. On-site you'll find an indoor pool and hot tub, decks with grills, a playground, and one of the namesake brooks. If your travel plans are flexible, keep an eye on the website, as they're constantly running specials on lodging.

There is one fantastic campground in the area: the ★ Balsam Mountain Campground (Milepost 458.2, Heintooga Spur Rd., 828/497-9270, www.nps.gov/grsm, reservations www.recreation.gov, mid-May-mid-Oct., $18), the highest campground in Great Smoky Mountains National Park at 5,310 feet. This primitive campground has 43 sites for tents and RVs, with a dedicated tent-only section. It's a beautiful isolated campground that's often overlooked as it's slightly off the beaten path. Because it's also a primitive campground (pit toilets, no showers), most of the year you won't have many neighbors here. If you're driving a vehicle you feel comfortable taking on forest roads, Balsam Mountain Road, sometimes called Round Bottom Road, continues on from the campground, making a nice trip through the forest down to Cherokee. It's about two hours but worth the drive.

GETTING THERE AND AROUND

U.S. 19 is the main thoroughfare in these parts, leading from Asheville to the Great Smoky Mountains National Park. If you're taking your time between Asheville, Boone, or parts north, the Blue Ridge Parkway is a beautiful, but slow, drive to this part of the state. Maggie Valley is also a reasonably short jog off I-40 via exits 20, 24, and 27.

Cherokee and the Qualla Boundary

The town of Cherokee is a study in juxtapositions: the cultural traditions of the Cherokee people, the region's natural beauty, a 24-hour casino, and community-wide preparation for the future. Cherokee is the seat of government of the Eastern Band of the Cherokee, who have lived in these mountains for centuries. Today, their traditional arts and crafts, government, and cultural heritage are very much alive, although their language seems to be disappearing. The Qualla ("KWA-lah") Boundary is not a reservation but a large tract of land owned and governed by the Cherokee people. Institutions like the Museum of the Cherokee Indian and the Qualla Arts and Crafts Mutual provide a solid base for the Eastern Band's cultural life. As you drive around, take a look at the road signs: Below each English road name is that same name in Cherokee, a beautiful script created by Sequoyah, a 19th-century Cherokee silversmith. This language, once nearly extinct, is being taught to the community's youth now, and there is a Cherokee language immersion school on the Qualla Boundary. This doesn't mean the language is not in danger; few Cherokee people speak it fluently.

The main street in Cherokee is a classic cheesy tourist district where you'll find "Indian" souvenirs—factory-made moccasins, plastic tomahawks, peace pipes, faux bearskins, the works. In a retro way, this part of Cherokee, with its predictable trinket shops and fudgeries, is charming.

Aside from its proximity to the Great Smoky Mountains National Park and the Blue Ridge Parkway, the biggest draw in town is Harrah's Cherokee Casino, one of the largest casino hotels in the state and home to a world-class spa. The 24-hour entertainment opportunities attract visitors from far and wide, some of whom stay on the property the whole time, while others take a break from the slap of cards and the flash of slot machines to experience the natural and cultural wonders of Cherokee.

Take all of this that you see—the casino, the tacky tourist shops, and the stereotyping signs—with a grain of salt, as they don't represent the true nature of the Cherokee people and their long history.

SIGHTS
Harrah's Cherokee Casino
The Eastern Band of the Cherokee operates **Harrah's Cherokee Casino and Hotel** (777 Casino Dr., 828/497-7777, www.harrahscherokee.com, 24 hours daily). This full-bore Vegas-style casino has more than 3,800 digital games and slot machines along with around 150 table games, such as baccarat, blackjack, roulette, and a poker-only room. Inside the casino complex is a 3,000-seat concert venue where acts like Alicia Keys and the Black Crows have performed, a huge buffet, and a grab-and-go food court next to the casino floor. Unlike in the rest of the state, smoking is allowed on the casino floor, though certain areas have been designated as nonsmoking. Inside the hotel portion of the casino are a restaurant, a Starbucks, and the **Mandara Spa,** which offers salon and spa services like massages and facials.

TOP EXPERIENCE

★ Museum of the Cherokee Indian
The **Museum of the Cherokee Indian** (589 Tsali Blvd., 828/497-3481, www.mci.org, 9am-5pm daily, $12 adults, $7 ages 6-12, free under age 6) was founded in 1948 and was originally housed in a log cabin. Today it is a well-regarded modern museum and locus of community culture. In the exhibits that trace the long history of the Cherokee people, you may notice the disconcertingly realistic mannequins. Local community members volunteered to be models for these mannequins, allowing

Cherokee

To River's Edge Outfitting, Smoky Mountain Tube & Raft, Wize Guyz Grille, and Native Brews

PETER'S PANCAKES & WAFFLES

LAMBERT BRANCH RD

RIVER'S EDGE MOTEL

TSALI BLVD

BJ'S DINER

OCONALUFTEE INDIAN VILLAGE

FIRE MOUNTAIN TRAILS

JOSEPH WASHINGTON DR

UNTO THESE HILLS

QUALLA ARTS AND CRAFTS MUTUAL

ACQUONI RD

Cherokee

1361

MUSEUM OF THE CHEROKEE INDIAN

Fair Grounds

FIRE MOUNTAIN OUTFITTERS

441

BIA HWY 1390

BIA HWY 316

Oconaluftee River

0   200 yds
0   200 m

441 19

TSALAGI RD

To Harrah's Cherokee Casino and Hotel

19

© MOON.COM

invasion of their homeland. It was also a time of great cultural advancement, including Sequoyah's development of the script to write the Cherokee language. The forced relocation of Native Americans called the Trail of Tears began near here, along the North Carolina-Georgia border, in the early 19th century. A small contingent of Cherokees remained in the Smokies at the time of the Trail of Tears, successfully eluding, and then negotiating with, the U.S. military, who were trying to force most of the Native Americans in the Southeast to move to Oklahoma. Those who stayed out in the woods, along with a few others who were able to return from Oklahoma, are the ancestors of today's Eastern Band, and their history is truly remarkable.

A favorite part of the museum are the stories, legends, and myths described on placards throughout the building. There's the story of a boy who became a bear and convinced his entire clan to become bears also. There's one about Spearfinger, a frightening creature that some say still lives in these woods today. And there are tales about Selu, the corn mother, and Kanati, the lucky hunter. Cherokee member and contemporary writer Marilou Awiakta has written widely about Selu, tying the past and present together with taut lines of thought that challenge our views on culture and technology.

★ Qualla Arts and Crafts Mutual

Across the street from the museum is the **Qualla Arts and Crafts Mutual** (645 Tsali Blvd., 828/497-3103, http://quallaartsandcrafts.com, 8am-5pm Mon.-Sat., 8am-4:30pm Sun.), a community arts co-op where local artists sell their work. The gallery's high standards and the community's thousands of years of artistry make for a collection of very special pottery, baskets, masks, and other traditional art. The Qualla co-op does a great service to this community by providing a year-round market for the work of traditional Cherokee artists, whose stewardship of and innovation in the arts are so important. The double-woven baskets are

casts to be made of their faces and bodies so that the figures would not reflect an outsider's notion of what Native Americans should look like. The Museum of the Cherokee Indian traces their history from the Paleo-Indian people of the Pleistocene, when the ancestral Cherokees were hunter-gatherers, through the ancient days of Cherokee civilization, and into contact with the European settlers.

A great deal of this exhibit focuses on the 18th-19th centuries, when a series of tragedies befell the Cherokee as a result of the especially beautiful, as are the carvings of the masks representing each of the seven clans of the Cherokee people (the Bird, Deer, Longhair, Blue, Wolf, Paint, and Wild Potato).

TOP EXPERIENCE

★ Oconaluftee Indian Village

Oconaluftee Indian Village (778 Drama Rd., 828/497-2111, www.cherokeehistorical. org, 9:30am-4:30pm Mon.-Sat. Apr.-Nov., $25 adults, $15 ages 6-11, free under age 6) is a recreated Cherokee Indian Village tucked into the hills above the town. Here, you'll see how the tribe lived in the 18th century. Tour guides in period costumes lead groups on walking lectures with stops at stations where you can see Cherokee cultural, artistic, and daily-life activities performed as authentically as possible. From cooking demos to flint knapping (for arrowheads and spear points) to wood carving and clay work, you'll get a look at how the Cherokee lived centuries ago. The highlight of the tour is the ritual dance demonstration showing a half-dozen dances and explaining their cultural significance.

RECREATION
Fishing

Cherokee has more than 30 miles of streams, rivers, and creeks ideal for fishing. The Eastern Band owns and operates a fish hatchery that releases around 250,000 trout into these waters every year, creating the perfect mix for fantastic fishing. Unlike in the rest of North Carolina, you don't need a North Carolina fishing license; you need a **tribal fishing permit** (www.fishcherokee.com, 1 day $10, 2 days $17, 3 days $27, 5 days $47, season permit $250, trophy waters permit $25 1-3 days, $75 annually), sold at a number of outlets in Cherokee. You'll find brook, brown, golden, and rainbow trout, and it's fly-rod only, so you need to have your cast down pat if you want to bring in a big one. There are both catch-and-release and catch-and-keep waters in the Qualla Boundary, but if you want to fish outside the boundary, you need a North Carolina or Tennessee fishing permit. Tennessee permits are only valid

inside the Great Smoky Mountains National Park boundaries in North Carolina.

If you're unsure of your fly-fishing skills or want a guide to take you to a hot fishing hole, talk to the folks at **Rivers Edge Outfitters** (61 Big Cove Rd., 828/497-9300, www.wnc-fishing.com, 8am-5pm Sun.-Thurs., 7am-6pm Fri.-Sat., $25-500). Their shop is fully stocked with all the gear and tackle you need for a day on the water, and they offer lessons in casting and fly tying as well as guided trips. You can go for a two-hour, half-day, or full-day wading trip on local waters; other options are half- and full-day float trips or wading trips on private waters nearby.

Mountain Biking

Fire Mountain Trails (778 Drama Rd., https://visitcherokeenc.com, free) has 10.5 miles of trails suitable for mountain bikers, as well as hikers and trail runners. Riders of all skill levels can get in a good session here, with beginner-friendly runs that will boost your confidence and some rip-roaring single-track runs that will have expert riders catching air and finessing their way through rock gardens. The trailhead is adjacent to the Oconaluftee Indian Village.

Just across the street from where you head up to Fire Mountain Trails is **Fire Mountain Outfitters** (516 Tsali Blvd., 828/750-4196, www.firemountainoutpost.com, 10am-5pm Sun.-Mon., 10am-6pm Wed.-Sat.), an outdoor gear shop with plenty of stuff to outfit you for a hiking, camping, or biking adventure. They've partnered with **Motion Makers Bicycle Shop** (www.motionmakers.com, 828/586-6925) for mountain bike sales, repairs, and rentals ($45-150 per day). If you're staying in Bryson City (it's only 15 minutes away), **Tsali Cycles** (35 Slope St., Bryson City, 828/499-9010, www.tsalicycles.com, 10am-5pm Mon.-Fri., 9am-4pm Sat., $30-50 adults,

---

1: the Museum of the Cherokee Indian entrance with *Sequoyah* sculpture by Peter Wolf Toth **2:** Native American arrowheads from Cherokee **3:** street sign in Cherokee and English **4:** fishing on the Oconaluftee River

$20-25 children) can get you set up with a mountain bike rental to use here or on the Tsali Trails closer to their home base.

Water Sports

For fun on the water, try **Smoky Mountain Tube and Raft** (1847 Tsali Blvd., 828/497-4545, http://cherokeetubeandraft.com, 10am-5pm daily Memorial Day-Labor Day weekend, weather permitting, $14, cooler tubes $10). It has mountains of tubes, so rent one and float down the Oconaluftee River for 2-3 hours. It also has a fleet of shuttle buses to pick you up a few miles downstream.

ENTERTAINMENT AND EVENTS

Of the several outdoor dramas for which North Carolina is known, among the longest running is Cherokee's *Unto These Hills* (Mountainside Theater, 688 Drama Rd., adjacent to Oconaluftee Indian Village, 866/554-4557, https://visitcherokeenc.com, 8pm Mon.-Sat. June-Aug. 15, $35-60 adults, $25-60 ages 6-12, free under age 6). Since 1950, Cherokee actors have told the story of their nation's history, from ancient times through the Trail of Tears. Every seat in the house is a good seat at the Mountainside Theater, and the play is enlightening. Be warned: There is some cannon fire and gunfire in the play.

Hear stories, learn dances, and interact with Cherokee storytellers at the **Cherokee Bonfire** (Oconaluftee Islands Park, Tsalagi Rd. and Tsali Blvd., 800/438-1601, https://visitcherokeenc.com, 7pm-8pm Sun., Mon., Wed., and Sat. May-Oct., free), at the intersection of U.S. 19 and U.S. 441. Bring your bathing suit and some water shoes; afterward, you may want to go for a wade or a quick dip in the Oconaluftee River, which is wide, rocky, and fun.

FOOD

Harrah's Cherokee Casino is home to one of the best restaurants in town, **Brio Tuscan Grille** (777 Casino Dr., 828/497-8233, www.brioitalian.com, 11am-10pm Sun.-Thurs., 11am-11pm Fri.-Sat., $10-36), which specializes in dishes from northern Italy. The food is great, the wine list is excellent, and the ambience makes you forget you're in a casino. There are other options in Harrah's, from the expected casino buffet to the grab-and-go-back-to-gaming food court, even **Guy Fieri's Cherokee Kitchen + Bar** (4pm-10pm Sun.-Thurs., 4pm-11pm Fri.-Sat., $13-35), whose burgers, wings, steaks, and ribs don't hide from bold flavor. **Wicked Weed Brewpub** (4pm-11pm Wed.-Fri., 11am-11pm Sat.-Sun., $8-34) has set up an outpost here where they pour their Asheville-brewed beers and serve smashburgers, hot chicken sandwiches, and even steaks and beef tartare.

With a focus on wings, pizza, and burgers, **Wize Guyz Grille** (68 Big Cove Rd., 828/497-2838, https://wizeguyzgrille.com, 11am-7pm Mon.-Thurs., 11am-8pm Fri.-Sat., $6-50) gives diners a good option away from the casino. Dozens of iterations of chicken sandwiches and burgers, a bevy of appetizers (pickle fries, anyone? Get two baskets), and 15 pizzas to choose from means you have options aplenty.

I'd be remiss if I didn't mention the best burger in town, which comes from a roadside trailer. **BJ's Diner** (840 Tsali Blvd., 828/497-4303, https://bjs-diner.business.site, 11am-6pm Mon.-Thurs., 11am-8pm Fri.-Sat., 11am-4pm Sun., $2-9) keeps it simple: burgers with or without cheese, hot dogs, chicken tenders, and a few sandwiches. They do have a bacon cheeseburger served on a grilled cheese (which you should definitely get), but that's about as far afield as they go. If there's room at the picnic tables, grab a seat as the Oconaluftee River flows by just a few feet away. You might just see a few elk wading by.

At **Sassy Sunflowers Bakery & Café** (1655 Aquoni Rd., 828/497-2539, 9am-4pm Mon.-Fri. Mar.-Dec., $3-10), you can get the usual coffee and pastry treats but also excellent soups and sandwiches. The chicken salad is especially good—and quite portable if you're hoping to picnic in the park later in the day. Just remember to bring a cooler.

Up early to hit the trail? Grab breakfast in town at **Peter's Pancakes & Waffles** (1384

Tsali Blvd., 828/497-5116, 6:30am-2pm daily, $2-11), where you can order flapjacks (the blueberry pancakes are a sure bet), eggs with bacon, or a biscuit sandwich. Offerings are cheap, filling, and tasty.

Native Brews Tap and Grill (1897 Tsali Blvd., 828/497-2739, www.native-brews.com, noon-9pm Mon.-Thurs., noon-10pm Fri.-Sat., 11am-9pm Sun., $9-30) has a quartet of their own beers—an IPA, pale ale, golden lager, and blond—as well as spiced ales (think hard root beer, cream soda, and lemonade) and hard seltzers on offer alongside their own label of vodka, gin, and whiskey. As you taste your way through the liquid offerings, you're going to need a snack or a meal. The Colossal Pretzel is a whopper of an appetizer (not quite a wagon wheel, but still huge), the sandwiches hit the spot, and there are full-size entrées if you are feeling more than peckish.

ACCOMMODATIONS

Cherokee has many motels, including the family-owned and aptly named **Rivers Edge Motel** (1026 Tsalil Blvd., 828/497-7995, www.riversedgecherokee.com, from $179), and an **Econo Lodge** (20 River Rd./U.S. 19, 828/497-4575, www.choicehotels.com, from $120).

★ **Harrah's Cherokee Casino Resort** (777 Casino Dr., 828/497-7777, www.harrahscherokee.com, $125-510) is, without a doubt, the best place to stay in Cherokee. The hotel's 1,800 rooms are spacious, comfortable, and well kept; the casino and a number of dining options are an elevator ride away; and the spa provides an added layer of amenities you don't find at other hotels in town.

There's something about visiting a place and living where the residents live, and ★ **Panther Creek Cabins** (Wrights Creek Rd., 828/497-2461, www.panthercreekresort.com, $75-325, 2-night minimum seasonally) gives you that chance. The 13 cabins range from private two-person affairs to larger lodges that could easily sleep eight. Just outside downtown Cherokee, the quaint cabins are quiet and comfortable. Pets are welcome in most cabins for a flat fee ($49 for the first dog, $39 for the second).

On the outskirts of Cherokee are a couple of RV parks. **Happy Holiday RV Park and Campground** (1553 Wolfetown Rd., 828/497-9204, www.happyholidayrv.com, tents $25-46, RVs $48-70, cabins $90-180) sits just to the east of town on 40 acres. They have more than 375 sites and a half-dozen cabins. There's a pool, an ice-cream parlor, and a little spot where you can grab a quick snack, and if you're a bluegrass lover, they have a small bluegrass festival here in the early June and early September. Just south of town is **Fort Wilderness Campground & RV Park** (284 Fort Wilderness Rd., Whittier, 828/497-9331, www.fortwilderness.net, tent sites $35-45, RV sites $40-60), with 130 sites on 11 acres. Even though it's technically in the town of Whittier, it's only 1.5 miles to Harrah's Casino and 7 miles from the entrance to Great Smoky Mountains National Park and the Blue Ridge Parkway.

INFORMATION AND SERVICES

The **Cherokee Welcome Center** (498 Tsali Blvd., 800/438-1601, www.visitcherokeenc.com, 8am-5pm daily) can help you with tickets, directions, and things to do and see. There's one radio station in Cherokee, **WNCC** (101.3), a country station, although you can pick up distant stations with a wider selection.

GETTING THERE

Cherokee is on a particularly pretty and winding section of U.S. 19 between Maggie Valley and Bryson City, 2.5 miles south of the southern terminus of the Blue Ridge Parkway. From the Blue Ridge Parkway, a six-minute drive south along U.S. 441 will take you to the center of Cherokee. Asheville is 1 hour and 10 minutes to the west via I-40 and U.S. 19. If you're coming from the Tennessee side of the Smoky Mountains, Gatlinburg is 1 hour west via Newfound Gap Road (U.S. 441), and Knoxville is 2 hours west via U.S. 441 and I-40. If you're coming up from the south, Atlanta is 2 hours and 45 minutes away via I-85, I-985, and U.S. 19.

Bryson City and the Nantahala Forest

To look at the mountains here, you'd think that the defining feature in this part of North Carolina would be the surrounding peaks, but you're only partly right. This is a land dominated by water: Smoke-thick fog crowds valleys in the predawn hours. The peaks stand ringed in clouds. Moss, ferns, and dense forests crowd the edge of rivers and streams. When you're in the Nantahala Gorge, it feels like you've stepped into a fairy tale. According to Cherokee legends, a formidable monster called Spearfinger lived here, as did a monstrous snake and even an inchworm so large it could span the gorge. Spearfinger and her cohorts haven't been seen in years, and the Nantahala River, which runs through the narrow gorge, attracts white-water enthusiasts.

Nearby Bryson City is a river town whose proximity to white water makes it a favorite haunt for rafters, kayakers, and other white-water thrill seekers. If you approach Bryson City from the north on U.S. 19, you're in for a strange sight: The banks of the Tuckasegee River are shored up with crushed cars.

SIGHTS
★ Great Smoky Mountains Railroad

The **Great Smoky Mountains Railroad** (GSMR, depots in Bryson City and Dillsboro, 800/872-4681, www.gsmr.com, from $45 adults, $34 children) is one of the best and most fun ways to see the Smokies. Using historic trains, the GSMR carries sightseers on excursions that average 4.5 hours and take passengers through some of the region's most beautiful scenery. Trips between Dillsboro and Bryson City, with a layover at each end for shopping and dining, follow the banks of the Tuckasegee River; round-trips from Bryson City follow the Little Tennessee and Nantahala Rivers deep into the Nantahala Gorge. Many other excursions are offered, including gourmet dining; wine-, beer-, and moonshine-tasting trips; rides on a steam locomotive; autumn leaf-peeping trips; and more. There are *Thomas the Tank Engine* and the *Little Engine That Could* trips for kids, and runs to and from river-rafting outfitters.

Museums

Inside Great Smoky Mountains Railroad's gift shop is the **Smoky Mountain Trains Museum** (100 Greenlee St., 800/872-4681, www.gsmr.com, generally 9am-4pm daily late May-Dec., 9:30am-4:30pm daily Jan.-late May, call ahead, $9 adults, $5 children, free with train ticket).

The **Fly Fishing Museum of the Southern Appalachians** (210 Main St., 828/488-3681, www.flyfishingmuseum.org, 9am-5pm Tues.-Fri., 10am-4pm Sat., free) tells the story of fly-fishing on the 14,000 miles of trout waters in North Carolina and across the southern Appalachians. Displays of hand-tied flies, antique rods and reels, drift boats, and even live fly-tying demos round out this free museum.

Across the street is the **Swain County Heritage Museum** (2 Everett St., 828/488-7857, www.swainheritagemuseum.com, 9am-5pm Mon.-Sat., 10am-4pm Sun. Apr.-Dec., 10am-5pm Mon.-Sat., 10am-4pm Sun. Jan.-Mar., free); downstairs is a Great Smoky Mountain Association Bookstore, and upstairs is a small but thorough museum telling the history of Bryson City and Swain County.

SPORTS AND RECREATION
★ Nantahala River Gorge

The stunningly beautiful Nantahala River Gorge, just outside Bryson City in the Nantahala National Forest, supports scores of river guide companies, many clustered along U.S. 19 west. Nantahala is said to mean "land of the noonday sun," and there are indeed parts of this gorge where the sheer rock walls above the river are so steep that sunlight only hits the water at the noon hour. Eight miles of the Nantahala River flow through the gorge over Class II-III rapids. The nearby Ocoee River is also a favorite of rafters, and the Cheoah River, when there are controlled water releases, has some of the South's most famous and difficult Class III-IV runs.

Outfitters and Tours

There's a lot to do in and around Bryson City beyond the borders of Great Smoky Mountains National Park. White-water rafting, kayaking, and tubing are popular ways to spend a day. Many river guide companies are located along U.S. 19. Other popular options are zip-lining, hiking, and mountain biking. Fortunately, several outfitters can help you arrange for guided tours, rentals, and just about anything else you need to make your time here memorable.

You can explore the mountains around Bryson City with the **Nantahala Outdoor Center** (13077 U.S. 19 W., 828/785-4846, www.noc.com, 8am-8pm daily, from $30), which offers a variety of adventure options that include white-water rafting, stand-up paddleboarding on the flat-water sections of the river, hiking, mountain biking, and zip-lining. Half-day, full-day, and overnight trips are possible, and excursions like the Rapid Transit combine a relaxing morning train ride with an afternoon rafting trip.

Carolina Bound Adventures (35 Slope St., 828/788-6885, www.carolinabound-adventures.com, from $39) has guide and concierge services for a variety of outings, including hikes, mountain bike rides, overnight camping trips, waterfall tours, and brewery and winery tours. The company can assist in planning just about any aspect of your getaway, even pet-sitting if you're planning on a long day.

River Adventures

In addition to river guide services on the nearby Nantahala and Little Pigeon Rivers and farther afield on the Chattooga (where the 1972 movie *Deliverance* was filmed) and Ocoee Rivers, **Wildwater Rafting** (10345 U.S. 19 W., 12 miles west of Bryson City, 866/319-8870, www.wildwaterrafting.com, $50-110) leads half- and full-day **Wildwater Jeep Tours,** excursions on back roads and through wilderness to waterfalls and old mountain settlements.

Endless River Adventures (14157 U.S. 19 W., Bryson City, 828/488-6199, www.endlessriveradventures.com, $45-159) guides trips on the Nantahala River, the tamest of the rivers around with Class II-III rapids; the Ocoee River, with bigger rapids and more technical challenges; and the Cheoah River, where big rapids—Class IV and above—await.

Fly-Fishing

The Smoky Mountains, especially the eastern grade of the Smokies, are laced with streams perfect for fly-fishing. Anglers from all over come to float, wade, camp, fish, hone their fly-tying craft, and learn the finer points of fly-fishing. The Tuckasegee River flows through downtown Bryson City, and many of its feeder streams and creeks are ideal spots to throw a line. At **Great Smokies Fishing** (www.greatsmokiesfishing.com) you'll find resources that include license and permit information; regulations; seasonal information; maps; write-ups on lakes, streams, and rivers; and an exhaustive list of guides. We've put a few of the best right here.

Fly Fishing the Smokies (Bryson City, 828/488-7665, www.flyfishingthesmokies.net, $200-850) has a number of guides and options for a day or more of fly-fishing the streams on the north shore of the lake and other trout waters. Go bass fishing on Fontana for a half day, wade the streams with them for a half-day or full-day outing, try a float trip, go fly-fishing in Great Smoky Mountains National Park, or up the ante with some backcountry camping and fly-fishing in the park.

The name says it all: **Mac Brown Fly Fish** (779 W. Deep Creek Rd., 828/736-1469, www.macbrownflyfish.com). Mac's been an outfitter, guide, instructor, and casting maestro since 1987, and he knows where to find the fish and exactly how to get them on his side of the water. He offers float trips ($625 pp) and wading trips ($575) on nearby waters.

Nantahala Fly Fishing Co. (Robbinsville, 828/557-1409, www.flyfishnorthcarolina.com, $200-350) provides guided fly-rod fishing trips and private half- and full-day lessons. If you've never held one of these odd fishing rods in your hands before, there's also a fly-fishing school (2 days, $600) and private instruction. Best of all, the company has a "No Fish, No Pay" guarantee.

Fly fishers who don't need a guide can check out a number of streams that are packed with fish, but be sure to inquire about regulations for individual streams. Some are catch-and-release, while a neighboring stream might be catch-and-keep, and some have regulations about the types of hooks you can use. Once you're ready to put your line in the water, try **Hazel Creek** on the north shore of Fontana Lake, where you'll find pristine waters and a good number of fish. Other nearby creeks, like **Eagle Creek** and any of the feeder creeks that empty into the lake, are prime spots as well.

Hiking and Mountain Biking

Great Smoky Mountains National Park has more than 800 miles of wilderness trails, and with around 40 percent of the park located in Swain County, more trails than you could hike in a week are within striking distance of Bryson City. **Deep Creek Loop** is a 4.9-mile loop that passes two waterfalls on its easy, mostly flat, track. You can also take the strenuous **Deep Creek Trail** to Newfound Gap Road, a 14.2-mile one-way hike that will require a return ride. The **Noland Creek Trail** is a fairly easy 6-mile trail near the end of the Road to Nowhere (a failed road-building project from the 1930s and 1940s). At the end of the Road to Nowhere, just past the tunnel, is the **Goldmine Loop Trail,** a 3.1-mile track that's beautiful and enjoyable. The nature and lake views are especially welcome after trekking through the

dark 0.5-mile tunnel on the way in (bring a flashlight; you won't regret it).

With all these mountains, you'd think mountain biking would be a big deal around here, and you'd be right. The **Tsali Recreation Area Trail System** (Tsali Rd./Hwy. 28, Robbinsville, www.fs.usda.gov, $2) is only 15 miles from Bryson City and draws riders throughout the year. Named for Tsali (SAH-lee), a Cherokee martyr who led the resistance to removal at the start of the Trail of Tears, the area has four loops constituting 42 miles of trails that trace courses across the mountains. These multiuse trails are rated as moderate, and if you're up for the challenge, give these fun flowy single-tracks a try. You'll share the road with hikers and equestrians, but there's a schedule: two trails for bikes, two for horses each day. More information on area mountain biking, including an overview map showing 15 more places to ride, is available at www.greatsmokies.com.

SHOPPING

Bryson City Outdoors (169 Main St., 828/341-6444, www.brysoncityoutdoors.com, 10am-6pm Mon.-Thurs., 10am-7pm Fri.-Sat., 11am-6pm Sun.) features a well-curated selection of outdoor gear and may be the friendliest little outdoor store you've ever shopped in. Everyone here is outdoorsy—active in hiking, mountain biking, white-water rafting, kayaking, paddleboarding, fly-fishing, rock climbing, you name it—and can help you get set up for just about any activity. Next door, the store operates **BCOutdoors Taproom** (10am-9pm Mon.-Sat., 11am-7pm Sun.), offering a dozen beers on tap—mostly North Carolina brews as well as some other regional beers—plus a great selection of bottles and cans. It's a fun place to hang out, enjoy a pint, swap trail stories or fish tales, and figure out tomorrow's adventure.

There are a number of T-shirt and souvenir shops in Bryson City, but **Appalachian**

1: fly-fishing on the Tuckasegee River **2:** rafters on the Nantahala River

Mercantile (158 Everett St., 828/488-2531, www.appalachianmercantile.net, 10am-6pm daily Apr.-Oct., call for hours Nov.-Mar.) is top on the list. Their selection doesn't overwhelm, and there's not as much souvenir flotsam as you'll find elsewhere; instead, the foodstuffs, playing cards, games, and toys have been winnowed down to the best in each category. The owner, Lance, was a backcountry guide in the area and then a location scout for the film industry; now he's an author of local histories and a shopkeeper, and he's ready with a story if you've got a minute to listen.

FOOD

The Bistro at The Everett Boutique Hotel (16 Everett St., 828/488-1934, www.theeveretthotel.com, 4:30pm-9pm Wed.-Sun., $10-38) serves an excellent dinner that is contemporary Appalachian in nature but includes one or two vegetarian-friendly dishes, typically noodle bowls. Regardless of what you order, the flavors will be on point and you'll find a cocktail, wine, or North Carolina beer to pair with it.

You can't beat breakfast at Everett Street Diner (126 Everett St., 828/488-0123, www.brysoncityrestaurant.com, 7am-2pm Mon. and Wed.-Sat., 7:30am-2pm Sun., $5-14), featuring filling options that won't weigh you down on the trail, like fluffy pancakes or biscuits and gravy. For lunch, you'll find great burgers, and the light lunch—a salad and half a sandwich—is a bargain. For a real treat—Bryson City gossip and local news—sit at the counter in back.

The Appalachian Trail passes only a few feet from River's End Restaurant (13077 U.S. 19 W., 828/488-7172, www.noc.com, 11am-7pm Wed.-Sun., $8-23) at the Nantahala Outdoor Center. Given its proximity to the trail (really a footbridge over the river, but on the trail nonetheless) and to the center's rafting, paddling, and hiking nexus, it's a popular spot for outdoorsy sorts. The menu reflects this with dishes like the Sherpa bowls (rice, veggies, and optional meat) that are packed with protein, calories, and carbs to fuel you through a day on the trail.

For coffee and a quick breakfast, lunch, or snack, visit Mountain Perks Espresso Bar & Café (9 Depot St., 828/488-9561, www.mtnperks.com, 7am-3pm Sun.-Mon. and Thurs., 7am-4pm Fri.-Sat., $2-16). They make a good cappuccino, and the quiche, wraps, and bagel sandwiches hit the spot whether you eat them in-house or take them on your park adventure.

Nantahala Brewing Brewpub (116 Ramseur St., 828/585-5885, www.nantahalabrewing.com, 3pm-10pm Mon.-Fri., noon-11pm Sat., noon-10pm Sun. Jan.-Feb., noon-10pm Sun.-Fri., noon-11pm Sat. Mar.-Apr., noon-11pm Sun.-Thurs., noon-midnight Fri.-Sat. May-Aug., noon-10pm Sun.-Thurs., noon-11pm Fri.-Sat. Sept.-Dec., $7-25) carries a full slate of Nantahala Brewing beer but also a menu of elevated pub grub. The salads are sizable and fresh, the pot roast and brown ale chicken are pleasant surprises, and the tacos and shareable plates exceed your bar food expectations.

Speaking of bars and bar food, Mountain Layers Brewing Company (90 Everett St., 828/538-0115, www.mountainlayersbrewingcompany.com, noon-9pm Mon.-Sat., noon-8pm Sun.) has an excellent rooftop deck overlooking the Tuckasegee River and a board of tasty beers to go with it. The Russian Imperial Stout, Dragon Tamer New England IPA, and Hazel Creek Blonde Ale are top-notch. Local food trucks stop by to trade food for money with hungry imbibers.

ACCOMMODATIONS

Bryson City has a surprising number of high-quality inns and bed-and-breakfasts. Overlooking Bryson City is the McKinley Edwards Inn (208 Arlington Ave., 828/488-9626, www.mckinleyedwardsinn.com, from $159), a lovely 12-room house and inn built in 1922. The grounds are magnificent, and breakfast, a drink, or just quiet time on the deck gazing at the mountains will convince you to come back again.

Built in 1923 and on the National Register

of Historic Places, the ★ Fryemont Inn (245 Fryemont St., 828/488-2159, www.fryemontinn.com, mid-Apr.-late Nov. $190-345, includes meals, late Nov.-mid-Apr. $115-215, no meals) has a cozy, rustic feel with chestnut-paneled guest rooms and an inviting lobby with an enormous stone fireplace. Suites and a log cabin that sleeps six are available.

★ The Everett Boutique Hotel & Bistro (16 Everett St., 828/488-1934, www.theeveretthotel.com, $219-369) has 10 suites, a rooftop hangout area, and an excellent on-site restaurant. Rooms are spacious, comfortable, and mountain chic, and the beds are so comfortable you might just want to move in. The hotel is in the former Bryson City Bank, built in 1908, and you can still see the vault door in the restaurant. It's as lovely a place to stay as you can imagine, and everything Bryson City has to offer is within a 10-minute walk.

Some river outfitters provide lodging, which can be a cheap way to pass the night if you don't mind roughing it. Many of the outfitters also offer camping on their properties. The Rolling Thunder River Company (10160 U.S. 19 W., 800/408-7238, www.rollingthunderriverco.com, $10-12 pp) operates a large bunkhouse with beds for its rafting customers. For large groups of 15 or more, it offers a free night in the bunkhouse Monday-Thursday. No alcohol is permitted here. Carolina Outfitters (715 U.S. 19, Topton, 828/488-9819, www.carolinaoutfitters.com, $80-100) offers a variety of accommodations, including two-room cabins, two-bedroom apartments, and three-bedroom cabins suitable for a large group.

Nantahala Cabins (580 Nantahala Cabins Lane, 828/488-1433, www.nantahalacabins.com, $175-325) has 10 cabins to rent, ranging from studios to three-bedroom cabins fit for a family or group. A few minutes down the road from Bryson City proper, closer to Almond, Watershed Resort (137 W. Watershed Rd., Bryson City, 877/784-0688, www.watershedresort.com, $90-700) rents cabins in just about any size, style, and configuration imaginable. There are pet-friendly cabins, cabins

with a modern flair, small cabins, and cabins fit for a family reunion. Want a hot tub or a jaw-dropping view? They've got you covered. You'll find some short-term openings here and there, but if you're planning on staying for a week or more, you'll want to book well in advance. These are excellent properties, and folks snap them up quick.

Camping

Among the nicest camping options available in Nantahala National Forest is Standing Indian Campground (90 Sloan Rd., Franklin, campground 828/524-6441, reservations 877/444-6777, www.recreation.gov, Apr.-Oct., $20-75). It has a nice diversity of campsites, from flat grassy areas to cozy mountainside nooks. Drinking water, hot showers, flush toilets, and a phone are all available on-site, and leashed pets are allowed. The campground is close to the Appalachian Trail and sits at an elevation of 3,400 feet.

Another nice campground is the Deep Creek Tube Center and Campground (1040 W. Deep Creek Rd., 828/488-6055, www.deepcreekcamping.com, Apr.-late Oct., campsites $31-60, cabins $99-325), with more than 50 campsites, 18 cabins, and access to Deep Creek. The creek runs right by many campsites, and you can go tubing ($7 per day). You can also go gem "mining" here, a great mountain tradition; bags and buckets of gem-enriched dirt are sold in the camp store. The best part is that the campground is within walking distance of Great Smoky Mountains National Park.

DEEP CREEK

Just south of Cherokee and just north of Bryson City, Deep Creek is a spot more popular with locals than visitors, but it's worth a stop. Deep Creek is relatively placid, aside from a couple of waterfalls farther upstream. If you're not into wading or tubing, don't worry; this is a lovely place to picnic and hike or even camp away from the crowds in some of the more popular spots in the park.

At the end of Deep Creek Road you'll find

the trailheads leading to the waterfalls. You'll also find the Deep Creek Campground (877/444-6777, www.recreation.gov, mid-Apr.-late-Oct., $25). There are nearly 100 campsites, many of which fill up with locals. If you want to camp here, arrive early or reserve well in advance.

Deep Creek Tube Center and Campground (1040 W. Deep Creek Rd., Bryson City, 828/488-6055, www.deepcreek-camping.com, campsites $31-60, cabins $99-325) is a charming collection of tent and RV campsites and cabins for rent; the two largest cabins sleep 10, and one is pet-friendly. As the name implies, they rent tubes (all-day $7) for use on Deep Creek. Rentals are cheap, so you can play in the water as long as you like.

There are two nice waterfalls to see here. Juney Whank Falls (yes, that's its name) is less than 0.5 miles from the Deep Creek Campground and cuts an impressive figure as it drops a total of 90 feet in two stages. Indian Creek Falls, 1 mile from the campground, is a stunning set of falls and cascades some 60 feet high.

ROAD TO NOWHERE

An odd place to visit is the so-called Road to Nowhere. Just south of the Deep Creek entrance outside Bryson City is a short stretch of highway leading north into GSMNP. Lonely, even spooky, the road is all that remains of a parkway planned to trace a path through the Smokies along Fontana Lake. Though construction was started on the parkway, it was abandoned. Today, the road stops quite abruptly about six miles inside the park, at a constructed stone tunnel. Hard feelings over the failed parkway have softened, but many families still hold a grudge against government officials who vowed to build a road along the lake to provide access to old family cemeteries.

Cars are prohibited from using the tunnel at the end of the Road to Nowhere, but visitors on foot can stroll through. After you pass through the tunnel, there's a marathon-length hike—seriously, it's 26 miles—weaving along the northern bank of Fontana Lake.

GETTING THERE AND AROUND

Bryson City can be reached via U.S. 19 and U.S. 74, if you're coming south from Maggie Valley (45 minutes) and Cherokee (15 minutes). It's 20 minutes to the Great Smoky Mountains National Park's Oconaluftee Visitor Center, just north of Cherokee. Asheville is 1 hour and 20 minutes east via U.S. 74 and I-40.

Waynesville and Vicinity

Waynesville, just west of Asheville and east of Cherokee, is the very definition of the word *quaint*. Writers have compared it to a Norman Rockwell painting with its storybook Main Street, busy with shops and lined with brick sidewalks and iron lampposts. This is an artistic little community where the art and craft galleries and studios are seemingly endless. In nearby Cullowhee, Western Carolina University is one of the mountain region's leading academic institutions as well as the location of the Mountain Heritage Center museum and Mountain Heritage Day festival.

WAYNESVILLE

Waynesville's downtown can keep a gallery-hopper or shopper happy for hours. Main Street is packed with studio artists' galleries, cafés and coffee shops, and a variety of boutiques.

Sights

One interesting stop in Waynesville is the **Museum of North Carolina Handicrafts** (49 Shelton St., 828/452-1551, www.sheltonhouse.org, 10am-3pm Thurs.-Sat. Apr.-Oct., $7 adults, $5 students, free under age 6). Consisting of a farmhouse, a barn, and gardens, the museum opened in 1980 and shows off the work of Native American and North Carolina heritage artists. This means mountain musical instruments, ceremonial items and crafts from Native American tribes, basketry, woodcarvings, quilts, and even antique farm tools. Tours of the museum are guided, so you'll hear plenty of stories to go with the items you see.

Shops and Galleries

Waynesville's galleries are many and varied, although the overarching aesthetic is one of studio art with inspiration in the environment and folk arts. Shops in the area feature local gems and necessities.

Blue Ridge Books & News (428 Hazelwood Ave., 828/456-6000, www.blueridgebooksnc.com, 9am-4pm Mon.-Fri., 9am-3pm Sat.) is a nice bookstore with specialties of regional interest and good coffee. A number of prominent Southern authors come through here to read and sign books, so check their schedule and ask about signed copies.

One of the several locations of **Mast General Store** (63 N. Main St., 828/452-2101, www.mastgeneralstore.com, 10am-6pm Mon.-Sat., 11am-6pm Sun. spring-fall, hours vary in winter) in Waynesville. While the stores are perhaps best known among vacationers for making children clamor for the candy kept in big wooden barrels, old-time dry-goods-store style, they have an even larger selection of merchandise for adults, including camping gear, such as top-brand tents, cookware, maps, and outdoors-oriented upscale clothing and shoes.

Twigs and Leaves (98 N. Main St., 828/456-1940, www.twigsandleaves.com, 10am-5:30pm Mon.-Sat., 1pm-4pm Sun., hours vary seasonally) carries splendid art furniture that is both fanciful and functional, pottery of many hand-thrown and hand-built varieties, jewelry, paintings, fabric hangings, mobiles, and many other beautiful and unusual items inspired by nature.

Artist Gretchen Clasby displays her work alongside the works of 83 additional artists at **Cedar Hill Studio** (196 N. Main St., 828/421-6688, https://cedarhillstudio.com, noon-5pm daily). This is the largest fine-arts gallery in Waynesville and the artists represented are from town, nearby, and the region, and their works span media and styles, so you're sure to find something that catches your eye.

The work at **Curatory Gallery** (120 Miller St., 828/356-5585, https://curatorygallery.art 4pm-9pm Thurs.-Fri., noon-5pm Sat., Sun. by appointment) is on constant rotation, but one thing stays the same: the artists here are

Waynesville

© MOON.COM

pushing their limits. Underrepresented artists, artists from marginalized communities and backgrounds, and artists who have a distinct voice and distinct message are found here, so come expecting some challenging, dazzling, conversation-starting pieces.

Food

Waynesville's ★ **Frogs Leap Public House** (44 Church St., 828/456-1930, http://frogsleap-publichouse.com, 5pm-9pm Tues.-Sat., $8-29)

serves an interesting menu that's quite sophisticated but not afraid of its Southern roots. Dishes like the wood-grilled sirloin tip in a bourbon-shallot demi and the spicy Korean pork belly sliders show a real adventurous spirit that diners appreciate, not just because it's ambitious but because it's excellent.

Waynesville Pizza Company (32 Felmet St., 828/246-0927, www.waynesvillepizza. com, 11am-9pm Mon. and Wed.-Fri., noon-10pm Sat., noon-9pm Sun., $7-13) makes some hand-tossed pizzas that have folks in these parts talking. Well, they're talking about the pizza when they're not devouring a Buffalo chicken sandwich, a classic reuben, or a burger from this casual spot.

The ever-popular Bogart's (303 S. Main St., 828/452-1313, www.bogartswaynesville. com, 11am-8pm Sun.-Thurs., 11am-9pm Fri.-Sat., $7-23) is locally famous for its filet mignon, although their local trout also has a good reputation. The menu is huge but very steak house-y; vegetarians will have a tough time, although a few dishes, like the chipotle black bean burger and the grilled portobello salad, are options.

If you're just passing through town and need a jolt of good strong coffee, visit Panacea (66 Commerce St., 303 S. Main St., 828/452-6200, http://panaceacoffee.com, 9am-3pm Wed.-Sun., $5-11) in the funky Frog Level neighborhood downhill from downtown. The proprietors give back to their community and trade fairly with those who supply their coffee. They stock beans, blends, and brews from all around the world.

Accommodations

Waynesville has quite a selection of luxury inns. The Andon-Reid Inn (92 Daisey Ave., 828/452-3089, www.andonreidinn.com, from $160, no pets or children) is a handsome turn-of-the-20th-century house close to downtown with five tranquil guest rooms, each with its own fireplace, and a sumptuous breakfast menu that could include sweet-potato pecan pancakes and pork tenderloin, homemade cornbread with honey butter, or the intriguing baked lemon eggs. With advance notice they can cater to special dietary needs.

For absolute tip-top luxury, try The Swag (2300 Swag Rd., 800/789-7672, www.theswag. com, starting at $885). Superb guest rooms and cabins of rustic wood and stone each have a steam shower, and several have saunas, wet bars, and cathedral ceilings. The menu is decidedly country and upscale, two things you wouldn't think go together, but they do, and quite nicely. The inn is at 5,000 feet elevation

in a stunning location at the very edge of the Great Smoky Mountains National Park.

Up on the Blue Ridge Parkway above Waynesville and quite close to Asheville is the fantastic ★ Pisgah Inn (Milepost 408.6, Blue Ridge Pkwy., 828/235-8228, www.pisgahinn.com, Apr.-Oct., $138-182), with motel-style accommodations surrounding an old lodge with a large family-style dining room and a Parkway gift shop. The inn is on a nearly 5,000-foot-high mountaintop, so the view is sensational. Trails lead from the inn to short pretty strolls and challenging daylong hikes. The restaurant (7:30am-10:30am, 11:30am-4pm, and 5pm-9pm daily) has a mesmerizing view and an appetizing and varied menu (breakfast $3-9, lunch $9-20, dinner $10-27) of both country cooking and upscale meals. The guest rooms are simple but comfortable, each with its own balcony and rocking chairs overlooking the valley, and with a TV but no telephone. The Pisgah is a perfect spot for resting, reading, and porch-sitting.

Information and Services

The Haywood County Tourism Development Authority (1110 Soco Rd., 800/334-9036, http://visitncsmokies.com) has a wealth of information about visiting Waynesville and surrounding towns. MedWest Haywood (262 Leroy George Dr., Clyde, NC, 828/456-7311, www.myhaywoodregional.com), accessible from the Lake Junaluska exit off U.S. 23/74, is the region's hospital.

SYLVA

The small town of Sylva, southwest of Waynesville, is crowned by the pretty Jackson County Courthouse, an Italianate building with an ornate cupola, kept under wistful watch by the requisite courthouse-square Confederate monument. Visitors should stop by the Jackson County Visitor Center (773 W. Main St., 800/962-1911, www.mountainlovers.com, 9am-5pm Mon.-Fri.) or visit them online to learn more about the communities here.

Sights

South of Sylva, the mysterious **Judaculla Rock** (off Caney Fork Rd., www.judacullarock.com) has puzzled folks for centuries. The soapstone boulder is covered in petroglyphs estimated to be at least 500 years old. The figures and symbols and squiggles are clearly significant, but as of yet are not understood. I'm fascinated with petroglyphs, and these are some of the most mysterious I've encountered. The soft rock has eroded and the pictures are not as clear as they were in generations past, but many of them can still be discerned. To reach the rock, drive south on Highway 107 eight miles past the intersection with Sylva's U.S. 23 Business. Make a left on Caney Fork Road (County Rd. 1737) and drive 2.5 miles to a gravel road. Turn left, and after just under 0.5 miles you'll see the rock on the right and a parking area on the left.

Shopping

Sylva's City Lights Bookstore (3 E. Jackson St., 828/586-9499, www.citylightsnc.com, 10am-6pm Mon.-Sat., 10am-3pm Sun.) is hardly a knockoff of the monumental Beat establishment in San Francisco with which it shares a name. Instead, it's a first-rate small-town bookstore with stock that has the novelty sought by vacationers and the depth to make regulars of the local patrons. In addition to the sections you'll find in any good bookstore, their selection of books of regional interest, including folklore, nature, recreation guides, history, and fiction and poetry by Appalachian and Southern authors, is excellent.

Founded by a pair of Appalachian Trail through-hikers, **Black Balsam Outdoors** (562 W. Main St., 828/631-2864, 10am-6pm Mon.-Sat., noon-5pm Sun.) will get you geared up for a trip into the woods whether you're looking for hard-core trail gear to use on your own through-hike or if you're in the market for a day-hike kit that will serve you for this trip to the Smokies and many more. They know their gear, how to use it, and where to go to give it a good workout, so don't hesitate to inquire about their favorite hikes in the area and the national park.

Food

The North Carolina mountains are experiencing a booming organic foods movement, and you'll find eco-aware eateries throughout the area. **Lulu's On Main** (678 W. Main St., 828/586-8989, www.lulusonmain.com, 11:30am-3pm and 5pm-8pm Mon.-Thurs., 11:30am-3pm and 5pm-9pm Fri.-Sat., $11-30) is one of the most acclaimed restaurants in the area. The menu is American gourmet at heart, with splashes of Mediterranean and Nuevo Latino specialties. Try the cheese ravioli with tofu, the beef short ribs, or the paella. They have plenty of vegetarian options.

At ★ **Ilda** (462 W. Main St., 828/307-2036, www.ildainsylva.com, 5pm-9pm Thurs.-Sun., $16-22) you'll find rustic Italian dishes with a little bit of Appalachian twang on a menu that's perfectly representative of chef Santiago Guzzetti and sommelier Crystal Pace, a husband-and-wife duo who found their way back to her hometown. The food here is nothing short of spectacular. Seasonal availability drives the individual ingredients in dishes, and the mushroom risotto, *mafaldini* (lamb bolognese with local greens), and rigatoni with nasturtium sausage all take advantage of what's fresh and on hand, but even in the depths of winter, the menu shines.

City Lights Café (3 E. Jackson St., 828/587-2233, www.citylightscafe.com, 8am-3pm Mon.-Sat., 9am-3pm Sun., breakfast $2-8, lunch and dinner $5-12), downstairs from the bookshop, has some excellent crepes, a mighty good biscuit, and fun tacos, and they serve wine and beer. It's a cool, casual spot to dine and relax with your book and a bottle of wine, or to see a small local act.

If you're in the mood for coffee and something light, try **White Moon** (545 Mill St., 828/331-0111, www.whitemoonnc.com, 8am-3pm Tues.-Sun., $3-11). White Moon is one street over from the main drag, so it would be easy to overlook, but that would be a mistake. Friendly folks serve coffee, café drinks, and a small but tasty breakfast and lunch menu. When you need your avocado toast fix, a savory breakfast bowl, or a sandwich, this is the spot.

Nightlife

It's a small town, so there's not a whole lot in the way of nightlife, but **Innovation Brewing** (414 W. Main St., 828/586-9678, www.innovation-brewing.com, noon-10pm Sun.-Thurs., noon-midnight Fri.-Sun.) has 22 beers in their regular rotation, with 10 on tap at any time. The Nitro Irish Stout, Nut Brown, and Midnight Rye-der Black IPA are mainstays, but they also make a few sours. Keep an ear out for live music in the taproom, as bands drop by often. If you're hungry, you're in luck: **Cosmic Carry-Out** (828/506-2830, www.cosmiccarryout.com, noon-9pm Mon.-Thurs., noon-10:30pm Fri.-Sat., 11am-9pm Sun., $4-12) has burgers, tacos, grilled-cheese sandwiches, and fries for your dining enjoyment.

Balsam Falls Brewing (506 W. Main St., 828/631-1987, www.balsamfallsbrewing.com, 11am-10pm Mon.-Thurs., 11am-midnight Fri., 10am-midnight Sat., 10am-10pm Sun.) came to Sylva by way of the Tampa, Florida, home-brew scene, where owners Corey and Laure Bryson got their start. But Balsam Falls is far from home brew. The pair went on to get their Cicerone certification (think sommelier for beer), and Corey's a certified beer judge, so the brews they put on draft are top-notch. Every beer has a fun name—Elvis Has Left the Brewpub, Fergus the Rat Chocolate Milk Stout, Petrified Dragon—and the variety runs the gamut from IPAs to barley wine to Russian imperials to lightly hopped American pale ales.

Lazy Hiker Brewing (617 W. Main St., 828/349-2337, www.lazyhikerbrewing.com, noon-10pm Mon.-Thurs., noon-11pm Fri.-Sat., noon-9pm Sun.) is based in Franklin, North Carolina, but has a taproom in Sylva. They keep a dozen taps flowing with styles across the spectrum, each well done, and each appealing to different palates and preferences. Sour fans will find a black cherry sour as well as a gose and a berlinerweiss on tap, but dedicated IPA fans will find drafts highlighting different hops. If you like something in between, they have brown ales, blonds, and other brews to choose from.

DILLSBORO

Next door to Sylva is Dillsboro, a river town of rafters and crafters. **Dogwood Crafters** (90 Webster St., 828/586-2248, www.dogwoodcrafters.com, 10am-6pm Mon.-Sat., 10am-4pm Sun.), in operation since 1976, is a gallery and co-op that represents around 100 local artists and artisans. While the shop carries some of the ubiquitous country-whimsical stuff, mixed in is the work of some very traditional Blue Ridge weavers, potters, carvers, and other expert artisans, making the shop well worth a visit.

In November, Dillsboro's population grows significantly when potters and pottery lovers descend on the town for the annual **Western North Carolina Pottery Festival** (828/586-3601, www.wncpotteryfestival.com). This juried pottery show features more than 40 potters, a street fair, and the Clay Olympics. The Clay Olympics are timed competitions to make the tallest cylinder or widest bowl, as well as blindfolded pot making. The competition may seem odd, but the crowd and the artists get into it, making the one-day festival worth seeing.

Recreation

Dillsboro River Company (18 Macktown Rd., 828/507-2428, www.northcarolinarafting.com, 9:30am-5:30pm daily May-Oct., tubing $20, guided trips $27-37), across the river from downtown Dillsboro, will set you afloat on the Tuckasegee (tuck-a-SEE-jee) River, a comparatively warm river with areas of Class II rapids; it's often referred to simply as "the Tuck." Dillsboro River Company rents rafts, "ducks," and inflatable and sit-on-top kayaks. If you'd like to hire a river rat, guides will be happy to lead you on tours twice daily, and for an extra fee you can share a boat with the guide. There are minimum weight restrictions

1

2

3

CHURCH ST.

JARRETT HOUSE
INN & RESTURANT

NANCY TUT'S
CHRISTMAS SHOP

FRONT ST.

4

NEW T
CHARTS

for these watercraft, so if you are traveling with children, call ahead to ask if the guides think your young ones are ready for the Tuck.

Nightlife

Sylva's Innovation Brewing has an outpost in Dillsboro, **Innovation Station** (40 Depot St., 828/226-0262, www.innovation-brewing.com, noon-midnight Mon.-Thurs., 11am-midnight Fri.-Sun.). Housed in a former train depot, it's got the right feel for this railroad town, and their generous taps—there are nearly three dozen—mean plenty of brews to choose from. Innovation also has a barrel-aging program here, and Dillsboro is home to their pilot brewhouse, so you'll likely find a few experimental brews to sample.

Food

★ **Haywood Smokehouse** (403 Haywood Rd., 828/631-9797, www.haywoodsmokehouse.com, 11am-8pm Wed.-Thurs., 11am-9pm Fri.-Sat., $8-26) is a funky little barbecue shack serving some fine western North Carolina 'cue, craft beers, and house-made smoked barbecue sauces. The menu is small, but if it's pork or chicken and it can be barbecued, it's here. The Haywood Smokehouse is biker-friendly, so don't be surprised if you see a line of Harleys outside.

It's not surprising to find a restaurant bragging about their farm-to-fork philosophy these days, even in a town as small as Dillsboro, but it is surprising to find one living up to that boast and delivering great food. ★ **Foragers Canteen** (42 Depot St., 828/631-4114, www.foragerscanteen.com, 11am-8pm Mon. and Wed.-Thurs., 11am-3pm Tues., 11am-9pm Fri., 10m-9pm Sat., 10am-8pm Sun., $8-25) has fried (or grilled if that's your thing) chicken sandwiches, some inventive tacos, great salads, and bowls (steak tips over mashed potatoes or smoked gouda grits? Yes, please).

Chow down on some Greek goodness at **Kostas Express Restaurant** (489 Haywood Rd., 828/631-0777, www.kostasexpress.com, 11:30pm-8pm Mon.-Thurs., 11:30am-8:30pm Fri.-Sat., $7-28). Not everything here is expressly Greek, but it's all done with a Greek twist. Gyros, pita wraps, and baklava share menu space with burgers, pasta dishes, steak, and even barbecue, and whatever you order, you'll leave full (maybe even with leftovers) and happy to come back for another meal.

If your sweet tooth is calling, give it a little satisfaction with a stop at **Dillsboro Chocolate Factory** (28 Church St., 828/631-0156, www.dillsborochocolate.com, 10am-5pm Mon.-Tues., 10am-7pm Wed.-Sat., noon-5pm Sun.). They have truffles, chocolate, fudge, candy, and other assorted sweets, many of which they make in-house.

Accommodations

The **Best Western Plus River Escape Inn & Suites** (248 WBI Dr., 828/586-6060, www.bwriverescape.com, from $135 Mar.-Aug., from $185 Sept.-Oct., from $115 Nov.-Feb.) isn't what you think of when you think chain hotel; it's much more. The rooms are more attractive and comfortable (and more frequently updated) than you'd expect, the big patio overlooking the river includes a firepit area, and the hotel is close to Dillsboro (walkable, in fact), the road to Cherokee, and the national park.

The ever-charming ★ **Dillsboro Inn** (146 N. River Rd., 828/586-3839, www.dillsboroinn.com, $125-225) sits perched on the banks of the Tuckasegee River, giving every room in the place great views. Rooms range from spacious efficiencies to suites to something more akin to a small apartment (which means plenty of room to spread out). There are nightly fires on the deck overlooking the river, a couple of the rooms are pet-friendly, and it's walkable to Dillsboro, making a visit to Innovation Station or Foragers Canteen that much easier.

1: Sylva's historic and lovely courthouse
2: Dogwood Crafters **3:** signs in Dillsboro
4: finishing the glaze on pottery at the Western North Carolina Pottery Festival

CULLOWHEE

The unincorporated village of Cullowhee ("CULL-uh-wee"), on Highway 107 between Sylva and Cashiers, is the home of Western Carolina University (WCU). The university's **Mountain Heritage Center** (Hunter Library, WCU campus, 828/227-7129, www. wcu.edu, 10am-4pm Fri.-Mon., 10am-7pm Thurs.) is a small museum with a great collection that will fascinate anyone interested in Appalachian history. The permanent exhibit *Migration of the Scotch-Irish People* is full of artifacts like a 19th-century covered wagon, wonderful photographs, and homemade quilts, linens, and musical instruments. The Mountain Heritage Center also hosts two traveling exhibits in addition to the permanent installation as well as the annual **Mountain Heritage Day** (www.mountainheritageday.com) festival (late Sept.), which brings together many of western North Carolina's best and most authentic traditional musicians and artisans in a free festival that draws up to 25,000 visitors.

GETTING THERE AND AROUND

Waynesville is easily reached from Asheville by heading west on I-40 and then taking either U.S. 23 or U.S. 74. The Blue Ridge Parkway also passes a little to the south of the town, near Balsam. Sylva is to the southwest of Waynesville on U.S. 23, and from there, Cullowhee is an easy drive down Highway 107.

Robbinsville and the Valley Towns

Between Robbinsville and the Georgia state line is another region at the heart of Cherokee life. Snowbird, not far from Robbinsville, is one of the most traditional Cherokee communities, where it's common to hear the Cherokee language and the arts, crafts, and folkways are flourishing. The burial site of Junaluska, one of the Eastern Band's most prominent leaders, is here.

As moving as it is to see the memorial to one of the Cherokee heroes, the town of Murphy is forever linked with tragedy for the Cherokee people and a dark incident in American history—the Trail of Tears. Around 16,000 Cherokee people, including warriors and clan leaders, men, women, children, the elderly, and the infirm, were forced to leave their homes in North Carolina, Tennessee, and Georgia. They were arrested and marched under guard to Fort Butler, here in Murphy, and from Fort Butler they were forced to walk to Oklahoma. You'll find the names of these people, many of whom died along the way, inscribed in Cherokee on a memorial at the L&N Depot in Murphy.

In addition to places of historic significance in Cherokee culture, this farthest southwestern corner of North Carolina has other compelling sights. Brasstown, a tiny village on the Georgia state line, is the home of the John C. Campbell Folk School, an artists' colony founded in 1925, where visitors can stroll among studios and along trails and stop at a gallery shop with some of the most beautiful crafts you'll find in the region. Back up toward Robbinsville, the relentlessly scenic **Cherohala Skyway** (www.cherohala. org) crosses 43 miles of the Cherokee and Nantahala National Forests. This road is a major destination for motorcyclists and sports-car drivers as well as day-trippers and vacationers.

ROBBINSVILLE

The whole southwestern corner of North Carolina is rich with Cherokee history and culture, and the Robbinsville area has some of the deepest roots of great significance to the Cherokee people. In little towns and crossroads a few miles outside Robbinsville, several hundred people known as the Snowbird community keep alive some of the oldest Cherokee ways. The Cherokee language is spoken here, and it's a place where some of the Eastern Band's most admired basket makers, potters, and other artists continue to make and teach their ancient arts. If you're visiting and want to enjoy an adult beverage, you'd better bring your own, as Graham County is North Carolina's one and only dry county.

Sights

Outside Robbinsville, in the ancient Stecoah Valley, is an imposing old rock schoolhouse built in 1930 and used as a school until the mid-1990s. It has been reborn as the **Stecoah Valley Center** (121 Schoolhouse Rd., Stecoah, 828/479-3364, www.stecoahvalleycenter.com), home of a weavers' guild, a native plants preservation group, a concert series, several festivals, and a great **Gallery Shop** (828/497-3098, 10am-4pm Mon.-Sat.) with local artisans' work. Concerts in the Appalachian Evening summer series, featuring area musicians, are preceded by community suppers of traditional mountain cuisine.

On Robbinsville's Main Street is the **Junaluska Memorial** (Main St., 0.5 miles north of the Graham County Courthouse), where Junaluska, a 19th-century leader of the Eastern Band of the Cherokee, and his third wife, Nicie, are buried.

Down a winding country road 14 miles outside Robbinsville, **Yellow Branch Pottery and Cheese** (1073 Old Yellow Branch Rd., 828/479-6710, www.yellowbranch.com, noon-5pm Tues.-Sat. Apr.-Nov., or by appointment) is a beautifully rustic spot for an afternoon's excursion. Bruce DeGroot, Karen Mickler, and their herd of Jersey cows produce graceful, functional pottery and prize-winning artisanal cheeses. Visitors are welcome at their farm and shop.

Recreation

The **Joyce Kilmer Memorial Forest** (5410 Joyce Kilmer Rd., 828/479-6431, www.grahamcountytravel.com), off Highway 143 west of Robbinsville, is one of the largest remaining tracts of virgin forest in the eastern United States, where 450-year-old tulip poplar trees have grown to 100 feet tall and 20 feet around. The forest stands in honor of Joyce Kilmer, a soldier killed in action in France during World War I. His poem "Trees" inspired this living memorial. The only way to see the forest is on foot, and a two-mile loop or two one-mile loops make for an easy hike through a remarkable forest.

a trail in Joyce Kilmer Memorial Forest

Junaluska

One of the most important figures in the history of the Eastern Band of the Cherokee is Junaluska, who was born near Dillard, Georgia, in 1776. During the wars with the Creek Indians 1812-1814, the Cherokee people fought beside U.S. forces, and it's said that the fierce young Junaluska saved the life of Andrew Jackson at the battle of Horse Shoe Bend in Alabama.

Twenty years later, Jackson, by then president, repaid Junaluska's bravery and the loyalty of the Cherokee people by signing the Indian Removal Act, which ordered that they, along with four other major Southern nations, be forced from their homelands and marched to the new Indian Territory of Oklahoma. Junaluska traveled to Washington and met with Jackson to plead for mercy for the Cherokee nation; his pleas were ignored, and in 1838, Junaluska joined 16,000 members of the Cherokee nation, who were force-marched close to 1,000 miles to Oklahoma. Midway across Tennessee, he led a failed escape attempt and was captured and chained; he completed the march in leg irons and manacles. It was during this time that Junaluska supposedly said, "If I had known what Andrew Jackson would do to the Cherokees, I would have killed him myself that day at Horse Shoe Bend." In 1841 he was finally able to leave Oklahoma and made the 17-day trip to North Carolina on horseback.

He spent his final years in Cherokee County, on land granted to him by the state of North Carolina. He and his third wife, Nicie, are buried at Robbinsville, at what is now the Junaluska Memorial and Museum. His grave was originally marked according to Cherokee tradition—with a pile of stones—but in 1910 the Daughters of the American Revolution commissioned a marker for his gravesite. During the dedication ceremony, Reverend Armstrong Cornsilk delivered a eulogy in the Cherokee language:

He was a good man. He was a good friend. He was a good friend in his home and everywhere. He would ask the hungry man to eat. He would ask the cold one to warm by his fire. He would ask the tired one to rest, and he would give a good place to sleep. Juno's home was a good home for others. He was a smart man. He made his mind think well. He was very brave. He was not afraid.

Juno at this time has been dead about 50 years. I am glad he is up above [pointing upward]. I am glad we have this beautiful monument. It shows Junaluska did good, and it shows we all appreciate him together—having a pleasant time together. I hope we shall all meet Junaluska in heaven [pointing upward] and all be happy there together.

The Joyce Kilmer Memorial Forest abuts the Slickrock Wilderness Area, and Slickrock Creek Trail is one of its longest trails. This 13.5-mile (one-way) trail starts out easy, but the final 5.5 miles are fairly strenuous. *Backpacker* magazine named this one of the toughest trails in the country several years ago, in part because the hike can be a 21.7-mile loop by connecting with the Haoe Lead, Hangover Lead, and Ike Branch trails. Be forewarned that this is a big trip, but it's rewarding, with views of waterfalls (the first is only a few miles in, on the easy part) and rhododendron thickets. Its name is apt: The rocks here can be incredibly slick.

On the Hangover Lead South Trail, the trailhead is adjacent to the parking area at Big Fat Gap (off Slick Rock Rd., about 7 miles from U.S. 129). The trail is only 2.8 miles long, but it's strenuous. The payoff is the view from the Haoe summit at 5,249 feet. There are backcountry campsites here, and the rule is to keep campsites 100 yards from streams and practice Leave No Trace guidelines.

A handy collection of trail maps for Joyce Kilmer Memorial Forest, Slickrock Creek, Snowbird Back Country, and Tsali Recreation Area is available from the Graham Chamber (http://grahamchamber.com). The maps provide a rough idea of the locations and routes of these trails, but they are not a replacement for topographic maps, which you should have with you while on any of these rugged or isolated trails.

Entertainment and Events

Every year on the Saturday of Memorial Day weekend in late May, the Snowbird Cherokee host the **Fading Voices Festival** in Robbinsville. The festival features a mound-building ceremony along with typical festival attractions—music, dancing, storytelling, crafts, and lots of food—but in the deeply traditional forms carried on by the Snowbird community. Contact the Junaluska Museum (828/479-4727) for more information.

Food and Accommodations

You can grab a really good steak or burger at **Moonshiner's Steakhouse** (2645 Tallulah Rd., 828/479-0708, www.moonshiners-steakhouse.business.site, 5pm-9pm Fri.-Sun., $10-26), one of the only steakhouses around. As at many of the restaurants and accommodations in these parts, you're likely to see a lot of motorcycles and sports cars in the parking lot because folks come from all over to ride several of the twisty mountain roads. Belly up to the big outdoor bar and enjoy some live music, or sit inside with your fellow travelers and talk bikes, road trips, and what your neighbors ordered.

The **Snowbird Mountain Lodge** (4633 Santeetlah Rd., 11 miles west of Robbinsville, 828/479-3433, http://snowbirdlodge.com, $310-525, meals included) was built in the early 1940s, a rustic chestnut-and-stone inn atop a 3,000-foot mountain. The view is exquisite, and the lodge is perfectly situated among the Cherohala Skyway, Lake Santeetlah, and the Joyce Kilmer Memorial Forest. Guests enjoy a full breakfast, picnic lunch, and four-course supper created from seasonal local specialties.

Another pleasant place to stay 15 miles north of Robbinsville is the **Tapoco Lodge Resort** (14981 Tapoco Rd., 828/498-2800, www.tapoco.com, rooms and suites $179-329, cabins $149-249). Built in 1930, the lodge is on the National Register of Historic Places, and it has the feel of an old-time hotel. Guest rooms in the main lodge and surrounding cabins are simple but comfortable, and the resort overlooks the Cheoah River, a legendary run for rafters several times each year when controlled releases of water form superfast rapids. Dine here at **Tapoco Tavern** (828/498-2800, 11am-8pm Sun.-Thurs., 11am-9pm Fri.-Sat., $9-36) on pizzas, steaks, trout, fried chicken, sandwiches, and salads.

The 39-acre **Iron Horse Motorcycle Lodge** (1755 Lower Stecoah Rd., 828/479-3864, www.ironhorsenc.com) caters to motorcyclists here to ride the Tail of the Dragon, Cherohala Skyway, and Blue Ridge Parkway and to explore a number of other notable routes in the area. A lodge ($99-165), bunkhouses ($36), fully outfitted cabins ($420-1,250) that sleep up to 20, covered wagons ($110), and tent ($20-30) and RV ($45-55) camping are available.

If you're RVing your way through the Smokies, the **Simple Life Campground** (88 Lower Mountain Creek Rd., 828/788-1099, www.thesimplelifecampground.com, Mar.-Nov., cabins $38-194, RVs $48-58, tents $22, pop-up campers $32) has cabins, RV sites, and tent sites with access to hot showers and Wi-Fi. This campground is near the Cherohala Skyway, Joyce Kilmer National Forest, and Lake Santeetlah.

HAYESVILLE, BRASSTOWN, AND MURPHY

Between Hayesville and Brasstown, you can get a really good sense of the art that has come out of this region over the years. These three small towns are along the Georgia border on U.S. 64.

Murphy River Walk

The **Murphy River Walk** is a three-mile trail along the Hiwassee River and Valley River, winding from Konehete Park to the Old L&N Depot through the charming tiny town of Murphy. It gives you the chance to see the town up close, and it's a great way to stretch your legs after a long ride.

After a walk along the river, take a look in some of the many antiques stores in Murphy.

Marketplace Antiques (41 Peachtree St., Murphy, 828/837-1060, 10am-5pm Mon.-Thurs., 10am-6pm Fri.-Sat., noon-4pm Sun.) and **Black & White Market** (40 Valley River Ave., Murphy, 828/516-1634, www.black-and-white-market.com, 10am-5pm Mon.-Sat.) will have you covered in the antiques department, and **Serenity Mountain Gift Shop** (35 Tennessee St., Murphy, 828/361-7543, 10:30am-5:30pm Tues.-Fri., 10am-5pm Sat.) has all the shirts, souvenirs, and gifts you'll want. If you're looking for beer, wine, or cigars, swing by **The Murphy Co.** (50 W. U.S. 64, Murphy, 828/516-1630, 12:30pm-5:30pm Mon.-Fri., noon-4pm Sat.).

John C. Campbell Folk School

One of North Carolina's most remarkable cultural institutions, the **John C. Campbell Folk School** (1 Folk School Rd., Brasstown, 800/365-5724, www.folkschool.org) was created by Northern honeymooners who traveled through Appalachia 100 years ago to educate themselves about Southern highland culture. John C. and Olive Dame Campbell, like other high-profile Northern liberals of their day, directed their humanitarian impulses toward the education and economic betterment of Southern mountain dwellers. John Campbell died a decade later, but Olive, joining forces with her friend Marguerite Butler, set out to establish a "folk school" in the Southern mountains that she and John had visited. She was inspired by the model of the Danish *folkehøjskole,* workshops that preserved and taught traditional arts as a means of fostering economic self-determination and personal pride in rural communities. Brasstown was chosen as the site for this grand experiment, and in 1925, the John C. Campbell Folk School opened its doors.

Today, thousands of artists travel every year to this uncommonly lovely remote valley, the site of an ancient Cherokee village. In weeklong and weekend classes, students of all ages and skill levels learn about the traditional arts of this region, such as pottery, weaving, dyeing, storytelling, and chair caning, as well as contemporary and exotic crafts such as photography, kaleidoscope making, bookmaking, and paper marbling. The website outlines the hundreds of courses offered every year, but even if you're passing through the area on a shorter visit, you can explore the school's campus. Visitors are asked to preserve the quiet atmosphere of learning and concentration when viewing the artist studios, but you can have an up-close look at some of their marvelous wares in the school's **Craft Shop** (bottom floor of Olive Dame Campbell Dining Hall, 10am-5pm Mon.-Wed. and Fri.-Sat., 10am-6pm Thurs.), one of the nicest craft shops in western North Carolina; you'll be wowed by what you find here. Exhibits about the school's history and historic examples of the work of local artists of past generations are on display at the **History Center** (8am-5pm Mon.-Sat., 1pm-5pm Sun.), next to Keith House.

There are several nature trails on campus that thread through this lovely valley. Be sure to visit the 0.25-mile **Rivercane Walk,** which features outdoor sculpture by some of the greatest living artists of the Eastern Band of the Cherokee. In the evenings you'll often find concerts by traditional musicians, or community square, contra, and English country dances. A visit to the John C. Campbell Folk School, whether as a student or a traveler, is an exceptional opportunity to immerse yourself in a great creative tradition.

Harrah's Cherokee Casino opened a location in Murphy in 2015: **Harrah's Cherokee Valley River Casino & Hotel** (777 Casino Pkwy., Murphy, 828/422-7777, www.caesars.com, $99-499) has 300 rooms and a huge 50,000-square-foot gaming floor with 70 table games and more than 1,000 slot machines. The dining options are mostly national chains. (Still, who comes to a casino to eat?)

Food

The western terminus of the North Carolina Barbecue Trail is in Murphy, and **Herb's Pit Bar-B-Que** (15725 W. U.S. 64, Murphy, 828/494-5367, 11am-7pm Thurs., 11am-8pm

Fri.-Sat., 11am-3pm Sun., $2-30) should be your first or last stop on it. Here you can sample more than the 'cue that pit masters in the deep mountains make—you can also order plates of tasty fried trout and chicken and thick steaks off the grill.

When you're hungry for something that's not barbecue, **Bistro Twenty Nine** (29 Tennessee St., Murphy, 828/361-0524, www. murphybistro29.com, 4pm-9pm Tues.-Sat., $9-32) serves some upscale but affordable meals in a surprisingly chic dining room. Warm lights, exposed brick, and local art make the perfect setting for a night out. On the menu you'll find steaks, crab cakes, burgers, shrimp scampi, and appetizers to satisfy a hungry hiker or someone ready to settle in for some good food, good company, and good conversation.

At **The Daily Grind & Wine** (46 Valley River Ave., Murphy, 828/835-7322, www. thedailygrindandwine.com, 8am-2pm Mon.-Tues. and Sat., 8am-8pm Wed.-Fri., breakfast $2-7, lunch $4-11), you'll find plenty of coffee and a great, cheap breakfast menu as well as a more filling lunch and snack menu loaded with sandwiches and salads, a very tasty, spicy black bean burger, and a Guinness beer brat that's top-notch. They also have a wine shop and bar serving wine and regional craft beer.

In nearby Hayesville, 15 miles east along U.S. 64, there are two spots to keep on your radar. **The Copper Door** (2 Sullivan St., Hayesville, 828/389-8460, http://thecopperdoor.com, 5pm-10pm Tues.-Sat., $16-48) is an upscale joint serving a nice selection of seafood, steaks, and other meat-centric dishes, but they can accommodate vegetarians and vegans. This elegant restaurant is run by a chef from New Orleans, and his influence is all over the menu, from crawfish to mussels to other French- and Creole-inspired creations.

Over at **Nocturnal Brewing Company** (893 U.S. 64 Business, Hayesville, 828/305-7337, www.nocturnalbrewing.com, 4pm-9pm Thurs.-Fri., 2pm-9pm Sat., $5-25), they have a solid burger, a really good lentil sloppy joe, and tempeh tacos if you're hungry, and the beer—saisons, goses, pale ales, and *bières de garde*—is proof positive that in North Carolina, there's a great brewery anywhere you go.

Tiger's Department Store & Chinquapins Ice Cream & Soda Bar (42 Herbert St., Hayesville, 828/389-6531, www.tigersandchinquapins.com, 9:30am-6pm Mon.-Sat.) has, in addition to clothing and gear, an **old-fashioned soda counter** (under $10) that provides some tasty refreshments.

GETTING THERE AND AROUND

This is the most southwestern corner of North Carolina, in some places as close to Atlanta as to Asheville. The drive from Murphy to Asheville is 2.5 hours along U.S. 74 and I-40, and to Atlanta the drive is closer to 3 hours. Robbinsville and Murphy are about 45 minutes apart along U.S. 129 and U.S. 74. It's 1 hour from Murphy to Bryson City, and the drive from Murphy to the Oconaluftee Visitor Center in Cherokee is 1.5 hours.

Background

The Landscape

GEOGRAPHY

North Carolina encompasses more than 50,000 square miles of land and water. The **Mountain Region** forms the western border of the state, with the Blue Ridge and Great Smoky Mountains, both subranges of the long Appalachian Mountain Range, undulating like the folds of a great quilt, running northeast-to-southwest from Virginia along the border with Tennessee and into the southwestern corner where the inland tip of North Carolina meets Georgia. This is a land of waterfalls, rivers and fast-flowing creeks, and rugged, beautiful peaks of smaller mountain configurations. Hemmed in among the peaks and hollows of the Blue Ridge and the Smokies are the Black Mountains, the Pisgah Range, and the Unka Range. The Black Mountains are only about 15 miles wide and are confined mostly to Yancey County, but they're the highest in the state, and 6 of the 10 tallest peaks in the eastern United States are here, including Mount Mitchell, the highest at 6,684 feet.

CLIMATE

Generalizing about North Carolina's climate is difficult. It's not as hot as at the equator and not as cold as at the poles, but beyond that, each region has its own range of variables and has to be examined separately.

The mountains are cool and winter can last a long time. Towns like Asheville and Boone can be blanketed in snow while less than 100 miles away the trees in Piedmont towns aren't even showing their fall colors. The coldest temperature ever recorded in North Carolina, -34°F, was recorded in 1985 on Mount Mitchell. Spring and fall can bring cool to temperate days and chilly nights, while summer days can hit the 80s, and the evenings bring a welcome relief.

North Carolina gets its fair share of hazardous weather to go along with beautiful summer days and crisp fall nights. **Tornadoes,** most common in the spring, can cause trouble any time of year. A rare November twister touched down in 2006, smashing the Columbus County community of Riegelwood, killing eight people and leaving a seven-mile swath of destruction. Even plain old **thunderstorms** can be dangerous, bringing lightning, flash flooding, difficult driving conditions, and even hail. **Snowstorms** are rare and usually occur in the mountains.

Plants

In the early 1700s, John Lawson, an English explorer who would soon be one of the first victims of the Tuscarora War, wrote of a magnificent tree house somewhere in the very young colony of North Carolina. "I have been informed of a Tulip-Tree," he wrote, "that was ten Foot Diameter; and another, wherein a lusty Man had his Bed and Household Furniture, and liv'd in it, till his Labour got him a more fashionable Mansion. He afterwards became a noted Man, in his Country, for Wealth and Conduct." Whether or not there was ever a tulip poplar large enough to serve as a furnished bachelor pad, colonial North Carolina's forests must have seemed miraculous to the first Europeans to see them.

FORESTS

Today, after generations of logging and farming across the state, few old-growth forests exist. In the Smoky Mountains, stands of old-growth timber, like the Joyce Kilmer Forest, are a sight to behold, and some of the trees almost validate Lawson's anecdote. Across the state, scores of specialized ecosystems support a marvelous diversity of plant and animal life. In the east, cypress swamps and a few patches of maritime forest still stand; across the Sandhills are longleaf pine forests; in the mountains are fragrant balsam forests and stands of hardwoods.

Because the state is so geographically and climatically varied, there's a greater diversity in tree species than anywhere in the eastern United States. In terms of land area, more than half of the land is still forested in the

Previous: City Hall in Asheville.

Piedmont and eastern North Carolina. In the Piedmont, oak and hickory dominate the hardwoods alongside bands of piney woods. In the mountains oak and hickory are also the rule, but a number of conifers, including pine and balsam, appear, too.

The science and profession of forestry were born in North Carolina: In the 1880s and 1890s, George W. Vanderbilt, lord of the manner at Biltmore, engaged Frederick Law Olmsted, who designed New York City's Central Park, to plan a managed forest of the finest, healthiest, and most hardy trees. Vanderbilt hired Gifford Pinchot and later Carl Shenck to be the stewards of the thousands of wooded acres he owned in the Pisgah Forest south of Asheville. The contributions these men made to the nascent field are still felt today and are commemorated at the Cradle of Forestry Museum near Brevard.

FLOWERS

Some of North Carolina's flora puts on great annual shows, drawing flocks of admirers—the gaudy azaleas of springtime in Wilmington, the wildflowers of the first warm weather in the hills, the rhododendrons and mountain laurel of the Appalachian summer. The Ericaceae family, a race of great woody bushes with star-shaped blossoms that includes azaleas, rhododendrons, and laurel, is the headliner in North Carolina's floral fashion show. Spring comes earliest to the southeastern corner of the state, and the Wilmington area is explosively beautiful when the azaleas are in bloom. The Azalea Festival, held annually for more than 50 years, draws hundreds of thousands of people to the city in early to mid-April, around the time that public gardens and private yards are spangled with azaleas.

The flame azalea makes a late-spring appearance on the mountainsides of the Blue Ridge and Great Smokies, joined by its cousins the mountain laurel and Catawba rhododendron in May and June. The ways of the rhododendron are a little mysterious; not every plant blooms every year, and there's no

surefire way of predicting when they'll put on big shows. The area's widely varying elevation also figures into bloom times. If you're interested in timing your trip to coincide with some of these flowering seasons, your best bet is to call ahead and speak with a ranger from the Great Smoky Mountains National Park or the Blue Ridge Parkway to find out how the season is coming along.

Around the end of April and into May, when spring finally arrives in the mountains but the forest floor is not yet sequestered in leafy shade, a profusion of delicate flowers emerges. Violets and chickweed emerge early on, as do the quintessentially mountainous white trillium blossoms and the Wake Robin, also a trillium, which looks something like a small poinsettia. Every year since 1950, around the end of April, the Great Smoky Mountains National Park has hosted the Spring Wildflower Pilgrimage, a weeklong festival featuring scores of nature walks that also reveal salamanders, birds, and wild hogs, along with workshops and art exhibits. Visit www.springwildflowerpilgrimage.org for upcoming events.

Surprisingly, one of the best places in North Carolina to view displays of wildflowers is along the major highways. For more than 20 years the state's Department of Transportation has carried out a highway beautification project that involves planting large banks of wildflowers along highways and in wide medians. The displays are not landscaped but are allowed to grow up in unkempt profusion, often planted in inspired combinations of wildly contrasting colors that make the flowerbeds a genuinely beautiful addition to the environment. The website of the state's Department of Transportation (www.ncdot.org) offers a guide to the locations and seasons of the wildflower beds.

FALL FOLIAGE

Arriving as early as mid-September at the highest elevations and gradually sliding down the mountains through late October, autumn colors bring a late-season wave of visitors to

Horticultural Havens

AROUND ASHEVILLE

Asheville is the home of the **North Carolina Arboretum,** a garden of more than 400 acres that borders the Pisgah National Forest and the Blue Ridge Parkway. Special collections include the National Native Azalea Repository and more than 200 bonsai. You can tour the arboretum on foot, by Segway, or on your bike, and you can even bring your dog on some of the trails.

At the **Biltmore Estate,** Frederick Law Olmsted created formal gardens of beauty to match the opulent mansion, and architect Richard Morris Hunt designed the conservatory where young plants are still raised for the gardens. Self-guided tours of the conservatory—and the walled, shrub, Italian, vernal, and azalea gardens—are all included in admission to the estate.

Asheville is also an excellent home base for excursions to other garden spots in the mountains. Don't miss the **Rivercane Walk** at the John C. Campbell Folk School in Brasstown, where modern Cherokee sculpture lines a path along Little Brasstown Creek. The **Mountain Farm Museum** at the edge of Great Smoky Mountains National Park demonstrates gardening methods used on the early mountain homesteads. The **Cradle of Forestry** in Pisgah National Forest explains how the science of modern forestry was born here in western North Carolina.

western North Carolina. Dropping temperatures change trees' sugar production, resulting in a palette of colors, while simple fatigue causes the green to fade in others, exposing underlying hues. Countless climatic factors can alter the onset and progress of leaf season, so the mountains blush at slightly different times every year. The latter weeks of October tend to be the peak; during those weeks it can be difficult to find lodging in the mountains, so be sure to plan ahead. Some of the best places for leaf peeping are along the Blue Ridge Parkway and in the Great Smoky Mountains National Park.

Animals

Among the familiar wildlife most commonly seen in the state, **white-tailed deer** are out in force in the countryside and in the woods; they populate suburban areas in large numbers as well. **Raccoons** and **opossums** prowl at night, happy to scavenge from trash cans and the forest floor. **Skunks** are common, particularly in the mountains, and are often smelled rather than seen. They leave an odor something like a cross between grape soda and Sharpie markers. There are also a fair number of **black bears,** not only in the mountains but in swamps and deep woods across the state.

In woods and yards alike, **gray squirrels** and a host of familiar **songbirds** are a daily presence. Different species of **tree frogs** produce beautiful choruses on spring and summer nights, while **fireflies** mount sparkly shows in the trees and grass in the upper Piedmont and mountains. Down along the southeast coast, **alligators** and **turtles** sun themselves on many a golf course and creekside backyard.

The town of Brevard, in the Blue Ridge south of Asheville, is famous for its population of ghostly **white squirrels.** They're regular old gray squirrels that live all over North America, but their fur ranges from speckled gray and white to pure bone-white. They're not albinos; it's thought that Brevard's white squirrels are cousins of a clan that lives in Florida and that their ancestors may have found their way to the Blue Ridge in a circus or with a dealer of exotic pets in the early 20th century.

The Carolina woods harbor colonies of **Southern flying squirrels.** It's very unlikely that you'll see one unless it's at a nature center or wildlife rehabilitation clinic because flying squirrels are both nocturnal and shy. They're also almost unspeakably cute. Fully extended, they're about nine inches long snout to tail, weigh about four ounces, and have super-silky fur and pink noses. Like many nocturnal animals, they have comically long whiskers and huge, wide-set eyes that suggest amphetamine use. When they're flying—gliding, really— they spread their limbs to extend the patagium, a membrane that stretches between their front and hind legs, and glide along like little magic carpets.

Also deep in the Smokies are some herds of **wild hogs,** game boar brought to the area about 100 years ago and allowed to go feral. The official line among wildlife officials is that **mountain lions**—in this region called panthers—have been extinct in North Carolina for some time. But mountain dwellers claim there are still panthers in the Blue Ridge and Smokies, and most people here have seen or heard one—their cry sounds like a terror-filled scream. There are even tales of a panther in the inland woods of Brunswick and Columbus Counties on the southeast coast.

REINTRODUCED SPECIES

In the 1990s and early 2000s a federal program to reestablish **red wolf** colonies in the Southeast focused its efforts on parkland in North Carolina. Red wolves, thought to have existed in North Carolina in past centuries, were first reintroduced to the Great Smoky Mountains National Park. They did not thrive, and the colony was moved to the Alligator River National Wildlife Refuge on the northeast coast. The packs have fared better in this corner of the state and now roam several wilderness areas in the sound country.

The Smokies proved a more hospitable place for the reintroduction of **elk.** Now the largest animals in the Great Smoky Mountains National Park, elk, which can grow up to 700 pounds, are most often observed in the Cataloochee section of the park, grazing happily and lounging in the mist in the early morning and at twilight.

BIRDS

Bird-watchers flock to North Carolina because of the great diversity of songbirds, raptors, and even hummingbirds across the state—a 2013 count put the number of species at 473—but the state is best known for waterfowl. In the sounds of eastern North Carolina, waterfowl descend en masse as they migrate. Hundreds of thousands of birds crowd the lakes, ponds, trees, marshes, and waterways as they move to and from their winter homes. Many hunters take birds during hunting season, but they're outnumbered by bird-watchers. Birders say that one of the best spots for birding in the state is around large, shallow **Lake Mattamuskeet** on the central coast, with 40,000 acres of water to attract incredible numbers of snow geese and tundra swans, Canada geese, and ducks. Just a few miles away, **Swan Quarter National Wildlife Refuge** is also a haven for ducks, wading birds, shorebirds, and their admirers.

While in eastern North Carolina, bird fanciers should visit the **Sylvan Heights Bird Park,** a remarkable park in the small town of Scotland Neck that's a conservation center and breeding facility for rare waterfowl from across the globe. Visitors can walk through the grounds, where large aviaries house bird species that, unless you're a world traveler and a very lucky birder, you're unlikely to see elsewhere. There are more than 170 species, and you can get quite close to most of them. Bring your camera; you'll have the chance to take shots you could never get in the field.

There are many books and websites about birding in North Carolina. One of the most helpful is the North Carolina Birding Trail, both a website (www.ncbirdingtrail.org) and a series of print guidebooks. Organized by region, these resources list dozens of top sites for bird-watching and favorite bird-watching events throughout the state. Another good resource is the Carolina Bird Club (www.carolinabirdclub.org).

AMPHIBIANS

Dozens of species of salamanders and their close kin, including mudpuppies, sirens, and amphiumas, call North Carolina home, and Great Smoky Mountains National Park harbors so many of them that it's known as the Salamander Capital of the World. Throughout the state, frogs and toads are numerous and vociferous, especially the many species of dainty tree frogs. Two species, the gray tree frog and the spring peeper, are found in every part of North Carolina, and beginning in late winter they create the impression that the trees are filled with ringing cell phones.

Hellbenders are quite possibly the strangest animal in North Carolina. They are enormous salamanders—not the slick little pencil-thin five-inch salamanders easily spotted along creeks, but hulking brutes that grow to more than two feet long and can weigh five pounds. Rare and hermetic, they live in rocky mountain streams, venturing out from under rocks at night to gobble up crayfish and minnows. They're hard to see even if they do emerge in the daytime because they're lumpy and mud-colored, camouflaged against streambeds. Aggressive with each other, the males often sport battle scars on their stumpy legs. They've been known to bite humans, but as rare as it is to spot a hellbender, it's an exponentially rarer occurrence to be bitten by one.

REPTILES

Turtles and snakes are the state's most common reptiles. Box turtles, found everywhere, and bog turtles, found in the Smokies, are the only land terrapins. A great many freshwater turtles inhabit the swamps and ponds, and on a sunny day every log or branch sticking out of fresh water will become a sunbathing terrace for as many turtles as it can hold. Common water turtles include cooters, sliders, and painted turtles. Snapping turtles can be found in fresh water throughout the state, so mind your toes. They grow up to a couple of feet long and can weigh more than 50 pounds. Not only will they bite—hard!—if provoked, they will actually initiate hostilities, lunging for you if they so much as disapprove of the fashion of your shoes. Even the tiny hatchlings are vicious, so give them a wide berth.

There are plenty of real snakes in North Carolina. The vast majority are shy, gentle, and totally harmless to anything larger than a rat. There are a few species of venomous snakes that are very dangerous. These include three kinds of rattlesnake: the huge diamondback, whose diet of rabbits testifies to its size and strength; the pigmy; and the timber or canebrake rattler. Other venomous species are the beautiful mottled copperhead and the cottonmouth or water moccasin, famous for flinging its mouth open in hostility and flashing its brilliant white palate. The coral snake is a fantastically beautiful and venomous species.

Most Carolina snakes are entirely benign to humans, including old familiars such as black racers and king snakes as well as milk, corn, and rat snakes. One particularly endearing character is the hognose snake, which can be found throughout North Carolina but is most common in the east. Colloquially known as a spreading adder, the hognose snake compensates for its total harmlessness with amazing displays of histrionics. If you startle one, it will first flatten and greatly widen its head and neck and hiss most passionately. If it sees that you're not frightened by plan A, it will panic and go straight to plan B: playing dead. The hognose snake won't simply lay inert until you go away, though; it goes to the dramatic lengths of flipping onto its back, exposing its pitiably vulnerable belly, opening its mouth, throwing its head back limply, and sticking out its tongue as if it had just been poisoned. It is such a devoted method actor that should you call its bluff and poke it back onto its belly, it will fling itself energetically back into the mortuary pose and resume being deceased.

History

ANCIENT CIVILIZATION

By the time the first colonists arrived and called this place Carolina, the land had already sustained some 20,000 years of human history. We know that Paleo-Indians hunted these lands during the last ice age, when there were probably more mammoths and saber-toothed tigers in North Carolina than people. Civilization came around 4000 BC, when the first inhabitants settled down to farm, make art, and trade goods. By the first century, Southern Woodland and Mississippian Indians were also living in advanced societies with complex religious systems, economic interaction among communities, advanced farming methods, and the creation of art and architecture.

When the Europeans arrived, there were more than a dozen major Native American groups within what is now North Carolina. The Cherokee people ruled the mountains while the Catawba, Pee Dees, Tutelo, and Saura, among others, were their neighbors in the Piedmont. In the east, the Cheraw, Waccamaw, and Tuscarora were some of the larger communities, while many bands occupied land along the Outer Banks and sounds.

CONQUEST

The first Europeans to land here were Spanish. We know conquistador Hernando de Soto and his troops marched around western North Carolina in 1539, but they were just passing through. In 1566, another band of Spanish explorers, led by conquistador Juan Pardo, came for a longer visit. They were making a circuitous trek in the general direction of Mexico, and along the way they established several forts in what are now the Carolinas and Tennessee. One of these forts, called San Juan, has been identified by archaeologists outside present-day Morganton in a community called Worry Crossroads. Although the

troops who were garrisoned for a year and a half at Fort San Juan eventually disappeared into the woods or were killed, it's theorized that they may have had a profound impact on the course of history, possibly spreading European diseases among the Native Americans and weakening them so much that, a couple of decades later, the indigenous people would be unable to repel the invasion of English colonists.

The next episode in the European settlement of North Carolina is one of the strangest mysteries in American history: the Lost Colonists of Roanoke. After two previous failed attempts to establish an English stronghold on the island of Roanoke, fraught by poor planning and disastrous diplomacy, a third group of English colonists tried their luck. Sometime between being dropped off in the New World in 1587 and one of their leaders returning three years later to resupply them, all of the colonists—including Virginia Dare, the first English person born in the Americas—had vanished into the woods. To this day, their fate is unknown, although a host of fascinating theories are still debated and probably always will be.

The disappearance of the Roanoke colonists did little to slow the process of the European conquest of North America. After the establishment of the Virginia colony in 1607, new English settlers began to trickle southward into Carolina, while Barbadians and Europeans from Charles Town (in present-day South Carolina) gradually began to populate the area around Wilmington. The town of Bath was established in 1706, and New Bern was settled shortly thereafter. The bloody Tuscarora War followed, and after a crushing defeat near present-day Snow Hill, in which hundreds were killed, the Tuscarora people retreated, opening the land along the Neuse River to European colonization.

COLONIALISM

The conflict between Europeans and Native Americans wasn't the only world-changing cultural encounter going on in the Southern colonies. By the middle of the 18th century, nearly 100,000 enslaved people had been brought to North Carolina from West Africa. By the end of the 18th century, many areas, especially those around Wilmington, had populations where enslaved African Americans outnumbered white people. Although North Carolina did not practice enslavement of people on as vast a scale as South Carolina, there were a handful of plantations with more than 100 enslaved people, and many smaller plantations and town homes of wealthy planters, merchants, and politicians with smaller numbers of enslaved people. Africans and African Americans were an early and potent cultural force in the South, influencing the economy, politics, language, religion, music, architecture, and cuisine in ways still seen today.

In the 1730s the Great Wagon Road connected Pennsylvania with Georgia by cutting through the Mid-Atlantic and Southern backcountry of Virginia and North Carolina. Many travelers migrated south from Pennsylvania, among them a good number of German and Scottish-Irish settlers who found the mountains and Piedmont of North Carolina to their liking. Meanwhile, the port of Wilmington, growing into one of the most important in the state, saw a number of Gaelic-speaking Scots move through, following the river north and putting down roots around what is now Fayetteville. Shortly before the American Revolution, a group of German-speaking religious settlers known as the Moravians constructed a beautiful and industrious town, Salem, in the heart of the Piedmont, which would later become Winston-Salem. Their pacifist beliefs, Germanic heritage, and artistry set them apart from other communities in colonial North Carolina, and they left an indelible mark on the state's history.

The 18th century brought one conflict after another to the colony, from fights over the Vestry Act in the early 1700s, which attempted to establish the Anglican church as the one official faith of the colony, through various regional conflicts with Native Americans and events that played out at a global level during the French and Indian War. At mid-century the population and economic importance of the Piedmont was growing exponentially, but colonial representation continued to be focused along the coast. Protesting local corruption and lack of governmental concern for the western region, a group of backcountry farmers organized themselves into an armed posse in resistance to colonial corruption. Calling themselves the Regulators, they eventually numbered more than 6,000. Mounting frustrations led to an attack by the Regulators on the Orange County courthouse in Hillsborough. Finally, a colonial militia was dispatched to crush the movement, which it did at the Battle of Alamance in 1771. Six Regulators were captured and hanged at Hillsborough.

REVOLUTION AND STATEHOOD

Many believe the seeds of the American Revolution were sown, tended, and reaped in New England, but the southern colonies, particularly North Carolina, played important roles before and during the rebellion. In 1765, as the War of the Regulation was heating up, the residents of Brunswick Town, the colonial capital and the only deep-water port in the southern half of the colony, revolted in protest of the Stamp Act. They placed the royal governor under house arrest and put an end to taxation in the Cape Fear region, sending a strong message to the crown and to fellow patriots hungry to shake off the yoke of British rule. In the ensuing years, well-documented events like the Boston Tea Party, the Battles of Lexington and Concord, and the signing of the Declaration of Independence occurred, but North Carolina's role in leading the rebellion was far from over.

After the Battles of Lexington and Concord, the colonies were aflame with patriotic fervor, and Mecklenburg County (around Charlotte) passed the first colonial declaration rejecting the crown's authority. By this time, North Carolina, like the other colonies, had formed a provincial government, and it was busy in the tavern at Halifax writing the Halifax Resolves, the first official action in the colonies calling for independence from Britain. On April 12, 1776, the resolves were ratified and delegates carried them to the Second Continental Congress in Philadelphia. Other delegates were so inspired that more such resolves appeared, ultimately the Declaration of Independence was written and ratified, and the revolution was on in earnest.

Although North Carolina may have been the first to call for independence, the state was divided in its loyalties. Among the most noteworthy Loyalists was the community of Highland Scots living in and around modern-day Fayetteville. Men from this community were marching to join General Cornwallis near Brunswick Town and Southport (then Smithville) when Patriots ambushed them at the bloody battle of Moore's Creek, killing 30 Scots and routing the Loyalist force.

North Carolinians fought all over the eastern seaboard during the Revolution, including about 1,000 who were with Washington at Valley Forge. The year 1780 brought fighting back home, particularly in the area around Charlotte, which a daunted General Cornwallis referred to as "the hornets' nest." The battle of Kings Mountain, west of Charlotte, was a pivotal moment in the war and particularly costly to the Loyalist forces. Cornwallis received another blow at the Battle of Guilford Courthouse; although technically a British victory, it weakened his forces considerably. By the time the war ended, thousands of North Carolinians were dead, and the treasury was far in debt—but North Carolina was now a state with the business of statehood to attend to. The capital was moved inland to Raleigh, and 20 miles away at Chapel Hill, ground was broken for the establishment of the University of North Carolina, the first state university in the country.

THE FEDERAL ERA

The early 19th century in North Carolina was a good deal more peaceful than the previous hundred years had been. The first decade of the 1800s saw a religious awakening in which thousands of North Carolinians became devout Christians. At the same time, the introduction of the cotton gin and bright-leaf tobacco were economic boons in the state, particularly the eastern counties. Railroads and plank roads made trade immeasurably more efficient, bringing new prosperity to the Piedmont.

There was also conflict, of course, in the early 19th century. Andrew Jackson's administration presided over the passage of the Indian Removal Act in 1830, which assigned reservations in the Indian Territory of present-day Oklahoma to the "Five Civilized Tribes" of the southeastern United States—the Cherokee, Choctaw, Creek, Chickasaw, and Seminole. Thousands of Cherokee people were forced out of western North Carolina, northern Georgia, eastern Tennessee, and Alabama and marched west on the Trail of Tears. About 4,000 died along the way. Another 1,000 or so Cherokee people, through hiding, fighting, and negotiation, managed to win the right to stay in North Carolina—an act of resistance that was the birth of the modern Eastern Band of the Cherokee, still centered around the town of Cherokee on the Qualla Boundary in North Carolina's Great Smoky Mountains. The Eastern Band of the Cherokee tell the story of their relocation in the enlightening outdoor drama *Unto These Hills*.

THE CIVIL WAR

Compared to South Carolina and a few other Southern states, North Carolina was considered politically moderate in the mid-19th century because it was less invested economically and politically in the enslavement of people. Combined with the knowledge that if secession became a reality, war would follow and North Carolina's tobacco and cotton fields would quickly become battlefields, secession was on the lips of everyone across the South. As some states voted to remove themselves from the Union, North Carolina's voters rejected a ballot measure authorizing a secession convention. As grand a gesture as that victory may have been, when fighting erupted at Fort Sumpter in Charleston Harbor, North Carolina's hand was forced and its secession was a reality. Secessionist governor John Ellis rejected Lincoln's call to federalize state militias, instead seizing control of the state and all federal military installations within its boundaries as well as the Charlotte Mint. North Carolina officially seceded on May 20, 1861, and a few weeks later Union ships began to blockade the coast. Roanoke Island in the Outer Banks fell, and a freedmen's colony (a home for enslaved people who had been freed or escaped) sprung up. New Bern, which fell in the spring of 1862, became a major focal point of Union military strategy and a thriving political base for freed and escaped African Americans. To the south, Fort Fisher, on the Cape Fear River just south of Wilmington, guarded the river's inlet and was crucial to the success of the blockade runners—smugglers whose speedy boats eluded the Union blockade. Fort Fisher kept Wilmington in Confederate hands until nearly the end of the war. When it finally did fall to Union forces in February 1865, it required what would be the largest amphibious assault in American military history until World War II. Wilmington was the last major port on the Confederacy's eastern seaboard, and its fall severed supply lines and crippled what remained of the Confederate Army in the area.

The varying opinions felt by Southerners about the Civil War, in the South also called the War between the States, was particularly strong in North Carolina, where today you'll still hear whites refer to it as the War of Northern Aggression or the War of Yankee Aggression. A symbol of the Lost Cause and of racial oppression—the confederate flag—is flown with pride rather than the shame it deserves. More than 5,000 African Americans from North Carolina joined and fought in the Union Army, and there were pockets of strong Union sentiment and support among white North Carolinians, especially in the mountains. Some 10,000 North Carolinians fought for the Union. Zebulon Vance, who won the 1862 gubernatorial election and served as governor through the duration of the war, was a native of Weaverville, near Asheville, and felt acutely the state's ambivalence toward the Confederacy. Much to the consternation of Richmond (the Confederate capital), Governor Vance was adamant in his refusal to put the interests of the Confederacy over those of his own state. Mountain communities suffered tremendously during the war from acts of terrorism by deserters and rogues from both armies.

The latter years of the Civil War were particularly difficult for North Carolina and the rest of the South. Approximately 4,000 North Carolina men died at the Battle of Gettysburg alone. After laying waste to Georgia and South Carolina, General William T. Sherman's army entered North Carolina in the spring of 1865, destroying homes and farms. His march of fire and pillage spared Wilmington, which is one reason the town contains such an incredible collection of Federal architecture. The last major battle of the war was fought in North Carolina, when General Sherman and Confederate General Joseph Johnston engaged at Bentonville. Johnston surrendered to Sherman in Durham in April 1865.

By the end of the war more than 40,000 North Carolina soldiers were dead—a number equivalent to the entire present-day population of the city of Hickory, Apex, or Kannapolis.

RECONSTRUCTION AND THE NEW SOUTH

The years immediately after the war were painful as well, as a vast population of newly free African Americans tried to make new lives for themselves economically and politically in the face of tremendous opposition and violence from whites. The Ku Klux Klan was set up during this time, inaugurating an era of horror for African Americans throughout the country. Federal occupation and domination of the Southern states' political and legal systems also exacerbated resentment toward the North. The state's ratification of the 14th Amendment on July 4, 1868, brought North Carolina back into the Union.

The late 1800s saw large-scale investment in North Carolina's railroad system, launching the industrial boom of the New South. Agriculture changed in this era as the rise of tenancy created a new form of enslavement for many farmers—Black, white, and Native American. R. J. Reynolds, Washington Duke, and other entrepreneurs built a massively lucrative empire of tobacco production from field to factory. Textile and furniture mills sprouted throughout the Piedmont, creating a new cultural landscape as rural Southerners migrated to mill towns.

THE 20TH CENTURY AND TODAY

The early decades of the 1900s brought an expanded global perspective to North Carolina, not only through the expanded economy and the coming of radio but as natives of the state scattered across the globe. About 80,000 North Carolinians served in World War I, many of them young men who had never before left the state or perhaps even their home counties. Hundreds of thousands of African Americans migrated north during what became known as the Great Migration. The communities created by Black North Carolinians in the Mid-Atlantic and the Northeast are still closely connected by culture and kinship to their cousins whose ancestors remained in the South. The invasion of the boll weevil, an insect that devastated the cotton industry, hastened the departure of Southerners of all races who had farmed cotton. The Great Depression hit hard across all economic sectors of the state in the 1930s, but New Deal employment programs were a boon to North Carolina's infrastructure, with the construction of hydroelectric dams, the Blue Ridge Parkway, and other public works.

North Carolina's modern-day military importance largely dates to the World War II era. Installations at Fort Bragg, Camp Lejeune, and other still-vital bases were constructed or expanded. About 350,000 North Carolinians fought in World War II, and 7,000 of them died.

A few old-timers remember World War II quite vividly because they witnessed it firsthand: German U-boats prowled the waters off the coast, torpedoing ships and sinking them with frightening regularity. These German submarines were often visible from the beach, but more often the evidence of their mission of terror and supply-chain disruption—corpses, wounded sailors, and the flotsam of exploded ships—washed up on the shore. More than 10,000 German prisoners were interned in prisoner-of-war camps, in some parts of the state becoming forced farm laborers. In Wilmington, just a few blocks from downtown, is an apartment complex that was part of a large prisoner-of-war compound for U-boat officers.

In the 1950s and 1960s, African Americans in North Carolina and throughout the United States struggled against the monolithic system of segregation and racism enshrined in the nation's Jim Crow laws. The Ku Klux Klan stepped up its pro-segregation efforts with political and physical violence against Native Americans as well as African Americans; in the famous 1958 Battle of Maxton, 500 armed Lumbee people foiled a Klan rally and sent the Knights running for their lives. Change arrived slowly. The University of North Carolina accepted its first African American graduate student in 1951 and the first Black undergraduates four years later. Sit-ins in 1960 at the Woolworth's lunch counter in Greensboro began with four African American men, students at North Carolina A&T. On the second day of their protest they were joined by 23 other demonstrators; on the third day there were 300, and by day four about 1,000. This was a pivotal moment in the national Civil Rights Movement, sparking sit-ins across the country in which an estimated 50,000 people participated. You can see the counter today at the International Civil Rights Center and Museum in Greensboro. Even as victories were won at the level of Congress and in the federal courts, as in *Brown v. the Board of Education* and the 1964 Civil Rights Act, actual change on the ground was inexorably slow and hard-won. North Carolina's contribution to the Civil Rights Movement continues to be invaluable for the whole nation.

The 2020 census showed that North Carolina's population is at 10.44 million and growing, making it the ninth most populous state in the U.S. The state continues to adapt and contribute to the global community, thanks in large part to larger cities like Charlotte and the university-, research-, and tech-rich Raleigh, Durham, and Chapel Hill area. It is now a place of ethnic diversity, growing especially quickly in Latino residents. In 2014 an estimated 9 percent of North Carolinians were Latino, and that number is still climbing. There are also significant communities of Dega, Hmong, and Montagnard people from Southeast Asia as well as Eastern Europeans, among many others.

Government and Economy

POLITICAL LIFE
Liberal Enclaves
Although historically a red state, North Carolina's large population of college students, professors, and artists has created several boisterous enclaves of progressive politics. The outspoken archconservative U.S. Senator Jesse Helms supposedly questioned the need to spend public money on a state zoo in North Carolina "when we can just put up a fence around Chapel Hill." The Chapel Hill area is indeed the epicenter of North Carolina's liberalism, with its smaller neighboring town of Carrboro at its heart. Would-be Democratic presidential candidates and politicians on the campaign trail regularly stop here to bolster support in the state.

Although you'll find a mixture of political views statewide, the Triangle is not the only famously liberal community. In Asheville, lefty politics are part of the community's devotion to all things organic and DIY. Significant pockets of liberalism also exist in Boone, the cities of the Triad, and Wilmington.

MAJOR INDUSTRIES
Over the last 20 years, North Carolina has experienced tremendous shifts in its economy as the industries that once dominated the landscape and brought wealth and development declined. The tobacco industry ruled the state's economy for generations, employing innumerable North Carolinians from field to factory and funding a colossal portion of the state's physical and cultural infrastructure. The slow decline of the tobacco industry worldwide from the 1980s changed the state dramatically, especially the rural east, where tobacco fields once went from green to gold every fall. Other agricultural industries, especially livestock—chickens and hogs—are still important in the east. The textile industry, a giant for most of the 20th century, suffered the same decline as manufacturers sought cheaper labor overseas. Likewise, the furniture industry slipped into obscurity. Today, the once-thriving fishing industry is in steep decline, largely due to globalization and overfishing.

While these staple industries have fallen off, new industries and fields have sprouted across the state. Pharmaceutical and biotech companies have set up in the Research Triangle, formed by Raleigh, Durham, and Chapel Hill. The film industry has made Wilmington a hub of feature film production, Charlotte is a major production center for television programming and commercials, and Raleigh is home to a number of visual-effects studios that contribute to films and TV. **High-tech** leaders such as Apple have set up in North Carolina, and other tech giants have followed, locating database and network centers here. Charlotte is second only to New York City among the country's largest **banking** centers. **Tourism** continues to grow and contribute in a major way to the state's economy. **Agriculture** remains relevant, though it is increasingly becoming more specialized, especially as demand for organic products and locally and regionally sourced products continues.

Tourism

North Carolina has always drawn visitors to its mountains and cities. As the economy evolves, tourism has become even more important. Mountain and beach landscapes sell themselves, but competition is strong to be the town visitors think of first. As **culinary tourism** gains momentum, so too do foodie destinations like **Asheville,** which was named "Beer City USA" from 2009 to 2012 and boasts some two dozen breweries and specialty beer shops along with more than 250 independently owned restaurants. **Heritage tourism** is also enormously important, with a number of guidebooks and driving trails established or under development to promote history, traditional music, folk arts, and literary achievements. The state's Department of Commerce estimates that nearly 46 million people visit North Carolina every year, bringing in more than $19 billion, and that close to 200,000 state residents work in industries directly related to and dependent on tourism.

DISTRIBUTION OF WEALTH

For the most part, North Carolina is basically working-class. Pockets of significant wealth exist in urban areas, and as more and more retirees relocate to North Carolina, there are moneyed people in the mountains and coastal counties. Extensive white-collar job availability makes the Triangle a comparatively prosperous region, with average household incomes in 2010 exceeding $60,000, much higher than the state's median household income of just over $46,000.

The state also experiences significant **poverty.** The proportion of people living in poverty has been rising in recent years, partly due to the ongoing worldwide economic slowdown but also due to the derailment of many of North Carolina's backbone industries. As recently as one generation ago, a high school graduate in small-town North Carolina could count on making a living wage in a mill or factory; nowadays those opportunities have dried up, and the poverty rate in 2017 was 14.7 percent. Even more distressing, the number of children living in poverty is just over 24 percent, climbing to 28 percent for children under age six.

The northeastern quadrant of North Carolina is the most critically impoverished, which points to **financial inequality** correlating to race, as the region has a significant African American population. Broken down by ethnicity, the data reveal that 10 percent of urban and rural whites live in poverty, while 20-30 percent of rural and urban Latinos, African Americans, and Native Americans live in poverty.

Several hardworking organizations and activists are trying to alleviate the economic hardship found in North Carolina. National organizations like **Habitat for Humanity** (www.habitat.org) and regional groups like the **Southern Coalition for Social Justice** (http://southerncoalition.org) and the **Institute for Southern Studies** (www.southernstudies.org) bring community activism and research to the state. There are also excellent North Carolina-based advocates in groups such as the **North Carolina Rural Economic Development Center** (www.ncruralcenter.org), the **North Carolina Justice Center** (www.ncjustice.org), the **Black Family Land Trust** (www.bflt.org), and **Student Action with Farmworkers** (http://saf-unite.org).

People and Culture

DEMOGRAPHICS

The ninth most populous state in the union, North Carolina's population of 10.44 million residents is slightly more than Michigan and New Jersey and slightly less than Georgia. More than two-thirds of North Carolinians are white, primarily of German and Scottish-Irish descent, and not quite one-quarter are African American. The state is about 9 percent Latino and has the seventh-largest Native American population of any state.

More than 40 percent of North Carolinians are between the ages of 25 and 59, but the older population is steadily rising, due in large part to the state's popularity with retirees. The majority—about 70 percent—of North Carolinians live in family groups, with married couples constituting about half of those and married couples with children making up almost one-quarter of households. Of the remaining one-third of the state's population who live in "nonfamily households"— that is, not with blood relatives or a legally recognized spouse—the vast majority are individuals living on their own. Unmarried couples, both straight and gay, have a much lower rate of cohabitation here than in more urban parts of the United States, but such households are common and accepted in the Triangle, Asheville, Charlotte, and other urban areas.

Indigenous People

Many Americans have never heard of the **Lumbee people** despite the fact that they are the largest Native American nation east of the Mississippi. This is in part due to the federal government's refusal to grant them official recognition, although the state of North Carolina does recognize them. The Lumbee are primarily based in and around Robeson County in the swampy southeastern corner of the state, their traditional home. In the Great Smoky Mountains, the town of Cherokee on the Qualla Boundary, which is Cherokee-administered land, is the governmental seat of the **Eastern Band of the Cherokee.** The Eastern Band are largely descended from those Cherokee people who escaped arrest during the deportation of the Southeast's Native Americans on the Trail of Tears in the 19th century, or who made the forced march to Oklahoma but survived and walked home to the mountains again. The Lumbee people and Cherokee people are both important cultural groups in North Carolina. Several other Native American communities are indigenous to the state as well; those recognized by the state are the **Waccamaw-Siouan, Occaneechi Band of the Saponi Nation, Haliwa-Saponi, Coharie, Sappony,** and **Meherrin.**

Latinos

North Carolina has one of the fastest-growing Latino populations in the United States, a community whose ranks have swelled since the 1990s, in particular as hundreds of thousands of **Mexican and Central American laborers** came to work in the agricultural, industrial, and formerly booming construction trades. Their presence in such large numbers makes for some unexpectedly quirky cultural juxtapositions, as in small rural towns that are now majority Latino or in Charlotte, where the Latino population has made Roman Catholicism the most common religion.

Non-Latino Immigrants

Significant numbers of non-Latino immigrants also live in North Carolina. Charlotte is a dizzying hodgepodge of ethnicities, where native Southerners live and work alongside **Asians, Africans,** and **Middle Easterners,** where mosques and synagogues and *wats* welcome worshipers just down the street from

What manner of man is a North Carolinian? How can you tell a Tar Heel? What ingredients went into his making? Is he different, and if so, how and why? There is no slide-rule answer to these questions, but it may be interesting to explore them. The Tar Heel is not a distinct species, but he may have some distinguishing marks. [We are] independent, courageous, resourceful, democratic, gregarious and individualistic, although we would use plainer words than these Latin terms to describe ourselves.... There is a progressive strain in this Tar Heel, a realistic and resourceful determination to get ahead with the work for a better way of life for himself and his fellows.... There is often a kindness in the voice which covers a lot of humanity in its acceptance of all sorts and conditions of men.... But there is no pouring Tar Heels into a mold. The point is that we are by preference and habit individualists, or what we call "characters."

Blackwell P. Robinson, ed., *The North Carolina Guide*, UNC Press, 1955.

Baptist churches and Houses of Prayer. Many **Hmong** and other **Southeast Asian** immigrants have settled in the northern foothills and the Piedmont Triad, and the dense thicket of universities in the Triangle attracts academics from around the world.

RELIGION

As early as the 17th century, North Carolina's religious landscape foreshadowed the diversity we enjoy today. The first Christians in North Carolina were Quakers, soon followed by Anglicans, Presbyterians, Baptists, Moravians, Methodists, and Roman Catholics. Native American and African religions, present in the early colonial days, were never totally quashed by European influence, and Barbadian Sephardic Jews were here early on as well. All of these religions remain today, with enrichment by the presence of Muslims, Buddhists, and an amazing mosaic of other Christian groups.

North Carolina claims as its own one of the world's most influential modern religious figures, Billy Graham, who was raised on a dairy farm outside Charlotte and experienced his Christian religious awakening in 1934. After preaching in person to more people around the world than anyone in human history, and being involved with every U.S. president since Harry Truman, Billy Graham died at his home in 2018 and is buried at the Billy Graham Library in Charlotte.

LANGUAGE

Few states can boast the linguistic diversity of North Carolina. North Carolina speech varies widely by region and even from county to county. These variations have to do with the historical patterns of settlement in a given area—whether Scots-Irish or German ancestry is common, how long Native American languages survived after the arrival of the Europeans, the presence or lack of African influence—as well as other historical patterns of trade and communication.

Of our distinct regional accents, the **Outer Banks brogue** is probably the best known. Much like the residents of the Chesapeake islands in Maryland and Virginia, "Hoi Toiders," as Outer Bankers are jokingly called, because of how they pronounce the phrase "high tide," have a striking dialect that resembles certain dialects in the north of England. "I" is rounded into "oi," the *r* sound is often hard, and many distinctive words survive from long-ago English, Scottish, and Irish dialects. Not dissimilar is the Appalachian dialect heard through much of the mountains. The effect is more subtle than in the Outer Banks, but "oi" replaces "I" in Appalachian English too, and *r*'s are emphasized. A telltale sign of upcountry origins is the pronunciation of the vowel in words like bear and hair, which in the mountains is flattened almost inside-out so that the words are pronounced something like "barr" and "harr." This is similar to mountain accents in Tennessee, West Virginia, Virginia, and Kentucky.

Piedmont Carolinians have a wide spectrum of linguistic influences. The heart of the state has been a cultural and commercial crossroads since the days of the Great Wagon Road, which brought 18th-century white settlers into the Southern backcountry; the magnetic influence of jobs in cigarette factories and textile mills drew rural Southerners from all over the region. The product of this linguistic mix-and-match is probably the closest thing in North Carolina to the generic Hollywood version of "the Southern accent," but Piedmont speech is far from homogenous within the region. For example, native central Carolinians are equally likely to call the Queen City "CHAR-lit" or "SHOLL-utt."

There are a great many smaller linguistic zones peppered throughout the state. Folks from up around the **Virginia border** in eastern North Carolina may have a distinctively Virginian accent. Listen for the classic telltale word *house*. Southside Virginians and their neighbors south of the state line will pronounce it "heause," with a flat vowel. **Cherokee English,** heard in the Smokies, combines the Appalachian sound with a distinctively Cherokee rhythm, while **Lumbee English,** spoken in and around Robeson County in the southeast, combines sounds somewhat like those of the Outer Banks or deep mountains with a wealth of unusual grammatical structures and vocabulary of unknown origin. Oft-cited examples are the Lumbee construction "be's," a present-tense form of "to be," and words like *ellick* for coffee and *juvember* for slingshot: "Get me some more ellick, please, if you be's going to the market." Residents of the **Sandhills**

area, bounded by the Uwharries to the west, Sanford to the north, and Southern Pines to the southeast, have a highly unusual rhythm to their speech—a rapid, soft, almost filigreed way of talking, delivered in bursts between halting pauses. Down around Wilmington and south to the South Carolina state line, African American English, and to a lesser extent white English, have some of the inflections of the **Gullah language** of the Lowcountry. These are only a few of the state's dialects, and even these have subvariations. Old-timers can pinpoint geographical differences within these categories—whether a Lumbee speaker is from Prospect or Drowning Creek, for example, or whether a Banker is from Ocracoke or Hatteras.

Of course, English is hardly the only language spoken here. If you visit Cherokee, you'll see that many street and commercial signs bear pretty, twisty symbols in a script that looks like a cross between Khmer or Sanskrit and Cyrillic; **written Cherokee** uses the script famously devised by **Sequoyah** in the early 19th century. Cherokee also survives as a spoken language, mostly among the elders in traditional communities such as Snowbird, near Robbinsville, and many younger Cherokee people are determined to learn and pass on their ancestral tongue, but the small pool of speakers points to the slow death of the language. **Spanish** is widely spoken throughout the state as the Latino population continues to grow rapidly, and within Latino communities here are many national and regional dialects of Spanish. Some Central American immigrants who speak indigenous languages arrive unable to understand English or Spanish. Anyone who doubts that newcomers to this country are dedicated to the task of integrating into American society need only consider the incredibly difficult task faced by such immigrants, who must first learn Spanish before they can enroll in ESL programs to learn English.

Understanding Local Lingo

North Carolina speech features delightful and sometimes perplexing regional vocabulary and grammar. Following are some of the common Carolinianisms most likely to stump travelers.

- **bless your/his/her heart:** A complex declaration with infinitely varied intentions, interpreted depending on context or tone. In its most basic use, "Bless your heart," is a sincere thank-you for a favor or a kindness paid. It's also an exclamation of affection, usually applied to children and the elderly, as in, "You're *not* 92 years old! You are? Well, bless your heart." Frequently, though, hearts are blessed to frame criticism in a charitable light, as in, "Bless his heart; that man from New York don't know not to shout."

- **buggy:** a shopping cart, as at a grocery store.

- **carry:** convey, escort, give a ride to. "I carried my mother up to the mountains for her birthday."

- **Coke:** any soft drink; may be called "pop" in the mountains.

- **come back:** often uttered by shopkeepers as a customer leaves, not to ask them to return immediately, but simply an invitation to patronize the establishment again someday.

- **dinner:** the midday meal.

- **evening:** not just the twilight hours, but all the hours between about 3pm and nightfall.

- **fair to middling:** so-so, in response to "How you?"; a holdover term from North Carolina's moonshining days, the term originally applied to grading 'shine by examining bubbles in a shaken mason jar.

- **fixing to:** about to or preparing to do something. "She's fixing to have a baby any day now."

- **holler:** hollow, a mountain cove.

- **Kakalak:** Carolina. (Also Kakalaky, Cakalack)

The Arts

As much as North Carolinians like to brag about the beaches and mountains and college sports teams, it's the artists across the state who help North Carolina distinguish itself. There is an incredibly rich and complex cultural heritage here that has strong support from the North Carolina Arts Council and a vast network of local and regional arts organizations. These groups have supplied inspiration, financial and emotional support, and sustenance for generations of remarkable musicians, writers, actors, and other artists.

LITERATURE

Storytelling seems to come naturally to Southerners. From the master storytellers of Jack Tales in the Blue Ridge to the distinguished journalists we see every night on television, North Carolinians have a singular gift for communication. Thomas Wolfe was an Asheville native, and O. Henry, whose real name was William Sidney Porter, was born and raised in Greensboro. Tom Robbins (*Even Cowgirls Get the Blues*) was born in Blowing Rock. Charles Frazier (*Cold Mountain*) is from Asheville. Sarah Dessen (*Just Listen*) is from Chapel Hill. Kaye Gibbons, Lee Smith, Fred Chappell, Randal Kenan, and Clyde

- **mash:** press, as a button. "I keep mashing the button, but the elevator won't come."

- **mess:** discombobulated, in a rut, not living right. "I was a mess until I joined the church."

- **mommocked:** exhausted, worn out. Used especially on the Outer Banks and in rural southeastern North Carolina.

- **piece:** a vague measure of distance, as in, "down the road a piece" (a little ways down the road) or "a fair piece" (a long way).

- **poke:** a bag, such as a paper shopping bag. Used especially in the mountains.

- **reckon:** believe, think. Often used in interrogative statements that end in a falling tone, as in, "Reckon what we're having for dinner." (That is, "What do you suppose is for lunch?")

- **right:** quite, very. Variations include "right quick" (soon, hurriedly), "right much" (often), and "a right many" or "a right smart of" (a great quantity).

- **sorry:** worthless, lame, shoddy. "I wanted to play basketball in college, but I was too sorry of an athlete."

- **supper:** the evening meal (as opposed to "dinner," the midday meal).

- **ugly:** mean or unfriendly, spiteful. Sometimes referred to as "acting ugly." "Hateful" is a common synonym.

- **wait on:** to wait for.

- **y'all:** pronoun used to address any group of two or more people.

- **yonder:** over there.

- **y'uns:** mountain variation of y'all.

Edgerton, leading lights in Southern fiction, are all natives or residents of North Carolina. Also closely associated with the state are Carl Sandburg, David Sedaris, Armistead Maupin, and Betsy Byars, who have all lived here at some point in their lives. Arts programs focused on creative writing have sprung up across the state, imbuing the literary scenes in towns like Wilmington, Greensboro, Asheville, and Chapel Hill with talented undergraduate and graduate students and their professors. Notable writers teaching creative writing programs include poet A. Van Jordan, essayist David Gessner, and novelist and short story writer Jill McCorkle. In 2021, a North Carolina novelist became the second in the state to receive the National Book Award (Charles Frazier was the first with *Cold Mountain*) when Jason Mott received the National Book Award for his novel, *One Hell of a Book,* making him the first Black author, second novelist, first graduate of UNC Wilmington's MFA program, and the first friend of mine to take home such an honor.

North Carolina has also given the world some of the giants of 20th-century journalism. Edward R. Murrow, Charles Kuralt, David Brinkley, and Howard Cosell were all sons of Carolina, and Charlie Rose carries their torch today.

MUSIC

It's hard to know where to begin when describing the importance of music to North Carolinians. Since the earliest days of recorded country music, North Carolinians have shared their songs with the world. Charlie Poole and Wade Mainer were among the first to record and became influential artists in the 1930s. By 1945, a banjo player named Earl Scruggs was helping to create what would become the quintessential sound of bluegrass music, particularly his three-fingered picking style. Bluegrass greats like Del McCoury helped further define the sound. Today, bluegrass is alive and well in North Carolina; Steve Martin's collaboration with the Steep Canyon Rangers sells out concerts around the world and garners awards at every turn, and the late Doc Watson's annual MerleFest is still going strong. Country musicians like Ronnie Milsap, Donna Fargo, Charlie Daniels, and Randy Travis made big names for themselves from the 1970s to the 1990s; more recently, Kellie Pickler and Scottie McCreery (of *American Idol* fame) and Eric Church have made waves on the country charts.

The growth of jazz and funk would be unimaginably different if not for a number of notable innovators that make North Carolina nearly as important as New Orleans to the development of these genres. John Coltrane was raised in High Point, Thelonious Monk was a native of Rocky Mount, Nina Simone hails from Tryon, and Dizzy Gillespie grew up just over the South Carolina state line but contributed greatly when he studied music in Laurinburg. In terms of funk music, what would the genre be without George Clinton, founder of Parliament and Parliament-Funkadelic? Saxophonist Maceo Parker and his brother, drummer Melvin Parker, played with Clinton and with South Carolina's favorite son and the Godfather of Soul, James Brown. Together they developed the classic funk sound and influenced the groove-driven side of soul music.

In North Carolina, you're never far from some good gospel music. On the coast, African American choirs blend spirituality and faith with showmanship and serious talent to perform beautiful, inspired sets. In the mountains, you're more likely to find gospel quartets and old-time gospel music, which is more inspired by bluegrass and traditional

music, at camp meetings and gospel sings on weekend nights. The state's Native American communities also have thriving gospel traditions of their own.

Artists that include James Taylor, Tori Amos, Clay Aiken, the Squirrel Nut Zippers, the Avett Brothers, Fred Durst (from Limp Bizkit), rapper and producer Jermaine Dupri, Corrosion of Conformity, Ben Folds Five, Daughtry, Southern Culture on the Skids, and Megafaun have all had a hand in shaping the state's musical legacy.

THEATER

Regional theater companies such as the venerable Flat Rock Playhouse near Hendersonville make great theater accessible in small towns and rural areas. Wilmington is home to Thalian Hall and the Thalian Association, a group founded in 1788 that was named the Official Community Theatre of North Carolina thanks to their long-running commitment to the arts in Wilmington. The North Carolina School for the Arts in Winston-Salem mints great actors and filmmakers, among other artists. The film and television industries have long recognized North Carolina as a hotbed of talent as well as a place with amazing filming locations.

For some reason, outdoor historical dramas have long flourished in North Carolina. The most famous is North Carolina playwright Paul Green's *Lost Colony*, which has been performed every summer since 1937 on Roanoke Island, except during World War II when German U-boats lurked nearby. The Cherokee people depict emblematic episodes in their history in the outdoor drama *Unto These Hills*, in production since 1950. The community of Boone has presented *Horn in the West* since 1952, and it is joined by Valdese and several other communities in North Carolina in turning to performance tableaux to commemorate their heritage. It's especially important to note that among the characteristics of outdoor drama in North Carolina is the fact that the cast, crew, and often the producers and playwrights are members of the communities whose stories the plays tell.

ARTS AND CRAFTS

Folk art and studio crafts show vitality in North Carolina. Several communities are known worldwide for their local traditions, and countless individual artists, studios, and galleries can be found across the state.

Seagrove, a miniscule town at the geographical center of the state, has been the home of hundreds of potters since the 18th century. What began as a commercial enterprise to turn out utilitarian products made for trade on the Great Wagon Road became an increasingly artistic form in the early 20th century. Skilled potters still work in Seagrove today, many of them descendants of founding members of the community. Wilson, between Raleigh and Wilmington, was home to Vollis Simpson, a folk artist and maker of internationally admired whirligigs that were named the Official Folk Art of North Carolina.

Cherokee craft is an important aesthetic school comprising a wide range of techniques and media such as wood- and stone-carving, fiber arts, traditional weaponry, and avant-garde sculpture and painting. Qualla Arts and Crafts Mutual, located in the town of Cherokee, has a wonderful sales gallery that will dazzle lovers of fine craft.

Asheville is an epicenter of the arts, the heart of a vast community of artists that stretches throughout western North Carolina and includes such major folk schools as John C. Campbell in Brasstown, near the Georgia state line, and Penland, close to Tennessee in the northeastern mountains. In Asheville you can see and purchase an infinite variety of crafts that include handmade baskets, quilts, furniture, clothing, jewelry, and iron architectural elements. The Southern Highland Craft Guild (www.southernhighlandguild. org), an old and accomplished organization, deserves a lot of the credit for the thriving health of the craft movement in western North Carolina. Its website has a great deal of information about contemporary master crafters and their work. On the coast, Wilmington, New Bern, Hatteras, and other towns have folk-art and fine-art artists and galleries.

As people become more accustomed to a world in which almost every object we see and use was mass-produced far away, we develop a deeper appreciation for the depth of skill and aesthetic complexity that went into the production of everyday objects in past generations. North Carolinians have always been great crafters of utilitarian and occupational necessities. As you travel through the state, keep an eye out for objects that you may not immediately recognize as art—barns, fishing nets, woven chair bottoms—but that were made with the skill and artistry of generations-old traditions. In North Carolina, art is everywhere.

Food

You'll probably have heard of North Carolina's most famous specialties—barbecue, Brunswick stew, and hush puppies—but are you brave enough to venture deeper into the hinterlands of Carolina cooking? Few snacks are more viscerally craved by locals, and more revolting to non-Southerners, than boiled peanuts. The recipe is simple: Green peanuts are boiled in their shells in bulk in water as salty as the chef deems necessary. Once they're soft and slimy, the peanuts are dumped into a strainer and are ready to eat. All you need to make them is a big kettle and a fire, so boiled peanuts are often made and sold in small bags at roadside stands, primarily in the Lowcountry and coastal plain, but increasingly in the mountains as well. Often these roadside stands are themselves folk art, with handmade signs reading "Bolit P-Nuts Here," with a collection of carvings or sculptures for sale in the bed of a truck nearby. To eat a boiled peanut, pick it up by the ends with your thumb and forefinger and place it lengthwise between your front teeth. Gently crack open the shell—don't bite through it—and detach the halves. Pry off half of the shell, and nip or slurp the peanuts out as if you're eating an oyster (boiled peanuts often show up at Lowcountry oyster roasts). Toss the shell out the window—chances are you're driving as you eat—and have another. Be sure you have a lot of something to drink close at hand, because you'll soon get thirsty.

Many cultures have a recipe that makes thrifty use of the leftover meat scraps that are too small, too few, or too disgusting to be served alone. For upper Piedmont Carolinians, particularly those of German ancestry raised in the wavy ribbon of towns between Charlotte and Winston-Salem, that delicacy is **livermush.** Some folks say that if you're from the Mid-Atlantic and are familiar with scrapple, you'll have a pretty good idea of what livermush is like. That's not true—livermush is much worse and tastes like some bitter combination of burning hair and pepper. Under North Carolina law (really), livermush must contain at least 30 percent hog liver, which is supplemented with sundry scraps from hog heads, sometimes some skin, and cornmeal. At the factory, it's mashed up and cooked in loaves. In the kitchen, it's sliced and fried. You can eat it at breakfast like sausage, in a sandwich, or even on a stick if you go to the annual livermush festivals in Drexel and Shelby. Should you try it? Yes, at least a bite; plenty of people like it.

In the eastern part of the state, a similar aesthetic underlies the creation of **hog hash,** best made directly after an old-time hog killing, when the animal's organs are pulled steaming hot out of the carcass in the frosty fall morning. The liver, lungs, and a variety of other organs and appendages are dumped in a kettle with potatoes, a liquid base (broth, milk, or just water), and some vegetables and seasonings. Unlike livermush, hog hash is served in bowls or tubs as a dark, musky stew; it's not common.

Up in the Blue Ridge Mountains, and across Appalachia, for that matter, the early spring is the season for **ramps,** sometimes called skunk cabbage—very pungent wild onions that grow along creek beds in the deep mountains. They're another of those foods passionately defended by those who grew up eating them but greeted with trepidation by outsiders. The reason they're feared by the uninitiated is their atomically powerful taste, which will emanate from every part of your body for days if the ramps are too strong or not prepared correctly. Ramps taste like a cross between regular onions, garlic, leeks, shallots, and kryptonite. When they're young, they're perfectly pungent—not too overwhelming, but still powerful enough to let you know they're in the dish. Folks skillet-cook them, fry them up in grease, boil them with fatback, or just chomp on them raw. For a special treat and a gentle introduction to ramps, stop in at the Stecoah Valley Center near Robbinsville, pick up a bag of the Smoky Mountain Native Plants Association's special cornmeal mix with dried ramps, and make yourself a skillet of deliciously tangy cornbread. You can also try them at the local ramps festivals held in Robbinsville and Cherokee in spring. A growing number of restaurants from Asheville to Wilmington are buying ramps and **morel mushrooms** from mountain foragers and preparing them every way from skillet fried to pickled, so ramp lovers can get a taste of this springtime mountain delicacy even on the coast.

You can read all about these and other acquired tastes at **NCFOOD** (www.ncfolk. org) or **Our State Eats** by *Our State* magazine (www.ourstate.com), two food blogs devoted to Carolina cooking, or on the **Southern Foodways Alliance** (www. southernfoodways.com) and **Dixie Dining** (www.dixiedining.com) websites.

Vegetarians and devotees of organic food, fear not; North Carolina is an unusually progressive state when it comes to healthy and homegrown grub. Nevertheless, if you want to avoid meat, you have to be cautious when ordering at a restaurant: Make sure the beans are made with vegetable oil rather than lard, ask if the salad dressing contains anchovies, and beware of hidden fish and oyster sauce. Traditional Southern cooking makes liberal use of fatback (cured pork fat) and other animal products; greens are often boiled with a strip of fatback or a hambone, as are most soups and stews. Even pie crusts are still made with lard in many old-time kitchens.

In the major cities, you'll find organic grocery stores. Earth Fare and Whole Foods are the most common chains, but there are also plenty of small independent markets. Farmers markets and roadside stands are so plentiful that they almost have to fight for space. Visit the state Department of Agriculture's **North Carolina Farm Fresh** (www.ncfarmfresh. com) for directories of farmers markets and pick-your-own farms and orchards.

Essentials

Getting There

AIR

The state where air travel began has more than 70 public airports, almost 300 privately owned airfields, and about 20 fly-in communities where residents share an airstrip and have their own hangar space. Nine airports have regularly scheduled passenger service, and two of them host international flights. The state's Department of Transportation estimates that more than 35 million people fly in and out of North Carolina every year. The main hubs are North Carolina's international airports.

The eighth-busiest airport in the country, **Charlotte Douglas International Airport** (CLT, 5501 Josh Birmingham Pkwy., Charlotte, 704/359-4013, www.cltairport.com) has more than 730 daily departures and is served by dozens of airlines. There are nonstop flights to 140 U.S. cities as well as international flights to Latin America and the Caribbean, London, Frankfurt, Munich, and Toronto. Parking is abundant and inexpensive, with parking shuttle buses operating from 5am. **Piedmont Triad Airport** (GSO, 1000 A Ted Johnston Pkwy., Greensboro, 336/665-5600, www.flyfrompti.com) serves the Greensboro and Winston-Salem area with flights to domestic destinations in the South, Midwest, and Mid-Atlantic.

There are several smaller airports around the state with regularly scheduled domestic passenger service, including, **Asheville Regional Airport** (AVL, 61 Terminal Dr., Fletcher, 828/684-2226, www.flyavl.com).

Private aircraft can fly to any of the state's 75 regional, county, and municipal air strips statewide; **NC Airports Association** (www.ncairports.org) has a full list with contact details, navigational information, airstrip specifications, and aerial photos. For historical reasons there are more municipal airports in the central and western parts of the state. When the state government started handing out grants for small public airstrips in the 1950s, there were already many surplus military airfields in the eastern part of the state, a legacy of World War II.

CAR

Several major interstate highways run through North Carolina, so if you're driving and would prefer that your trip be efficient rather than scenic, you've got several choices. From anywhere along the eastern seaboard, I-95 slices through the eastern third of the state, providing easy access to the beaches, which are mostly one or two hours east of I-95, and to the Triangle area, under an hour west of I-95 via U.S. 64, U.S. 70, or I-40. From the north, you may choose to veer southwest at Richmond, Virginia, on I-85; this is an efficient route to Durham and Chapel Hill as well as to the Triad and Charlotte regions.

I-40 starts in Wilmington and runs west to Barstow, California. It's a fast road all the way through North Carolina, although weather—ice in the fall, winter, and spring, and fog any time of year—may slow you down considerably between Knoxville, Tennessee, and Asheville. U.S. 64 and I-77 connect North Carolina to the Midwest. I-77 cuts through the toe of Virginia in the mountains and runs straight to Charlotte, while U.S. 64 meanders east through the Triangle all the way to Roanoke Island and the Outer Banks. From the Deep South or Texas, the best bet is I-20 to Atlanta, and from there I-85 to Charlotte, or U.S. 19 or U.S. 23 if you're going to the mountains.

There are no checkpoints at the state line to inspect vehicles for produce or animals, but sobriety checkpoints are established and staffed throughout the year.

BUS

Travel around North Carolina can be accomplished easily and cheaply by bus. **Greyhound** (800/231-2222, www.greyhound.com) offers daily service to many towns and cities, with the exception of the Outer Banks and mountain towns other than Asheville, but you can access that region via the Tennessee cities close to the state line, including Knoxville and Johnson City. Before you reserve bus tickets, be sure to check out special discounts on the Greyhound website. There are often regional promotions as well as special "Go Anywhere" fares as low as $29 each way with 14-day advance booking, for example, as well as regular discounts for students and seniors.

These days, the large buses used by Greyhound and its local subsidiaries are clean

Previous: Cades Cove Loop Road in Great Smoky Mountains National Park.

and comfortable, and if you make a reservation ahead of time, you can choose your seat. One word of caution is that some bus stations are located in seedy parts of town, so make sure taxi service is available at your destination station after dark.

TRAIN

Although it does not currently serve the mountains or the coast, **Amtrak** (800/872-7245, www.amtrak.com) is a great way to get to and around central North Carolina. The main New York-Miami *Silver Service* and *Palmetto* trains pass through North Carolina following the I-95 corridor. The New York-New Orleans *Crescent* stops at both Winston-Salem and Charlotte. The *Carolinian* runs from New York to Charlotte by way of Raleigh.

Getting Around

CAR

North Carolina's highway system, with the largest network of state-maintained roads in the country and a good interstate highway grid, provides access to the whole state. I-95 crosses north-south, demarcating the eastern third of the state, and I-85 runs northeast-southwest from north of the Triangle area through Charlotte. I-40 is the primary east-west route, from Wilmington through the Smoky Mountains to Knoxville, Tennessee. The highest speed limit, which applies to some rural interstate highways and four-lane roads, is 70 mph. Highways in developed areas have much lower speed limits, and in residential areas it's a good idea to keep it under 25 mph.

You can take your pick of car-rental agencies at the major airports at Charlotte, Winston-Salem, and Raleigh-Durham; there are fewer choices at smaller regional airports. There are also car-rental pickup and drop-off offices in many towns. Rental car companies in North Carolina include **Alamo** (800/462-5266, www.alamo.com), **Avis** (877/222-9075, www.avis.com), **Budget** (800/218-7992, www.budget.com), **Dollar** (800/800-4000, www.dollar.com), **Enterprise** (800/261-7331, www.enterprise.com), **Hertz** (800/654-3131, www.hertz.com), **National** (877/222-9058, www.nationalcar.com), **Thrifty** (800/847-4389, www.thrifty.com), and **Triangle Rent-A-Car** (800/643-7368, www.trianglerentacar.com). To rent a car you must be at least 25 years old and have both a valid driver's license and a credit card, although some companies will accept a cash security deposit in lieu of credit.

For getting around town in every city of a reasonable size, you can always use rideshare services like Uber (www.uber.com). Service will be limited in small towns and rural areas, but check the website or the app for available drivers in your destination.

On the other side of the state, driving in the Great Smoky Mountains and Blue Ridge can be difficult in bad weather, and roads can be icy in winter. The major interstate highways that cross the mountains are fast, and if you're traveling from one major town to another, U.S. 19, U.S. 74, and U.S. 421 are also fast. On smaller highways, count on much slower traveling. The Blue Ridge Parkway, while geographically direct, is very slow. The maximum speed is 45 mph, but there are few stretches of the Parkway where it's safe to drive that fast; add to that the frequent braking of sightseers, and traffic can crawl. Numbered roads in the mountains are often similar, with surprise hairpin turns and narrow cliff-side shoulders. Allow plenty of time to get from point to point; on some roads it'll take you an hour to cover 20 miles. In the mountains you have to take it slow and be alert to weather and wildlife. If you find a local driver tailgating you, find a place to pull over and allow the faster drivers to pass.

Driving Trails

The state of North Carolina and a variety of regional organizations have created a wonderful network of automobile "trails"—thematic itineraries showcasing North Carolina's treasures. Check out the destinations on this sampling of trails.

- **Asheville Ale Trail:** http://ashevillealetrail.com
- **Blue Ridge Music Trails:** www.blueridgemusic.org
- **Cherokee Heritage Itinerary:** www.ncfolk.org
- **Civil War Traveler:** www.civilwartraveler.com
- **Core Sound Itinerary:** www.ncfolk.org
- **Discover Craft North Carolina:** www.discovercraftnc.org
- **Family Frolic in Winston-Salem:** http://visitwinstonsalem.com/Family
- **Haw River Wine Trail:** www.hawriverwinetrail.com
- **Historic Albemarle Tour:** www.historicalbemarletour.org
- **Homegrown Handmade Art Roads and Farm Trails:** www.homegrownhandmade.com
- **North Carolina Scenic Byways:** www.ncdot.gov/travel/scenic
- **North Carolina Wine Country:** www.visitncwinecountry.com
- **Pottery Itinerary for the Seagrove Area:** www.ncfolk.org
- **Quilt Trails of Western North Carolina:** www.quilttrailswnc.org
- **Trail of Tears National Historic Trail, North Carolina Chapter:** www.arch.dcr.state.nc.us/tears
- **Western North Carolina Cheese Trail:** http://wnccheesetrail.org
- **Yadkin Valley Wine Country:** www.yadkinvalleywinecountry.com

Highway Safety

Write "*HP" (*47) on a sticky note and affix it to your dashboard. That's the direct free hotline to the North Carolina Highway Patrol, which will send help if you're trouble. North Carolinians don't hesitate to report aggressive, reckless, or drunk motorists to the highway patrol, and you might be reported by another driver if you're tailgating, speeding, weaving, or driving aggressively. What passes for normal driving in many parts of the United States is regarded as aggressive driving in the South.

Pull well off the road and turn on your hazard lights if you have an accident. If you can't safely pull your vehicle out of traffic, at least get away from the roadway. A distressing number of motorists with disabled vehicles as well as pedestrians are struck and killed by cars every year.

Some rules to remember while driving in North Carolina: Wearing your seat belt is required by law; child safety seats are mandatory for anyone under age 8 or weighing less than 80 pounds; and if it's raining hard enough to need windshield wipers, you must also use your headlights.

Weather Considerations

If you're driving in the mountains in the morning or at night, you may run into heavy **fog.** Because the clouds perch on and around mountaintops, you may find yourself in clear weather one moment and only seconds later in a fog with little visibility. It can be dangerous and frightening, but if this happens, slow down, keep an eye on the lines on the road, watch for other cars, and put on your low beams. As in any kind of bad weather, it's always best to find a safe place to pull off the road and wait for the weather to improve. Fog can dissipate as quickly as it appears.

In the winter you could encounter icy roads in any part of the state, and up in the mountains you may hit **ice and snow** three seasons of the year. Many Southerners on the coast and in the Piedmont tend to panic when snow is forecast; folks in the mountains manage to keep their wits about them no matter the weather. In anticipation of a half-inch dusting of snow, schools and businesses may close, fleets of sand and salt trucks hit the highway, and residents mob the grocery stores. This overreaction to snow makes the roads a little safer because many folks are more likely to stay home, but those who do drive in winter weather are less likely to know how to drive on ice than the average Yankee or Midwesterner. That can make the roads hazardous, so even if you are an experienced snow driver, stay alert.

While North Carolinians from the mountains are more experienced at driving in snowy or icy weather, the roads themselves can be dangerous. The safest plan is to avoid driving in the mountains in bad weather. If you must go, keep in mind that mountain roads, even highways, may close—especially those maintained by the National Park Service, including the Blue Ridge Parkway and the roads in Great Smoky Mountains National Park. The National Park Service offers the following advice: "When driving downhill on slippery mountain roads, shift to a lower gear (2, 1, or L on automatic transmissions) to avoid using brakes more than necessary. Leave extra room between you and the vehicle in front of you. Be aware that icy sections persist on mountain roads even when the weather is warm in the lowlands."

The other weather concern is rain. In spring and fall, you can encounter thunderstorms in all parts of the state, and these are usually run-of-the-mill storms, but heed any weather warnings you hear or see. Summer and early fall is hurricane season, and while most people think of hurricanes as coastal events, the torrential rains brought on by a hurricane (or tropical system of any sort) can cause flash flooding, high winds, and heavy rains as these systems move inland. Whether you're on the coast or in the mountains and you learn there is a hurricane on the way, follow the directions of civil authorities and be safe. If you're on the coast, familiarize yourself with hurricane evacuation routes (they're marked on highways and in local literature) and follow directions.

Wildlife on the Road

A final note about highway travel: Be conscious of wildlife. Deer, rabbits, turtles, foxes, coyotes, raccoons, and opossums litter the highways. Head-on collisions with deer can be fatal to both species, and smaller animals die because drivers are going too fast to avoid them. If you see an injured animal and are able to help it without putting yourself in danger, you'll find a phalanx of wildlife rehabilitators throughout the state to give it the care it needs.

The large number of deer in urban and rural areas makes them frequent victims of highway accidents. In clear weather when there's not much oncoming traffic, use your high beams so that you'll see them from farther away. If you see a deer cross the road in front of you, remember that they usually travel in small herds, and there may be several more nearby.

Road Etiquette

Certain informal rules of road etiquette apply in North Carolina, and they help make driving less stressful. North Carolina drivers willingly let other vehicles get in front of them, whether merging onto the highway or exiting a parking lot. Wave to say thanks when someone lets you in; positive reinforcement helps keep these habits alive. Folks will often wave at drivers in oncoming traffic on two-lane country roads, and there is an expectation of a quick wave from drivers and pedestrians as well. It's not a big production; simply lift two or three fingers off the steering wheel. A general rule of thumb is that if you're able to discern the facial features of someone outside your car, waving to that person is appropriate.

Drivers are legally obligated to pull over to let emergency vehicles pass. There's also an old tradition of pulling over to allow funeral processions to pass. Very few drivers are willing to merge into or cross a train of cars headed for a funeral, but in rural areas you will still see drivers pulling all the way off the road and waiting for a procession to pass before resuming driving. It's meant as a gesture of respect to the deceased and the mourners.

In all of these situations, safety should be the top priority. You don't need to wave or make eye contact with someone you feel is threatening, and don't pull off the road if there's no safe place to do so. But if you show courtesy to other drivers when you're able, you'll find that traffic karma will work its way back around to you when it's needed.

BUS

Municipal bus services operate in larger towns and some of the more popular tourist areas. The state **Department of Transportation** (www.ncdot.gov/nctransit) maintains information on the state's 99 public transportation systems, including those that serve rural counties.

BICYCLE

Before the Wright brothers made history as the first aviators, they were bicycle men. With its temperate climates, abundance of scenic roads, and full spectrum of terrain, North Carolina is bicycling heaven. There are hundreds of organized bicycling events every year, many of them in support of charities, and they welcome participants from all over. The most popular bike events are held spring to fall, including a six-day Ocracoke Vacation Tour from New Bern to the tip of the Outer Banks, regular scenic rides through wine country, and rides along the Blue Ridge that include a five-day bicycling vacation starting in Blowing Rock.

Each month except December has as many as a dozen public cycling events, including January's New Year's Day Breakfast Ride in Jacksonville, February's Frostbite Tour in Raleigh, and March's Rumba on the Lumber 5K Run and Bike Ride in Lumberton. In April there's the annual Circle-the-Bald Bike Ride, starting in Hayesville, and in May, Wilkesboro's Burn 24 Hour Challenge, a team relay endurance challenge. June has bicycling events as part of the North Carolina Blueberry Festival in Burgaw; July has North Wilkesboro's Hurt, Pain, and Agony Century Race; and August has a Beginner Skills Bicycling Camp in Asheville. In late September is the state-spanning Annual Mountains to the Coast Ride that even goes to the islands of the Outer Banks by ferry; approximately 1,000 cyclists take part. In October there's Rutherfordton's Tour de Pumpkin, and in November, the North Carolina Horse Country Tour takes place. For a full roster of routes, trails, and events, see the **Traveling by Bicycle** page maintained by the North Carolina Department of Transportation (www.ncdot.gov).

Baggage cars on **Amtrak**'s *Piedmont* trains are equipped with bicycle racks; call 800/872-7245 to reserve bike space on a train. You can also take your bicycle on any of the seven **North Carolina Ferries** (800/293-3779, www.ncdot.gov/ferry).

TRAIN

North Carolina has good rail connections among the major cities in the central part of the state. **Amtrak** (800/872-7245, www.amtrak.com) serves North Carolina with its *Silver, Carolinian, Crescent,* and *Palmetto* trains; cities served include Raleigh and Durham, High Point, Winston-Salem, Gastonia, Kannapolis, and Charlotte. *Piedmont* trains connect Raleigh to Charlotte twice daily with stops in several Piedmont towns in between.

Conduct and Customs

GREETINGS

Common courtesy, such as saying "please" and "thank you," being deferential to the elderly, and demonstrating concern for others, is hardly particular to the South. No matter where you're from, chances are your parents raised you to "act like folks," as people say here. The difference is that in North Carolina and elsewhere in the South, manners are somewhat more ritualized.

If you're unfamiliar with Southern ways, the thing you may find strangest is the friendliness of strangers. When passing a stranger on the sidewalk or in a corridor, riding together in an elevator, or even washing hands in the restroom, eye contact and a quick greeting are usually in order. Most common greetings are "Hey," "How you doing," and "How you," spoken as a statement rather than a question. The reply is usually equally casual: "Doing good, how about you," pronounced with just four syllables, "Doin' good, 'bout you," again spoken as a statement rather than a question. Often that's the end of the conversation, although passengers on elevators sometimes wish each other a good day when one gets out. In these encounters, eye contact needn't be lingering, there's no expectation of false pleasantries, and there is certainly no obligation to engage someone who makes you uncomfortable.

It's standard courtesy in a retail or similarly casual transaction to inquire as to the wellbeing of the person serving you. It takes little time, especially when delivered in the spoken shorthand most Southerners use. For instance, a cashier at McDonalds in another part of the country might greet you with "What would you like?" or simply wait for your order and not speak until asking for your money. The transaction here would more likely start with the "How you," "Doin' good, 'bout you," exchange. With that two- or three-second dialogue, a bit of human warmth and mutual respect is shared.

It's expected that people hold doors open for each other and thank each other for doing so. In addressing someone elderly that you don't know well, the standard courtesy is to use a title, Mr. or Ms., with the last name, or in friendlier situations, Mr. or Ms. with the first name. The South was way ahead of the curve in adopting the "Ms." designation; Southerners have always pronounced both "Mrs." and "Miss" as "miz." North Carolinians will likely address you as "ma'am" or "sir" regardless of your age; it doesn't mean they think you're old.

TIPPING

Besides restaurant servers, tip motel and hotel housekeeping staff, bartenders, cab drivers, bellhops, redcaps, valet parking staff, and other service workers. Standard tipping rates are 20 percent for meals, 15 percent for a taxi ride, and $1 per piece of luggage for a redcap or porter, although tipping extra for good service is always gracious and appropriate.

Travel Tips

TRAVELERS OF COLOR

North Carolina is a predominantly white state, with just a touch over 70 percent of our population of 10.44 million identifying as white. Nearly a quarter, 22 percent, identify as Black, 9.8 percent as Latino, 2.3 percent as Asian, and 1.6 percent as Native American. Generally, more rural areas tend to have higher populations of white residents, lower concentrations of other races and ethnicities, and more conservative worldviews. The urban areas—the cities and communities with large university or college presences—are more diverse and politically liberal.

Visitors of color will find themselves welcome and warmly received in every part of the state, though I can't say they'll find every individual in every community welcoming them with open arms. The unfortunate truth is that too many North Carolinians take pride in flying the flag of the Confederate army and espousing political sentiments that aren't in keeping with the richness and diversity that makes the United States great. Fortunately, these troubling truths do not make the state unsafe for visitors. There are no significant instances of violence against visitors or in general.

In Asheville, the **Racial Justice Coalition** (www.rjcavl.org) maintains a list of organizations working on race- and equality-based issues. These include the Asheville-Buncombe NAACP, which maintains an active social media presence; SONG, an acronym for **Southerners on New Ground** (www.southernersonnewground.org); and the **ACLU of Western North Carolina** (www.acluofnorthcarolina.org). The North Carolina Chapter of the **NAACP** (866/626-2227, www.naacpnc.org) has resources in every corner of the state.

LGBTQ+ TRAVELERS

North Carolina offers no legal protection against discrimination based on sexual orientation or gender identity, and, like in most states, hate-crimes statutes do not address violence targeting victims because of their sexual orientation or gender identity. Despite all this, don't close the book on North Carolina. While some laws may be retrogressive, the people are not; much of North Carolina is LGBTQ+-friendly.

Despite being a red state, North Carolina has a strong purple streak. Metropolitan areas have active and open queer communities with numerous organizations and social groups, publications, human rights advocacy services, and community centers. Like anywhere in the United States, smaller and more rural communities are less likely to be gay-friendly, although there are exceptions and pleasant surprises. As a general rule, a couple perceived as same gender will attract little attention holding hands on Durham's 9th Street, Asheville's Patton Avenue, or Weaver Street in Carrboro, but they may not be received warmly at Big Al's Shuckin' Shack in Back Water Creek (not a real place, but you get the idea).

Travelers planning to visit North Carolina can learn a great deal about community resources and activities at **QNotes** (www.q-notes.com), **North Carolina Pride** (www.ncpride.org), and **NC Gay Travel** (http://ncgaytravel.com).

SENIOR TRAVELERS

North Carolina has attracted a tremendous number of retirees in recent years, especially in the mountains and coast. It's also an increasingly popular destination for older travelers. For those who want to visit the state through organized programs, **Road Scholar** (www.roadscholar.org) is a great choice. Tours and classes are available throughout the state;

the offerings in the mountains are particularly rich, with a great variety of courses and hands-on workshops about Appalachian culture and crafts. The North Carolina chapter of AARP (866/389-5650, www.states.aarp.org) is a good resource for senior issues and information. VisitNC (800/847-4862, www.visitnc.com) can also answer questions about activities and accessibility.

WOMEN TRAVELING ALONE

Women from other parts of the country might find male strangers' friendliness a little disconcerting, but keep in mind that while some of them may be flirting with you, it's just as likely that they are simply being courteous. When a Southern man holds a door open for you, offers to help you carry something, or even calls you "honey," "darlin'," or "dear heart," it usually implies no ulterior motives

and isn't intended to be condescending; he's probably just showing that he was raised up right. Again, manners should never preclude safety, so if some sketchy character is coming on to you in a way that gives you the creeps, trust your instincts.

TRAVELERS WITH DISABILITIES

Access North Carolina (800/689-9090, TDD 919/733-5924, www.ncdhhs.gov) is an excellent up-to-date guide on the accessibility of hundreds of cultural, recreational, historical, environmental, and commercial sites of interest and a goldmine for travel planning. Download a copy or phone to ask for the current edition, published by the state Department of Health and Human Services. The guide is set up by region and county, and sites and venues are described and rated in terms of accessibility.

Health and Safety

CRIME

As nice a place as North Carolina is, it's not immune to crime. Common sense about safety applies, particularly for women. Lock your doors immediately when you get into the car, park in well-lit areas as close as possible to your destination, and don't hesitate to ask a security guard or other trustworthy type to see you to your car. Don't carry too much cash on you. Pepper spray might save your life if you're attacked, whether by a person or by a bear.

Note that 911 emergency phone service is available everywhere in the state, but cell phone signals are not dependable everywhere. The deep mountains and more remote parts of western North Carolina and isolated stretches of the coast are more likely to have cell-phone dead zones.

SPECIAL WEATHER CONCERNS

Hurricanes

Hurricanes are a perennial danger, but luckily there tends to be plenty of warning when one is approaching. The Atlantic Hurricane season runs June-November, but North Carolina generally sees the highest hurricane activity late in the season, in September-October. Evacuation orders should always be heeded, even if they are voluntary. It's also a good idea to leave sooner rather than later to avoid being trapped in traffic when the storm hits. The state Department of Crime Control and Public Safety (www.nccrimecontrol.org) posts a map online every year showing evacuation routes. You'll also see evacuation routes marked along the highways.

Tornadoes

Tornadoes can happen in any season and have killed people here in recent years. Pay close attention to tornado watches and warnings, and don't take chances: Find a safe place to shelter until the danger is over.

ANIMAL THREATS

There are a handful of dangerous creatures across the state, ranging in size from microscopic to monstrous, that can pose risks to health and safety. Be on the lookout for mean bugs: **Ticks** can carry Lyme disease and Rocky Mountain spotted fever, both serious and lingering conditions. Most likely to climb on you if you are walking through brush or bushes but liable to be lurking about anywhere, ticks come in many sizes and shapes, from barely visible pinpoint-size to that thing that looks like a grape hanging off your dog's neck. Wear insect repellent if you're going to be tramping around outside, and check your body and your travel companions thoroughly—your clothing as well as your skin—for stowaways. They'll attach themselves to any soft surface on your body, but they particularly like people's heads, often latching on to the scalp an inch or so behind the ears. If you find a tick on you or on a human or canine companion, don't remove it roughly, no matter how freaked out you are. Yanking can leave the tick's head buried in your skin, increasing the risk of infection. Grasp the tick in a pinching motion, and pull slowly but firmly. You may have to hang on for several moments, but eventually it will decide to let go. Dab the bite with antiseptic, and over the next several weeks be alert for a bull's-eye-shaped irritation around the bite and for flu-like symptoms such as fever, achiness, malaise, and fatigue. If you have any of these signs, visit your doctor for a blood test.

Mosquitoes can carry West Nile virus, La Crosse encephalitis, and eastern equine encephalitis. Wear insect repellent and clothing that covers your arms and legs to avoid bites. Although not disease vectors, **fire ants** are among the state's most feared insects. It's easy to stumble onto one of their nests, and before you realize what you've stepped in, they can be swarming up your legs and biting you. Certainly this is a painful and frightening experience, but it's also potentially dangerous if you're allergic. There have been documented cases in recent years of adult humans being swarmed and killed by fire ants. Watch where you step, and keep an eye out for areas of disturbed ground and turned-up soil. Sometimes their nests look like conventional anthills, sometimes like messy piles of dirt, and other times just soft spots on the ground.

Another reason to mind where you tread: snakes. The vast majority of snakes in North Carolina are harmless and shy, but we do have a few pit vipers. **Copperheads** are quite common in every part of the state and in wooded or semi-wooded terrain—even in backyards, where they can lurk in bushes and leaf piles, under porches and in storage sheds, and in the walls of a house. They have a gorgeous pattern of light and dark brown splotches, which makes them incredibly difficult to spot against the ground in fall. Copperheads are usually less than three feet long. Their bite is poisonous but usually not fatal.

Found in the eastern half of the state and up into the Sandhills, **cottonmouths**—also called water moccasins—are very dangerous. They range in color from reddish brown to black, can grow up to 5.5 feet long, and are easily mistaken for harmless water snakes (and vice versa). They sometimes venture into the woods and fields, but cottonmouths are most commonly seen on or near water. Be especially careful walking along creek beds or in riverside brush. When threatened, they display the inside of their mouths, which are a startling and beautiful cottony white. Their bite is potentially lethal.

Coral snakes are endangered in North Carolina, but if you're going to be in the woods in the southeastern quarter of the state, keep an eye out. These jewel-toned snakes are generally small and slim, rarely more than a couple of feet long. Like the harmless scarlet king snake and scarlet snake, coral snakes have alternating bands of red, yellow, and black. The way to tell coral snakes from their harmless kin is to note the order of colors. On coral snakes, the yellow bands separate the

Coronavirus in North Carolina

At the time of writing in 2022, North Carolina had mostly stabilized from the effects of the coronavirus, but the situation is constantly evolving.

Now more than ever, Moon encourages readers to be courteous and ethical in their travel. Be respectful to residents and mindful of the evolving situation in your chosen destination when planning your trip. Get vaccinated if your health allows, and if possible, test regularly before, during, and after your trip to ensure you continue to test negative for Covid-19.

On the whole, North Carolina weathered the coronavirus storm well, with widespread—but not total—mask use, social distancing, and reduced hours/capacity for businesses; the state's appetite for vaccines and boosters varied (with mask and vaccine use drawn roughly along political and urban/rural lines), but today most residents are vaccinated and boosted. Predictably, the hospitality industry was hit hard by quarantines and shutdowns forcing the closure of smaller businesses and the delay of new business openings, but also impacting staffing at hotels, restaurants, breweries, bars, and more (a problem that endures today).

LOCAL CONDITIONS AND RESTRICTIONS

Check local websites for local restrictions and the overall health status of your destination and your point of origin. If you're traveling to or from a Covid-19 hotspot, or anticipate potential cancellations or quarantine requirements, you may want to reconsider your trip.

Some destinations may require proof of vaccination or a recent, negative Covid test result before arrival; other tests and potentially a self-quarantine period, once you've arrived; or proof of a negative test to re-enter your original point of departure. You may also be required to wear a mask and/or provide proof of vaccination or a negative Covid test to enter indoor businesses such as restaurants, bars, and museums. For proof of a negative Covid test, a PCR test is often required. It's a good idea to research places that offer tests in your destination, and possibly make some testing appointments, before your trip.

TRAVEL REQUIREMENTS

If you plan to fly, check with your airline and the destination's health authority for updated travel requirements. Some airlines may be taking more steps than others to help you travel safely. Check their websites for more information before buying your ticket, and consider an early or late flight to limit exposure. Flights may be more infrequent, with increased cancellations.

At present, mask requirements for visitors are few and far between. Airlines and airports are following CDC guidance and internal policies, meaning that masks are optional for travelers, and on public transportation, it's much the same. Many rideshare and public transportation drivers and employees will wear masks, but they're not required for you.

PLANNING YOUR TRIP

Check the website of any venues you wish to patronize to confirm opening hours and to learn about any specific visitation requirements, such as testing, mask, and vaccination policies; mandatory reservations; or limited occupancy. Check Google, the venue's website, and even their social media to get the most up-to-date information on hours and whether they're open. And when in doubt, reach out to a business and ask; most are responsive to queries about their hours over social media.

black and the red, whereas on their imitators, red and black touch. An adage advises, "Red and black, friend of Jack; red and yellow, kill a fellow." Coral snakes can also be identified by their sinister black snouts, making them look like cartoon burglars, whereas scarlet snakes and scarlet king snakes have red clown noses. That's a lot to remember in that instant of panic when you notice a coil of red and yellow and black stripes at your feet looking up at

More than ever, it's a good idea to plan your meals and accommodations and make reservations well in advance. You may want to consider restaurants with outdoor dining options picnic areas and parks for to-go meals, or find accommodations where you can cook meals on your own (which is another great way to connect with your destination). Small towns and out-of-the-way destinations (like the villages and hideaways on the coast, along the Blue Ridge Parkway, and in the deep mountains) continue to have issues with staffing at restaurants, bars, and similar businesses, so arrive early, be patient, and be flexible with your plans. Service disruptions and difficulty landing a table isn't limited to small businesses, though, and it's possible you'll experience these in cities and at typically well-staffed destinations. For those must-see places and must-eat restaurants, do yourself a favor and make reservations before you arrive.

Expect general disruptions. Events may be postponed or cancelled. Some tours and venues may require reservations, enforce limits on the number of guests, operate during different hours than the ones listed, or be closed entirely. Be diligent and continue to research all the way up to your time of departure, as things are likely to change. Across most of North Carolina's outdoor destinations—our beaches, state and national parks, and in forests and on trails—you'll find increased use, which means limited parking and more folks sharing the great outdoors with you.

WHAT TO PACK

Pack hand sanitizer, a thermometer, and plenty of face masks. Though cloth masks may be sufficient for local requirements, a well-fitting N95, KN95, or KF94 mask is generally considered more effective at reducing the risk of transmission of Covid-19. If possible, stock up on at-home rapid tests to take throughout your travels.

Be prepared for possible closures and reduced services over the course of your travels. Consider packing snacks, bottled water, a cooler, or anything else you might need to limit the number of stops along your route.

RESOURCES

- World Health Organization: https://www.who.int/emergencies/diseases/novel-coronavirus-2019/travel-advice

- CDC: https://www.cdc.gov/coronavirus/2019-ncov/travelers

- International Air Transport Organization: https://www.iatatravelcentre.com/world.php

- U.S. State Department: https://travel.state.gov/content/travel/en/traveladvisories/ea/covid-19-information.html

- New York Times Coronavirus Map: https://www.nytimes.com/interactive/2020/world/coronavirus-maps.html

- North Carolina Department of Health and Human Services COVID-19 information page: https://covid19.ncdhhs.gov

- State of North Carolina COVID-19 information hub: https://www.nc.gov/covid19

you testily. Rather than stopping to figure out if the snake is friend or foe, it's better just to quickly step away. Coral snakes' venom works on its prey's respiratory system, and it can kill humans. They're cousins of cobras and are some of the most beautiful snakes in these parts, but locals fear them more intensely than the huge, lumpy-headed, tusky-fanged vipers that appear more threatening.

There are also three poisonous native

rattlesnakes: The **eastern diamondback rattlesnake** is the largest of rattlesnakes and can grow to nearly six feet long and as fat around as an adult human's arm. They are extremely dangerous—powerful enough to catch and eat rabbits, and willing, if provoked, to kill a person. Eastern diamondbacks are rare but can be found in the southeastern sandy swamp counties. Also large are **canebrake rattlers,** more formally known as timber rattlers. They are found throughout the state, including the mountains. Their bite can be fatal to humans. To make them even scarier, they too can grow to nearly six feet in length, and in cold weather they like to congregate in large numbers to hibernate. **Pygmy rattlesnakes** are found along the state's coastline, up into the Sandhills, and around Crowder's Mountain. Generally up to about 1.5 feet long, pygmies are also venomous.

Bear attacks are rare and usually defensive, but considering that the creatures can weigh up to 800 pounds, caution would seem to be indicated. They are present in the woods in various parts of the state, especially up in the mountains and in the deep swamps and pocosins along the coast. They're quite shy and apt to gallop into the brush if they see a human coming. They will investigate potential meals, though, so securing your food when camping is crucial. If your car is nearby, lock the food in it; otherwise, hoist it into a tree with a rope, too high to reach from the ground and out of reach from the tree trunk. The National Park Service recommends the following course of action if a bear approaches you. First, try backing away slowly. If the bear follows, stand your ground. If it continues to menace you, try to scare it: Make yourself look bigger and more threatening by standing on a rock or next to your companions. Try waving sticks and throwing rocks. In the extremely unlikely event that you actually find yourself in hand-to-hand combat with a bear, remember the Park Service's advice to "fight back aggressively with any available object." Your chances of seeing a bear in North Carolina, much less being threatened by one, are pretty slim.

DISEASES AND NATURAL THREATS

Among the invisible villains here is **giardia,** a single-celled protozoan parasite that can be contracted by drinking untreated water. Hikers and campers should avoid drinking from streams unless they first boil the water vigorously for at least one minute. Filtering water with a filter of 0.1-1 micron absolute pore size or chemically treating it with iodine or chlorine is less reliable than thorough boiling.

There's a fairly high incidence of **rabies** in North Carolina's raccoons, bats, foxes, groundhogs, and skunks. If you're bringing a pet into the state, be sure that its vaccinations are up to date. If you plan to go hiking with your dog, it may even be wise to bring a copy of its rabies vaccination certificate in case you have to prove its immunity. If you are bitten by a wild animal, seek medical help immediately, even if you're out in the woods. Rabies is deadly to humans, and it's extremely important to start treatment immediately.

HEALTH PRECAUTIONS
Emergencies

As elsewhere the United States, calling 911 in North Carolina will summon medical help, police, or firefighters. On the highway, blue road signs marked with an "H" point the way to hospitals, but if you're experiencing a potentially critical emergency, it's best to call 911 and let the ambulance come to you. There are plenty of rural places in the state where cell-phone coverage is spotty to nonexistent, so if you have a medical condition from which an emergency could arise, keep this in mind.

Summer Weather

Heat, humidity, and air pollution often combine in the summer to create dangerous conditions for children, the elderly, and people with severe heart and lung conditions. Even if you're young and healthy, don't take chances in the heat. Carry drinking water with you, avoid exertion and being outside in the hottest part of the day, and stay in the shade. Even young, healthy people can die from the heat. Remember that even if it doesn't feel very warm outside, children and pets are in grave danger when left in cars. Temperatures can rise to fatal levels very quickly inside closed vehicles, even when it's not terribly hot outside.

Information and Services

MONEY

For international travelers, currency-exchange services can be found in the big cities at some major banks and at currency-exchange businesses. Numerous money-transfer services, from old familiars like Western Union to a multitude of overseas companies, are easily accessible. The easiest place to wire or receive money is at a grocery store—most have Western Union or a proprietary wiring service—or at a bank. Banking hours vary by location and chain, but most are closed on Sunday and federal holidays. ATMs are located at most bank branches as well as in many grocery stores and convenience stores.

COMMUNICATIONS AND MEDIA

Newspapers and Radio

North Carolina has several major newspapers, including the Asheville *Citizen-Times* (www.citizen-times.com). Alternative papers like the *Mountain Xpress* (www.mountainx.com), available in print and online, cover the state's counterculture. Among the many local and regional radio stations are a number of NPR affiliates. There are few parts of the state where you won't be able to tune in to a clear NPR signal.

Magazines

Our State magazine (www.ourstate.com) is a widely distributed monthly that tells the stories of people, places, and history across North Carolina. As a travel resource, it will give you a feel for the people you're likely to encounter, but it will give you an even better idea of places to eat and towns you may not have thought to visit. Their website has an extensive collection of archived stories arranged by topic. In most larger cities in North Carolina it isn't hard to find magazines covering the local arts scene or guiding area parents to the best the town has to offer for kids. Look at news racks outside grocery stores and on street corners to pick up free publications like *North Brunswick Magazine* in and around Brunswick County; *Wilma!* And *Wrightsville Beach Magazine* in Wilmington; and *O. Henry Magazine* in Greensboro. Online, there's no better resource than **NC Tripping** (www.nctripping.com), a travel-centric website run by dear friends.

Internet Access

Internet access is widespread. Coffee shops are always a good place to find Wi-Fi, usually free but sometimes for a fee. A few small towns have free municipal wireless access. Most chain motels and major hotels offer free wireless access, and smaller hotels and bed-and-breakfasts often do too. This is true for some remote areas as well. The deep mountains are the most difficult place to get a reliable internet connection, but you'll probably be able to get online at your place of lodging or the coffee shop in town.

Cell Phones

Cell phone coverage is not consistent across North Carolina. You'll get a signal in all of the cities and most areas in between. Up in the mountains, you may have a good signal on one side of a ridge and none on the other. Driving along the Blue Ridge Parkway, you'll find that signals come and go. Spotty cell-phone coverage is a safety issue; if you're treed by a bear or run out of gas on a backwoods track, 911 may be unreachable.

MAPS AND VISITOR INFORMATION

Among the best sources for travel information in North Carolina is the state's tourism website, VisitNC (www.visitnc.com). They maintain an up-to-date list of festivals and events, tours and trails, and almost anything else you may want to know. Also excellent is the magazine *Our State* (www.ourstate.com), available at grocery stores, drugstores, and bookshops. Their website monitors upcoming events as well.

North Carolina Welcome Centers, located at several major highway entry points to the state, are sources for more free brochures and maps than one person could carry. They are located at the Virginia state line on I-77 near Mount Airy, on I-85 in Warren County, and on I-95 in Northampton County; at the Tennessee state line on I-26 in Madison County and on I-40 in Haywood County; and along the South Carolina state line on I-26 in Polk County, I-85 in Cleveland County, I-77 just outside Charlotte, and I-95 in Robeson County.

For basic planning, the maps on the VisitNC website will give you a good sense of the layout of the state and its major destinations. Many areas are experiencing rapid growth, particularly around Charlotte and the Triangle, so if your map is even a little out of date, you may not know about the newest bypass. For features like mountains, rivers, back roads, and small towns that don't change, atlas-style books of state maps are useful. My own favorite is DeLorme's *North Carolina Atlas & Gazetteer.*

Resources

Suggested Reading

TRAVEL

Daniels, Diane. *Farm Fresh North Carolina.* Chapel Hill: UNC Press, 2011. This guidebook will help you find the perfect place to pick apples, cut Christmas trees, visit a pumpkin patch, pick a bushel of blueberries, and shop at every farmers market across the state. You'll find recipes from chefs and farmers as well.

Duncan, Barbara, and Brett Riggs. *Cherokee Heritage Trails.* Chapel Hill: UNC Press, 2003; online companion at www.cherokeeheritage.org. A fascinating guide to both the historic and present-day home of the Eastern Band of the Cherokee in North Carolina, Tennessee, and Georgia, from ancient mounds and petroglyphs to modern-day arts co-ops and sporting events.

Eubanks, Georgann. *Literary Trails of the North Carolina Mountains: A Guidebook.* Chapel Hill: UNC Press, 2007. This book and its companion books, *Literary Trails of the North Carolina Piedmont: A Guidebook,* 2010, and *Literary Trails of Eastern North Carolina: A Guidebook,* 2013, introduce fans of Southern literature to the places that produced and inspired various scribes. Also included are the best bookstores and book events across the state.

Fussell, Fred, and Steve Kruger. *Blue Ridge Music Trails of North Carolina: A Guide to Music Sites, Artists, and Traditions of the Mountains and Foothills.* Chapel Hill: UNC Press, 2013. A guide to destinations—festivals, restaurants, oprys, church singings—in the North Carolina mountains where authentic bluegrass, old-time, and sacred music can be experienced by visitors. An accompanying audio CD allows you to continue to hear the music. The exceptional photography by Cedric N. Chatterley in this book and in *Cherokee Heritage Trails*—reproduced in full color—and the depth of context conveyed make these two guides worth buying even if you're not touring the region.

NC Tripping. www.nctripping.com. Useful, constantly updated, and focused on the best of what the Tar Heel State has to offer, this is a great resource for visitors. Follow Carl and Christina and their family across the state. Responsive in their community on social media, they are always fun to run into on the road.

North Carolina Atlas and Gazetteer. Yarmouth, ME: DeLorme, 2012. Since I was a Boy Scout, I have always been partial to DeLorme's state atlases. This series represents in great detail the topography and other natural features of an area, giving far more useful and comprehensive information than the standard highway map.

Our State. www.ourstate.com. For a lively and informative look at North Carolina destinations and the cultural quirks and treasures you may find in your travels, *Our*

State magazine is one of the best resources around. The magazine is easy to find, sold at most bookstores and even on grocery store and drugstore magazine racks. It covers arts, nature, folklore, history, scenery, sports, and lots of food, all from a traveler's perspective.

HISTORY AND CULTURE

Cecelski, David. *The Waterman's Song: Slavery and Freedom in Maritime North Carolina.* Chapel Hill: UNC Press, 2001. A marvelous treatment of the African American heritage of resistance in eastern North Carolina, describing how the region's rivers and sounds were passages to freedom for many enslaved people.

Powell, William S. *North Carolina: A History.* Chapel Hill: UNC Press, 1988. A readable, concise account of our fascinating and varied past.

Powell, William S., and Jay Mazzocchi, editors. *Encyclopedia of North Carolina.* Chapel Hill: UNC Press, 2006. A fantastic compendium of all sorts of North Carolina history, letters, and politics. If you can lift this mammoth book, you'll learn about everything from Carolina basketball to presidential elections to ghosts.

Setzer, Lynn. *Tar Heel History on Foot: Great Walks through 400 Years of North Carolina's Fascinating Past.* Chapel Hill: UNC Press, 2013. This book sends you on a series of short walks in all parts of the state—coastal and mountain, city and country, historic sites and state parks—to discover the history of the state. The walks are arranged by theme and location, making it simple to find one near you.

SPORTS

Blythe, Will. *To Hate Like This Is to Be Happy Forever: A Thoroughly Obsessive, Intermittently Uplifting, and Occasionally Unbiased Account of the Duke-North Carolina Basketball Rivalry.* New York: Harper, 2007. A highly entertaining book about the hatred between partisans of UNC and Duke, describing how the famous basketball rivalry brings out the best and worst in the fans.

Thompson, Neal. *Driving with the Devil: Southern Moonshine, Detroit Wheels, and the Birth of NASCAR.* New York: Broadway Books, 2008. The creation story of a great sport, the rise of stock-car racing from moonshiners' getaway wheels to a multibillion-dollar industry.

Internet Resources

NEWSPAPERS

North Carolina newspapers have unusually rich online content and are great resources for travel planning.

Asheville Citizen-Times
www.citizen-times.com
A good online edition for this Asheville-based paper.

Mountain Xpress
www.mountainx.com
Also covering the Asheville area, with a politically progressive and artistically countercultural bent—much like Asheville itself.

Mountain Times
http://mountaintimes.com
Weekly newspaper covering Boone and the High Country.

ARTS AND CULTURE

North Carolina's arts and history have an ever-growing online dimension, telling the story of the state in ways that paper and ink simply can't.

North Carolina Folklife Institute
www.ncfolk.org

The website will fill you in on the many organizations across the state that promote traditional music, crafts, and folkways. You'll also find a calendar of folk life-related events in North Carolina and travel itineraries for weekends exploring Core Sound, the Seagrove potteries, and Cherokee heritage in the Smokies.

NCFood
www.ncfolk.org/category/food

This wonderful food blog, maintained by the Folklife Institute, features articles about the culinary back roads of the state.

North Carolina Arts Council
www.ncarts.org

The Arts Council provides information about performing arts, literature, cultural trails, galleries, and fun happenings.

North Carolina ECHO
www.ncecho.org

ECHO stands for "Exploring Cultural Heritage Online," and this great site has links to hundreds of online exhibits and brick-and-mortar museums.

Carolina Music Ways
www.carolinamusicways.org

A lively guide to the extremely varied musical traditions of the North Carolina Piedmont.

Blue Ridge Heritage Area
www.blueridgeheritage.com

This resource has a huge amount of mountain-area travel information and an ever-growing directory of traditional artists of all kinds in the Carolina mountains.

Southern Highland Craft Guild
www.southernhighlandguild.org

An Asheville-based regional arts giant with an extensive online guide to craftspeople throughout the region.

Our State
www.ourstate.com

The online companion to this print publication provides expanded coverage of the history, people, food, and arts across North Carolina. An extensive archive of stories lets you look back several years for the best the state has to offer.

OUTDOORS

Great online resources exist for planning outdoor adventures in North Carolina, where rich arts and blockbuster sports are matched by natural resources.

North Carolina Sierra Club
http://nc2.sierraclub.org

Find information about upcoming hikes and excursions as well as an overview of the state's natural areas and environmental issues.

North Carolina Birding Trail
www.ncbirdingtrail.org

Covering bird-watching across the state, this site contains information about dozens of pristine locations and active flyways along the coast, in the Piedmont, and in the mountains.

Carolina Canoe Club
www.carolinacanoeclub.com

A clearinghouse of statewide canoeing resources.

Carolina Kayak Club
www.carolinakayakclub.org

A repository for flat-water kayaking information, resources, trails, and activities across the state.

CanoeNC
www.canoenc.org
A nice starting point for planning a flat-water paddling trip in eastern North Carolina.

North Carolina Sportsman
www.northcarolinasportsman.com
Covering hunting and fishing news, destinations, and seasonal trends across the state.

Friends of the Mountains-to-Sea Trail
www.ncmst.org
Find details, hike-planning tools, and resources for a day or longer on the 1,000-mile-long Mountains-to-Sea Trail that crosses North Carolina.

NC Hikes
www.nchikes.com
All things hiking-related, including trails in every corner of the state, books, and trip recommendations.

Index

List of Maps

Photo Credits

All interior photos © Jason Frye except: title page: © Appalachianviews | Dreamstime.com; page 2 © Carol R Montoya | Dreamstime.com; page 6 © (top right) Jerry Coli | Dreamstime.com; (bottom) Jon Bilous | Dreamstime.com; page 7 (bottom left) Guoqiangxue | Dreamstime.com; pages 8-9 © Jon Bilous | Dreamstime.com; page 10 © Linda Mohammed; page 13 © Eddydegroot | Dreamstime.com; page 15 © Eric Krouse | Dreamstime.com; page 16 © Jon Bilous | Dreamstime.com; pae 17 © Sayran | Dreamstime.com; page 18 © Sean Pavone | Dreamstime.com; page 19 © (top left) Volgariver | Dreamstime.com; page 29 © (top left) Jon Bilous | Dreamstime.com; (top right) Jill Lang | Dreamstime.com; (bottom) Jill Meyer | Dreamstime.com; page 48 © (right middle) Jerry Coli | Dreamstime.com; page 71 © (right middle) Jon Bilous / 123rf.com; (bottom) Kevin M. Mccarthy | Dreamstime.com; page 81 © (top) Moonborne | Dreamstime.com; (bottom) Jon Bilous | Dreamstime.com; page 95 © (top) Jon Bilous | Dreamstime.com; (left middle) James Vallee | Dreamstime.com; page 101 © (top left) Steven Prorak | Dreamstime.com; (top right) Anton Foltin | Dreamstime.com; (bottom) Jill Lang | Dreamstime.com; page 113 © (left middle) Tony Laidig | Dreamstime.com; (right middle) Deebrowning | Dreamstime.com; (bottom) Deebrowning | Dreamstime.com; page 119 © (top) Shester171 | Dreamstime.com; (bottom) Evaulphoto | Dreamstime.com; page 131 © Jilllang | Dreamstime.com; page 136 © Robert Hainer/123rf.com; page 158 © Dfikar | Dreamstime.com

MAP SYMBOLS

▤	Expressway	○	City/Town	✈	Airport	⚲	Golf Course
▨	Primary Road	◉	State Capital	✗	Airfield	🅿	Parking Area
▨	Secondary Road	✹	National Capital	▲	Mountain	▤	Archaeological Site
▦	Unpaved Road	✪	Highlight	✦	Unique Natural Feature	⛪	Church
- - - -	Trail	★	Point of Interest			⛽	Gas Station
⋯⋯	Ferry	•	Accommodation	⌇	Waterfall		
◆-◆-	Railroad	▼	Restaurant/Bar	⛰	Park		Glacier
▨	Pedestrian Walkway	■	Other Location	🚩	Trailhead		Mangrove
▥	Stairs	Ⓐ	Campground	⛷	Skiing Area		Reef
							Swamp

CONVERSION TABLES

°C = (°F - 32) / 1.8
°F = (°C x 1.8) + 32
1 inch = 2.54 centimeters (cm)
1 foot = 0.304 meters (m)
1 yard = 0.914 meters
1 mile = 1.6093 kilometers (km)
1 km = 0.6214 miles
1 fathom = 1.8288 m
1 chain = 20.1168 m
1 furlong = 201.168 m
1 acre = 0.4047 hectares
1 sq km = 100 hectares
1 sq mile = 2.59 square km
1 ounce = 28.35 grams
1 pound = 0.4536 kilograms
1 short ton = 0.90718 metric ton
1 short ton = 2,000 pounds
1 long ton = 1.016 metric tons
1 long ton = 2,240 pounds
1 metric ton = 1,000 kilograms
1 quart = 0.94635 liters
1 US gallon = 3.7854 liters
1 Imperial gallon = 4.5459 liters
1 nautical mile = 1.852 km

**MOON ASHEVILLE & THE
GREAT SMOKY MOUNTAINS**
Avalon Travel
Hachette Book Group
1700 Fourth Street
Berkeley, CA 94710, USA
www.moon.com

Editor: Kimberly Ehart
Acquiring Editor: Nikki Ioakimedes
Series Manager: Kathryn Ettinger
Copy Editor: Christopher Church
Graphics and Production Coordinators:
  Lucie Ericksen, Rue Flaherty
Cover Design: Toni Tajima
Map Editor: Kat Bennett
Cartographers: Erin Greb, Natalie Higginbotham,
  John Culp, Stephanie Poulain
Indexer: Greg Jewett

ISBN-13: 978-1-64049-752-8

Printing History
1st Edition — 2016
3rd Edition — April 2023
5 4 3 2 1

Front cover photo: Boardwalk through Graveyard
  Fields, Blue Ridge Parkway, near Asheville © Bill
  Gozansky/www.robertharding.com
Back cover photo: North Carolina Arboretum in
  Asheville © Jill Lang | Dreamstime.com

Printed in Thailand for Imago